Generic Tools, Specific Languages

This is the CreateSpace version of the book. Except for the Dutch summary, my CV, and some of the front matter missing from this edition, it is identical to the original thesis book.

This thesis is accepted by the promotors:
Prof. Dr. A. van Deursen
Prof. Dr. E. Visser

Doctoral Committee:

Rector Magnificus	voorzitter
Prof. Dr. E. Visser	Delft University of Technology, promotor
Prof. Dr. A. van Deursen	Delft University of Technology, promotor
Prof. Dr. K. G. Langendoen	Delft University of Technology
Prof. Dr. Ir. P. Jonker	Delft University of Technology
Prof. Dr. F. Steimann	Fernuniversität Hagen
Prof. Dr. J.J.M. Hooman	Radboud University Nijmegen
Prof. Dr. K. Ostermann	Universität Marburg

Development of mbeddr was supported by the German BMBF, FKZ 01/S11014.

Acknowledgments

First and foremost I want to thank the mbeddr team. While the idea for *Generic Tools, Specific Languages* and mbeddr was mine, realizing a system of this scope and size is impossible for one person alone. This is true in terms of the necessary amount of work, but also in terms of the necessary (more detailed) ideas and concepts that need to be tackled during realization. Hence I am grateful to the mbeddr team: Bernd Kolb (who was the mother of the project if I am the father), Dan Ratiu (who contributed his experience for formal methods), Domenik Pavletic (who implemented the debugger and fought with the build server), Kolja Dumman (who joined after the research project, but nonetheless made his mark on mbeddr), Sascha Lisson (who built the support for prose and tables in MPS in his spare time before we hired him into the mbeddr team where he now deals with MPS details), Zaur Molotnikov (who helped with the formal methods), Federico Tomassetti (who worked on the initial variant-aware legacy code importer) as well as Stephan Eberle, Birgit Engelmann, Stefan Schmierer, Aykut Kilic, Daniel Stieger and Bernhard Merkle who actually used mbeddr to build real software systems and provided critical feedback. Finally, I want to thank Bernhard Schätz for helping with the formal aspects of the research project and just generally for his support!

I also want to thank Wolfgang Neuhaus as a representative of itemis management for giving us the freedom to work on an innovation project like mbeddr. While we did get government funding as part of the LW-ES research project, Domenik, Bernd and myself spent much more time on mbeddr than what was backed by government funding. Without these additional resources, mbeddr would not be where it is today. Similarly, I want to thank Swaminathan Gopalswamy and Sundu Sundaresan, both of Siemens PL (LMS), for indirectly supporting the continued development of mbeddr through their investment into ACCEnT (which builds on top of mbeddr).

I also want to thank the JetBrains MPS team. They created a very powerful tool that was used as the platform for mbeddr, and they supported (and continue to support) us relentlessly. They answered questions, discussed and fixed bugs, and reprioritized the MPS roadmap to better fit our needs. Without this close collaboration, mbeddr would not have been possible. In particular, I want to thank the team lead Alexander Shatalin (who was tirelessly available via Google Chat and Skype), Konstantin Solomatov (who was Alexander's predecessor and helped start the mbeddr project) as well as Sergey Dmitriev (JetBrains founder and president, as well as the originator of MPS).

I want to thank Eelco Visser and Arie van Deursen for giving me the chance to pursue a PhD remotely, and based on my own ideas. Even though remote collaboration isn't always easy I enjoyed the experience thoroughly and learned a lot. And I am sure my writing has become less "sales-oriented" in the process :-) Thank you very much! I also want to thank Eelco's research group for always welcoming me in Delft, for inspiring discussions on language engineering and for the occasional help with the PhD process.

I am glad to have a great committee consisting of Jozef Hooman, Pieter Jonker, Koen Langendoen, Klaus Ostermann and Friedrich Steimann (plus, of course, Eelco and Arie). Thank you for serving, and thank you for the feedback!

I also want to thank Tamara Brusik, the TU Delft's Office of the Beadle and again, Eelco Visser, for helping me with the remoteness of the thesis. For example, Tamara and Eelco printed the thesis three times and brought it to the Beadle's Office, and the Beadle's Office agreed to do some of the process via phone instead of me showing up in the Office in person. Thank you!

I want to thank Eugen Schindler for translating the Summary at the end of the thesis into Dutch – a small piece of the overall puzzle that made a big difference.

Steve Rickaby, who has copyedited all my English language books before, has also performed his magic with regards to fixing problems with my English on this text. Thank you very much, Steve!

Last but not at all least, I want to thank Nora who often just saw my back hunched over the notebook, because I was coding for mbeddr, or writing a paper or this thesis. Apparently she also had to suffer through any number of look-at-this-new-thing-we-built-and-praise-me episodes. Thank you for your patience, support and love!

Markus Völter
April 2014
Stuttgart, Germany

The cover and back cover pictures are in line with the covers of my previous books *DSL Engineering* and *Model-Driven Software Development* in that they show gliders. The picture on the cover shows as ASH-26E breaking away from a Duo Discus, from which the photo was taken. The back cover shows the same Duo Discus flying closely behind the ASH-26E, from which I took the picture. I think both pictures were taken on the same autumn day over the Schwäbische Alb in Southern Germany.

iv

Contents

Part I

Generic Tools, Specific Languages

Introduction

Abstract — *Adapting tools to a particular domain is expensive, and the adaptation is often not very deep. To address this challenge,* Generic Tools, Specific Languages *shifts the focus from building and adapting* tools *(windows, buttons, algorithms) to building and adapting* languages *to a domain. The thesis applies the approach to embedded software development: mbeddr is an extensible set of integrated languages for embedded software development built with JetBrains MPS language workbench. The evaluation of mbeddr suggests that it is a productive tool for embedded software development. The evaluation of the development of mbeddr itself suggests that MPS is a suitable platform for* Generic Tools, Specific Languages, *and that the approach in general is worthwhile.*

1.1 OVERVIEW AND CONTRIBUTION

This section provides an overview of the thesis. It starts out by describing the contribution and the research methodology. It then discusses mbeddr, the primary artifact built during the dissertation and explains its context, embedded software engineering. A discussion of the technologies used for building mbeddr – language engineering, projectional editing and JetBrains MPS – follows. The section concludes with an overview of the results.

Contribution   Today's software engineering tools are hard to adapt to specific domains. A major reason is that while platforms such as Eclipse support easy extension of the *tool* (views, editors, buttons, menus) they do not easily support the extension of the data formats or *languages* that underlie a tool. The contribution of this thesis is the introduction and evaluation of a new approach to developing domain-specific software engineering tools called *Generic Tools, Specific Languages*. It shifts the focus from adapting the engineering *tool* to adapting the underlying *languages* to solve the problem of tool adaptation. It relies on language workbenches (the generic tool) and recent advances in language engineering, particularly, user-friendly projectional editing. The problem of tool extensibility, the *Generic Tools, Specific Languages* approach and the way it is evaluated is discussed in Chapter 2. The specific research questions that arise from the approach (domain-specific extensibility, language modularity and projectional editing, tool scalability, implementation efforts and the learning curve) are introduced and motivated in Section 2.6.

Methodology   As part of the dissertation, the *Generic Tools, Specific Languages* approach has been applied to embedded software engineering, resulting in a

3

tool called mbeddr[1]. mbeddr provides a set of extensions to C, plus a number of other languages relevant to embedded software engineering. The evaluation of the *Generic Tools, Specific Languages* rests on two pillars. First, the fact that mbeddr could be built at all is a validation of the technical feasibility of the approach. Chapter 10 evaluates the experience of building mbeddr, based specifically on a number of research questions introduced in Section 2.6. The second pillar evaluates whether mbeddr is an improvement in terms of the tooling for embedded software development. Only if useful tools can be built with *Generic Tools, Specific Languages* is the approach worthwhile. Chapter 5 investigates this question based on six challenges in embedded software development discussed in Section 3.2. The validation uses empirical, qualitative data obtained during the mbeddr-based development of six embedded software systems.

According to the categorization of different kinds of research contributions put forth by the Call for Papers[2] of ICSE 2014, the core contribution of this thesis is *technological*. It introduces a new modeling language and tool. The evaluation of the usefulness of the contribution is mainly backed by clear arguments extracted from practical use of the system; this applies to both mbeddr, as well as to language engineering and JetBrains MPS. The thesis also has an *empirical* component, in the sense that qualitative empirical evidence is gathered and evaluated from building mbeddr (Chapter 10) and a number of mbeddr-based applications (Chapter 5). The thesis does not contain a systematic case study because the realities of the LW-ES research project in which mbeddr was developed did not permit such a systematic study. The thesis also has a *methodological* component, in that it advocates general principles on how to build domain-specific software development tools. Finally, the thesis contains a new *perspective* on embedded software development using language engineering and highly integrated tools.

mbeddr   mbeddr implements the *Generic Tools, Specific Languages* paradigm for embedded software development, based on the MPS language workbench. mbeddr supports the incremental, modular extension of C. It ships with a set of extensions relevant to embedded software, such as interfaces and components, state machines and physical units. mbeddr provides multi-paradigm programming for C, in which different abstractions can be used and mixed in the same program. The availability of a first-class language construct for important abstractions in embedded software also makes programs more analyzable, because the application logic is expressed at an appropriate abstraction level. To exploit this benefit, mbeddr also includes formal analyses for some of the extensions; model checking of state machines, verifying determinism of decision tables and verifying interface contracts are examples. Finally, mbeddr supports process concerns such as documentation, requirements and product line variability, all based on language engineering. mbeddr's features are discussed in detail in Chapter 4.

---

[1] http://mbeddr.com

[2] http://2014.icse-conferences.org/research

As a consequence of being built on top of a language workbench, mbeddr allows third parties to create modular extensions of C or of existing extensions, without modifying any existing languages. Users can also build additional languages that are not related to (or just reference or generate to) C code, but which are nonetheless important for a particular domain-specific engineering environment. Examples of such extensions are shown at the beginning of Chapter 10.

mbeddr has been developed in the LW-ES research project[3]. However, mbeddr is not a research prototype, it is a mature system that has been (and continues to be) used to develop real-world software. mbeddr is open source software, licensed under the Eclipse Public License, is hosted by `eclipse.org` and continues to be actively developed even though the LW-ES research project has ended.

Embedded Software Development   Embedded software development is a good candidate for demonstrating the *Generic Tools, Specific Languages* paradigm. While some kinds of embedded software are developed with (rather generic) modeling tools, a significant share of embedded software is developed in C. The main reason for using C in embedded software is that it is very good for low-level concerns: direct access to memory and pointer arithmetic are available, and well-written C code can compile to quite small and efficient binaries, which is important in many embedded software systems. However, C also has well-known drawbacks: some of C's flexibility is considered dangerous in the context of safety-critical systems, it is hard to build higher-level custom abstractions, and excessive – and sometimes unavoidable – use of the C preprocessor can lead to completely unmaintainable and hard-to-analyze software. Section 3.2 introduces six challenges of embedded software development today; these form the basis of the evaluation of mbeddr in Chapter 5.

mbeddr attempts to solve these issues by using language engineering. By supporting multiple domain-specific extensions to C, different aspects of the overall system can be implemented with different, adequate abstractions. All of these are integrated semantically by being embedded in (and generating to) C programs, which are then compiled with existing tool chains. The extensions are also integrated in terms of the tool, because all languages and language extensions live in the same IDE (integrated development environment), the language workbench. This avoids the tool integration issues commonly found in embedded development projects that use different specialized tools for different aspects of the overall system. The state of the art in embedded software development and its tools is discussed relative to mbeddr in Section 3.4.

Language Engineering and Language Workbenches   Language modularization and composition are important ingredients of language engineering. These techniques refer to the ability to combine language modules into new,

---

[3] This project has been funded by the German BMBF (01 | S11014), and included itemis AG, fortiss GmbH, Sick AG and BMW Car IT. It ran from July 2011 to June 2013.

composite languages without invasively changing any of them. While language composition involves structure, syntax, type system, semantics and the IDE, the syntactic aspect has historically been a challenge, due to the limited compositionality of grammars, grammar classes and parsing. Section 7.5 discusses historic and alternative contemporary approaches for language engineering. mbeddr relies especially on language *extension*, in which additional language constructs are added to a known base language. Chapter 7 contains a classification of language composition approaches, among them extension.

Language workbenches are tools tailored for language engineering; they also support the development of rich IDEs for the engineered languages, with features such as syntax coloring, code completion, go-to-definition and find-references as well as model search, refactoring, debugging or visualization. Language workbenches are the *generic tool* in *Generic Tools, Specific Languages*. The term *language workbench* was introduced by Fowler [2005], even language workbench-like tools have a much longer history, which is discussed in Section 7.5.

Projectional Editing   Projectional editing refers to an approach of language and IDE implementation in which user interactions with the code leads to a change in the program AST (abstract syntax tree) *directly*. It is similar to a graphical diagram editor. In a UML tool, for example, when a user drags a class onto the canvas, the tool does not draw the class shape and a parser "parses the graphics" to build the AST (this is essentially what happens in textual IDEs). Instead, when the class is dropped onto the canvas, the in-memory data structure that represents the model gets a new instance of `uml::Class`, and a projection engine then renders the graphics. *There is never any transformation from concrete syntax to abstract syntax*, only the other way round. This means that the concrete syntax can be ambiguous (in terms of parsing), and it can use notations that cannot be parsed at all, such as mathematical symbols, tables or graphics.

mbeddr, and more generally, the *Generic Tools, Specific Languages* paradigm, exploit these characteristics to provide rich notations and flexibly combinable languages for the application developer.

It is important to point out that the benefits of projectional editing do not come for free. For textual notations, the editor feels a little different than regular text editors, and programs are not stored as plain text, but instead as a serialized AST, typically XML. Section 6.2 discusses how MPS addresses these problems, and Sections 5.3.2 and 5.3.4 report on whether this works in practice. In summary, MPS takes some time to get used to, but most developers then report that they can work productively with the editor.

JetBrains MPS   JetBrains MPS[4] is an open source projectional language workbench developed over the last ten years by JetBrains. It provides a comprehensive environment for language engineering, supporting language aspects such as concrete and abstract syntax, type systems and transformations,

---

[4] http://jetbrains.com/mps

as well as IDE aspects such as syntax highlighting, code completion, go-to-definition, find-usages, diff and merge, refactoring and debugging. MPS uses a projectional editor; in contrast to historical projectional editors, MPS has managed to improve editor usability to the point where it can be used productively. Some of the ways it achieves this are discussed in Section 6.2 as part of the general introduction to MPS in Chapter 6.

MPS has *not* been developed as part of this thesis. However, mbeddr is the first case in which MPS has been used to build a rich, multi-paradigm development tool based on the *Generic Tools, Specific Languages* approach. Chapters 8 and 9 explain how mbeddr is built on top of the JetBrains MPS language workbench.

MPS was chosen as the basis of this research because, through its projectional editor, it promises unparalleled language composition features and flexible domain-specific notations. Both are important cornerstones for *Generic Tools, Specific Languages*. The experience with mbeddr shows that, despite a few shortcomings, MPS can meet these expectations. Chapter 10 provides the details.

Results   The results are promising from an embedded software development perspective and from the perspective of language engineering. Chapter 5 contains the evaluation from the application developer's perspective; the following is a summary. mbeddr was used for implementing several systems, from relatively small examples to non-trivial commercial applications. Just using the existing extensions (interfaces, components, state machines, units) leads to better code quality and higher developer productivity. In particular, testing, which can be a challenge for embedded software, is simplified significantly as a consequence of better modularity and better abstractions. Also, testing can be backed up by using the integrated formal analyses, further increasing confidence in the code. Using the integrated requirements tracing and documentation facilities helps to improve the evolvability of the developed systems when requirements change or new developers are brought in. The fact that all systems built so far could be run on their intended target devices indicates that the overhead incurred by mbeddr cannot be prohibitive. Finally, the system scales to reasonable sizes; systems in the order of 100,000 SLOC can be implemented without running into performance issues.

Chapter 10 evaluates the development of mbeddr from a language engineering perspective; again, the following is a summary. The effort for building the mbeddr languages were moderate, and the result was a productive environment for developing embedded software. While the learning curve for MPS (and for comparable tools) is steep, once a developer has mastered it, they have access to a powerful set of capabilities. The notion of *modular* and *incremental* language extension works: mbeddr's default extensions have been built as independent, modular extensions of the C base language and can be used together in the same program. As part of all the projects done with mbeddr, we have also built project-specific modular extensions such as abstractions for processor registers, or languages for specifying messages for custom communication protocols. The efforts were limited (from hours to a few days) and covering these efforts in real-world projects was feasible. Projectional editing has turned out to be the right choice. It contributes to the practically unlimited language extensibility, and non-textual notations such as tables or mathematical symbols add to the readability of mbeddr code. Application developers report that, after a few days of changing editing habits, the editor works well; some even report that they prefer it over regular textual editors.

Conclusion   The results indicate that *Generic Tools, Specific Languages* works for non-trivial applications. Projectional editing, and in particular MPS, have proved to be a suitable foundation for the approach, even though MPS still has a few limitations and problems, discussed in Section 10.6. This is also backed up by the fact that mbeddr has been chosen by Siemens PL (LMS) as the basis for their new commercial embedded software engineering tool. Finally, the *Generic Tools, Specific Languages* approach is generalizable beyond embedded software. The mbeddr project team is currently in the process of using the same approach in the financial domain, where a set of interconnected DSLs are being developed to design and configure insurance products. Some details on the uses of *Generic Tools, Specific Languages* beyond mbeddr are discussed in Section 11.3.

1.2   MY PERSONAL CONTRIBUTION

The notion of *Generic Tools, Specific Languages* is mine. It has grown out of my experience with model-driven development and domain-specific languages. Also, the idea of applying this approach in embedded software development is my own. I built the original prototype of mebddr, called MEL, and discussed in the MoDELS 2010 paper [Voelter, 2010]. I was also the person who initiated the grant proposal that led to LW-ES research project in which the current version of mbeddr was developed. However, the implementation of mbeddr was much too big to be done by one person. The effort was split mainly between Bernd Kolb, Daniel Ratiu, Domenik Pavletic and myself. My role was to provide overall guidance for the project and implement many of the languages and extensions discussed as part of this thesis.

1.3   PUBLICATIONS

This thesis builds on other publications written during the dissertation period, mostly journal, conference and workshop papers. The first paper *Embedded Software Development with Projectional Language Workbenches* [Voelter, 2010] was published at MoDELS 2010. It is based on an early predecessor of mbeddr called the Modular Embedded Language (MEL). MEL was built on an earlier version of JetBrains MPS, and the example system implemented with it was a Lego Mindstorms robot. While that prototype was very basic, the paper introduces the idea of using language engineering to build embedded software development tools.

A more thorough treatment of the idea was presented at SPLASH/Wavefront 2012 in a paper titled *mbeddr: an Extensible C-based Programming Language and IDE for Embedded Systems* [Voelter et al., 2012]. It is based on the then-current state of the mbeddr implementation discussed in this thesis. It contains a much more thorough and systematic treatment of the challenges in embedded software development and how language engineering can help to solve them. It describes the extensions available in mbeddr in a fair amount of detail, and discusses how they are implemented.

A third paper was published in 2013 in the Journal of Automated Software Engineering, *mbeddr: Instantiating a Language Workbench in the Embedded Software Domain* [Voelter et al., 2013]. As the title suggests, this paper shifts the perspective from language engineering to tool development, and hence is closest to the theme of this thesis. The paper also contains a preliminary validation of the approach based on the systems that had been built with mbeddr at the time.

At GTTSE 2011 I published a paper called *Language and IDE Development, Modularization and Composition with MPS* [Voelter, 2011]. It is not directly related to mbeddr, but instead proposes a systematic approach to language modularization and composition. It illustrates these approaches with examples based on MPS. The understanding gained from writing this paper significantly influenced the design and implementation of mbeddr and *Generic Tools, Specific Languages* in general.

Finally, a paper for SPLC 2011 called *Product Line Engineering using Domain-Specific Languages* [Voelter & Visser, 2011] systematically explores the differences between feature models and DSLs in the context of product lines, and argues when and why DSLs are superior. The paper uses parts of mbeddr as an example; the work that went into it also informed the product line support available in mbeddr.

A number of papers address the integration of formal methods into mbeddr, and the underlying philosophy of exploiting language engineering to better support the use of formal methods in practice. The first was published at the FormSERA Workshop 2012 and is called *Language Engineering as Enabler for Incrementally Defined Formal Analyses* [Ratiu et al., 2012]. It introduces the idea and illustrates the concept with three of mbeddr's integrated formal methods: completeness and consistency checking of decision tables, model-checking for a dialect of state machines, and consistency checking of feature models. The second paper was published at the MoDeVVa 2012 workshop and is called *Implementing Modular Domain Specific Languages and Analyses* [Ratiu et al., 2012]. It introduces and illustrates the notion of using language engineering to support reuse of parts of the implementations of different formal analysis techniques in mbeddr. Finally, in a paper titled *Using Language Engineering to Lift Languages and Analyses at the Domain Level* [Ratiu et al., 2013], published at the 2013 edition of the NASA Formal Methods Symposium, we illustrate the integration of C-level model checking into the mbeddr system, once again exploiting language engineering to facilitate the approach.

Other aspects of mbeddr are also discussed in workshop papers. This includes requirements management and tracing [Voelter et al., 2013], the integration of structured programs and prose [Voelter, 2013] and extensible debuggers [Pavletic et al., 2013].

Finally, some aspects of this thesis have also been discussed in the book *DSL Engineering* [Voelter et al., 2013], published by me and a few collaborators in early 2013.

1.4 A NOTE ON STYLE

In this document I use "I" to refer to me as the author (as in "I will show in Section 2 how to ...". I use "we" when referring to the mbeddr team as a whole (as in "We have added support for ...").

Summary *— This thesis proposes a new approach to developing software engineering tools called* Generic Tools, Specific Languages. *It relies on language workbenches and language engineering to create productive development environments for different domains. The thesis proposes the approach, and validates it with the mbeddr tool for embedded software development. Chapter 2 discusses the current state of the art in tools, points out challenges, and shows how* Generic Tools, Specific Languages *address these challenges. Chapter 3 introduces the field of embedded software and shows how mbeddr addresses challenges in this field. The chapter concludes with a comparison of mbeddr to other approaches for embedded software engineering.*

Generic Tools, Specific Languages

Abstract — *Tools play an important role for many aspects of software engineering. Domains-specific tools, i.e., tools that are adapted to a particular domain, can be even more useful. However, building domain-specific tools, or adapting generic tools to a particular domain, is expensive. An important reason for this cost is that even those tools that are adaptable usually only adapt the tool's functionality and UI, but not the underlying data structures. This chapter lays out the paradigm of* Generic Tools, Specific Languages, *which addresses this challenge by casting data as languages and using language engineering and language workbenches to enhance adaptability.*

2.1 THE ROLE OF TOOLS

Tools play an important role in the development of software, and as the complexity of software increases the role of tools grows in importance. There are many ways in which tools can be classified, for example based on the task they support (discussed in this section), whether they are command-line tools or UI tools (Section 2.2), they are general-purpose or domain-specific (Section 2.3). Adequate tools have the potential to improve productivity [Bruckhaus et al., 1996] and support developers in various ways [Heitmeyer, 2006; Broy et al., 2010]:

Tools automate tedious tasks.   Language-aware editors automate some aspects of programming, such as generating getters and setters for fields in Java. Using code completion, they help to avoid typos and reduce the number of keystrokes developers have to type. Tools enable the use of non-textual languages such as UML, dataflow models or state charts. Refactoring tools help restructure the code and improve its internal structure. Continuous integration servers automatically build software and execute tests.

Tools automate the creation of derived artifacts.   Compilers create optimized binaries from sources. They can also generate derived artifacts such as interface descriptions or data structure descriptions needed by subsequent tools. Code generators generate source code from models. More generally, in model-driven software development [Stahl & Voelter, 2006], tools are essential for modeling, transformation and code generation.

Tools ensure the well-formedness of content.   Checking for structural correctness of programs or XML documents is an example. They also run type checks in the background, keeping developers aware of type violations.

Tools help verify critical properties of the system. Tools can establish metrics about software, providing a measure of complexity or other properties. Tools can check for violations of style guides or architectural guidelines. They can perform analysis of safety properties by analyzing the code, for example by using model checking.

Tools help find and fix bugs. Tools can insert tracing code into programs that help collect data used for finding bugs. Debuggers help to animate programs, allowing developers to step through and understand their execution. Profilers can be used to find performance bottlenecks. Quick fixes suggest how to fix type system or structural errors as the developer writes the code.

Tools support development processes. They can help create reports or other documents related to the system itself, such as FMEA or FTA analyses. They can be used to manage requirements or documentation, and establish traces between code or models and requirements. Tools can also create visualizations of the structure or other aspects of the system. Version control tools help with managing versions and releases of systems.

2.2 COMMAND-LINE VS. GUI TOOLS

The distinction between command-line and GUI tools is important, since the rest of this thesis and the *Generic Tools, Specific Languages* approach focuses on GUI tools.

Command-Line Tools Command-line tools are optimized for batch processing: they take a file as input and produce another file as output, the transformation from source to target being tool-specific. Examples include transformation tools such as compilers, which take program source code as input and translate it into machine code, and analysis tools, which take source data as input and output the result of the analysis; an example would be a symbolic model checker such as NuSMV[1]. Traditionally, command-line tools have been used interactively in software development, possibly together with a text editor to edit sources and view results. The developer uses the operating system's console to invoke the tools. Also, command-line tools play an important role in the context of Agile software development and DevOps [Humble & Molesky, 2011] where they are automatically run on integration servers to continuously compile, test, build and package software.

GUI Tools GUI tools provide a graphical user interface (GUI) with which users can interact in a much richer way compared to command-line tools. They usually let users work in and arrange multiple windows or editors, provide rich ways of inspecting or viewing data, and often support different representations of the same core data. Examples include IDEs (such as

---

[1] http://nusmv.fbk.eu/

Eclipse[2] plus JDT[3] or CDT[4], as well as IntelliJ IDEA[5]), modeling tools (such as the MagicDraw UML[6] tool or the Ascet SD[7] embedded software development tool), or complete engineering environments (such as Vector's Preevision[8] or Wolfram's Mathematica[9]). For the mainstream developer, GUI tools have replaced command-line tools as the dominant means for developing systems. However, underneath the GUI surface, many GUI tools still use trusted command-line tools. For example, Eclipse CDT can use the `gcc` compiler.

2.3 DOMAIN-SPECIFIC TOOLS

Many tools are relatively generic, which means that they do not make many assumptions about the specific context in which they are used. This is true for command-line tools and GUI tools alike. For example, `make` can be used to automate all kinds of build processes, not just compilation of source code, and MagicDraw can be used to model all kinds of systems based on (profiled) UML. This genericity leads to a lack of domain-specific abstractions, which, in turn, leads to limited productivity. A recent study by Whittle et al. [2013] in the context of model-driven engineering (MDE, [Schmidt, 2006]) tools states:

> Our interviews show that the tool market is focused only on supporting models at an abstraction level very close to code, where the mapping to code is straightforward. This is clearly somewhat removed from the MDE vision. Unfortunately, there is also a clear gap in the way that vendors market their tools and their real capabilities in terms of this low-level approach. As a result, many MDE applications fail due to expectations that have not been managed properly.

There are several reasons for this genericity. The first one is business-related: generic tools can be sold more broadly, and so the investment for developing such tools can be amortized more easily. Customers may even prefer buying generic tools because they can "standardize" on them, reducing training cost by leveraging their users' experience throughout the organization. The second reason for generic tools relates to the fact that a tool vendor may not actually know all the various contexts in which a tool may be used, and so the vendor is not able to incorporate all these (unknown) requirements. Even seemingly simple domains such as refrigerators or controllers for electrical motors are extremely deep and require lots of specific experience and know-how.

In addition to the often infeasibly expensive way of building domain-specific tools from scratch, it is also possible to build generic tools that are exten-

---

[2] http://eclipse.org

[3] http://www.eclipse.org/jdt/

[4] http://www.eclipse.org/cdt/

[5] http://www.jetbrains.com/idea/

[6] http://www.nomagic.com/products/magicdraw.html

[7] http://www.etas.com/en/products/ascet_software_products.php

[8] http://vector.com/vi_preevision_en.html

[9] http://www.wolfram.com/mathematica/

sible, or adaptable to specific domains, or to compose domain-specific tool chains by integrating existing tools. The above-mentioned study has found a clear need for domain-specific adaptation of tools, and points out that current tools are very limited in this respect:

> The majority of our interviewees were very successful with MDE but all of them either built their own modeling tools, made heavy adaptations of off-the-shelf tools, or spent a lot of time finding ways to work around tools. The only accounts of easy-to-use, intuitive tools came from those who had developed tools themselves for bespoke purposes. Indeed, this suggests that current tools are a barrier to success rather than an enabler [..] Complexity problems are typically associated with off-the-shelf tools. Of particular note is accidental complexity – which can be introduced due to [..] [a] lack of flexibility to adapt the tools to a company's own context [..] Our interviews point to a strong need for tailoring of some sort: either tailor the tool to the process, tailor the process to the tool, or build your own tool that naturally fits your own process. Based on our data, it seems that, on balance, it is currently much easier to do the latter. Some tool vendors actively prohibit tailoring to the process, but rather a process is imposed by the tool for business reasons.

In tool integration, a set of existing tools are combined in a way that leads to a domain-specific tool chain. According to both Wasserman [1990] and Thomas & Nejmeh [1992], three different styles of tool integration can be distinguished: data integration, control integration and presentation integration. A historical perspective on tool integration can be found in Brown & Penedo [1992].

Data Integration   Data integration is the most common form of tool integration. Tools exchange data, usually using files, and it is the responsibility of the user of the tools to exchange the *right* set of data at the *right* step in the development process. Data integration also comprises cases in which references (usually by qualified name or ID) between data from different tools are established and kept in sync. The synchronization is done by one of the tools, or by a third party tool.

XML is used widely for such integration architectures. For example, Khare et al. [2001] discuss a system in which architecture models are exchanged based on agreed-upon XML schemas. In modeling tools, metamodel based data integration is used widely [Burmester et al., 2004; Amelunxen et al., 2008]. In the Eclipse world, Ecore models and EMF files are often used for this purpose. The importance of model transformations for integrating tools that do not use compatible metamodels is discussed by Tratt [2005], and the approach described by Königs & Schürr [2006] proposes automatic, rule-based triggering of such transformations as data is exchanged between tools. Kramler et al. [2006] also propose transparent transformation, but this time using semantic technologies at the metamodel level. Finally, a tool integration platform for multi-disciplinary development that goes further than exchanging files is proposed by El-khoury et al. [2005]. It provides database-based functionalities found in product data management and software configuration management systems.

Control Integration   Control integration attempts to solve the problem of data integration, which is that it is the responsibility of the user of the tools to exchange the right set of data at any particular step in the development process. In control integration, tools "invoke" other tools through different mechanisms. Brown [1993] proposes message-passing, and Blanc et al. [2005] suggest a middleware called ModelBus, which relies on standardized descriptions of the "interfaces" of models to support interoperability. Control integration usually involves some kind of data integration as well, since the above-mentioned invocation typically involves the exchange of data.

Presentation Integration   Presentation integration refers to the case in which different tools run "in the same window". Usually, such integration happens on the basis of open platforms. Many of the mainstream IDEs (such as Eclipse, Visual Studio[10], NetBeans[11] or IntelliJ) are such platforms, with Eclipse being the most sophisticated and most widely used. Yand and Jiang discuss the Eclipse case in some detail [Yang & Jiang, 2007]. While in principle, presentation integration is independent of data and control integration (completely independent tools can run in the same GUI), presentation integration is typically used together with the other two. On Eclipse, for example, the plugin framework supports running different plugins in the same Eclipse window (presentation integration) and it supports calling APIs provided by other plugins (control integration); EMF often serves as a common baseline for data integration.

Tool Extension   Tool extension is a special case of presentation integration, in which a particular tool is extended with additional, domain-specific features. Tool extension is similar to presentation integration in the sense that the result will be a tool that is integrated even in the GUI. However, presentation integration is symmetric in that one integrates a set of *independent* tools into a coherent tool chain; all participating tools are equal. Tool extension is asymmetric: one tool is special and serves as the base for which extensions are developed. The extensions are developed specifically for that base tool and are typically not reusable with other base tools. Often tools are specifically built to be extended; such tools are called *extensible*. They typically define *extension points*, locations in the platform or plugin code that explicitly allow extension. If the base tool has an adequate set of extension points and the GUI framework is flexible enough, useful domain-specific tools can be built. Once again, because of its flexible plugin architecture, Eclipse [Yang & Jiang, 2007] is the most-widely used platform on which extensible tools are built. However, other engineering tools such as Simulink also provide extension APIs; for example, Dziobek et al. [2008] describe an extension for variant handling.

---

[10] http://www.microsoft.com/visualstudio/eng/
[11] https://netbeans.org/

In spite of the existence of extensible tools, there are still problems with extensibility; this is discussed in this section. Tools work with data that has to conform to certain formats: a C compiler expects valid C programs, a UML tool expects the model file to be valid XMI and `make` expects `tabs` in very specific places. Unless their input data conforms to these specific formats, the tools cannot process the data. They may report useful errors (a C compiler will report syntax errors in a program in meaningful way) or they may just not work (opening a corrupted XMI file with a UML tool will probably just fail). Notice the use of the words *syntax error* and *corrupted*: they imply that a user has made a *mistake*, by not encoding the input data in a way that conforms to the data format's specification. However, the user may not have made a mistake; the user may have intended to add additional information to the input data, to be processed by the particular tool or by additional tools in a tool chain.

To extend tools meaningfully, it is not enough to extend the way data is processed. It is also essential to be able to extend the data itself, and hence the language used to encode the data. The following subsections look at several examples of how extension of the data format is essential – and how this is a problem with today's tools. In anticipation of later chapters of this thesis, this section relies on the C programming language as an example data format[12].

2.4.1 *Example 1: Physical Units:*

As the first example of this problem, consider the following valid C program fragment:

```
// in file example.c
int distance = 10;
int time     = 1;
int speed    = distance / time;
```

This program makes certain assumptions about the physical correctness of the calculation: dividing distance by time results in speed ($v = \frac{s}{t}$). From the perspective of the C language and compiler, the following calculation is also correct:

```
int speed   = time / distance;
```

The compiler would not flag an error. This is because the information about units is not present in the code. So even if a custom analyzer was written and plugged into a command-line tool chain or into a UI tool, it could not perform the analysis, because the necessary information is not part of the data!

To solve this problem, the input to the analysis tool that is part of a custom tool chain, perhaps running before the C compiler, would have to be

---

[12] C is not typically considered a data format, but rather a language. Section 2.5 discusses the relationship between the two notions

extended. Since the C grammar is fixed, one way to do this is to use special-purpose comments starting with /*#, and make the checking tool aware of this convention:

```
int/*#m*/ distance  = 10 /*#m*/;
int/*#s*/ time       = 1 /*#s*/;
int/*#mps*/ speed   = distance / time;
```

However, this approach has many problems and limitations. First, it is syntactically ugly. Second, there is no IDE support for entering the units, unless one also builds a special IDE, which is a lot of work. Third, potential unit errors are only shown when the special tool runs, not directly in the IDE (in other words, control integration cannot easily be provided). Finally, the separate checker does not just have to parse out the units, it also has to parse the remaining C program, because the context in which the units occur is relevant. For example, adding two distances results in a distance (m), whereas multiplying two distances results in an area (m^2). An alternative solution to the unit problem could be built with macros:

```
UT(int, m) distance = UV(10, s);
UT(int, s) time      = UV(1, s);
UT(int, mps) speed   = distance / time;
```

The UT and UV macros mark types and values as having units. The macros are defined so as to eliminate the units as the preprocessor runs, so the program can be compiled as regular C code. The specialized checker, however, would use them to infer unit information. While the approach is a little bit more robust, because the units themselves can be defined as enum literals or constants, the checker is just as complicated, since it still has to be an external tool that has to understand all of C, plus the macros. A third approach would use external XML to add metadata to programs:

```
<unitdeclarations>
  <unit name="m" for="distance"/>
  <unit name="s" for="time"/>
  <unit name="mps" for="speed" calculateAs="m/s"/>
</unitdeclarations>
<programmarkup file="example.c">
  <globalvar name="distance" unit="m"/>
  <globalvar name="time" unit="s"/>
  <globalvar name="speed" unit="mps"/>
</programmarkup>
```

However, this has problems as well. First, the source file and the XML file have to be synchronized (as is typical in data integration). While this could be supported by a special tool, there is a more fundamental problem: there is no reasonable way to refer to literals (as in 10) to specify a unit for them. Since they have no name, they are not easily referenceable; line numbers and offset are too brittle with regards to program changes.

To solve the problem of adding units to C in a meaningful way, real language extension is necessary[13]. If real language extensions were available, the unit-aware program could be written like this:

```
int/m/ distance  = 10 m;
int/s/ time      = 1 s;
int/mps/ speed   = distance / time;  // with the unit mps defined
                                     // elsewhere as m/s
```

The definition of the extension would define that units can be attached to types and expressions, and nowhere else. The type system of the host language would be extended to check type compatibility and compute resulting units ($mps = \frac{m}{s}$). The compiler would be extended to ignore the units. No separate tool is necessary.

The last example shows mbeddr's syntax for units. The details are discussed in Section 4.3.

2.4.2 Example 2: State Machines

A popular means for specifying discrete behavior, especially in embedded software, is to use state machines. Even though the approach is popular, implementing state machines in plain C is tedious and error-prone, since it requires the encoding of the state machines with lower-level abstractions. There are two main idioms for implementing state machines[14]: switch-based and array-based. The switch-based variant encodes states and input events as integers or enums and then uses a switch-statement to implement the behavior. The following pseudocode illustrates the approach:

```
// a state machine that transitions into S2
// when E1 is received while the machine is in S1
void execute_StateMachine( Event_Enum evt ) {
  switch (currentState) {
    case S1: switch (evt) {
             case E1: if ( guard for E1 in S1 ) {
                        // execute exit actions for S1
                        currentState = S2;
                        // execute entry actions for S2
                        break;
                      }
             }
    case S2: ...
      ...
  }
}
```

---

[13] This is certainly true for C. Some object-oriented languages allow solving the problem – to some degree or another – with the means of OO abstractions and some syntactic tricks.

[14] As a consequence of the popularity of state machines, a huge number of other approaches exist. A very sophisticated one is Quantum Leaps: http://www.state-machine.com/index.php.

The array-based variant uses nested arrays to represent the state machine's transition matrix. The transition matrix is a table in which the columns represent the current state and the rows represent input events. The remaining cells represent the state to which the state machine transitions if an event `row` is received while the machine is in state `col`[15]. The states and events are encoded as sequential integers, so they can be used to directly index into the array. This has the desirable property of executing in constant time $O(1)$.

```
// a state machine that transitions into S2
// when E1 is received while the machine is in S1
// -1 means "do nothing".
                        //  S1  S2  S3 ...
int[N_EVT][N_STATE] = { {    1, -1, -1 }    // E1
                        {   -1, -1, -1 }    // E2
                        ...
                                       };
```

In addition to being tedious and error-prone, both approaches have the problem that the structure of the original state machine is lost. This is not just a problem for program comprehension and maintenance, but in addition, symbolic model checkers [Burch et al., 1992] that can prove various properties about the state machine (such as reachability of states, transition nonambiguity and custom safety properties) cannot be used on this low-level representation. Instead, C-level model checkers [Clarke et al., 2004] have to be used. These are much more cumbersome to use and suffer from the state space explosion problem.

It is much better to represent state machines as first-class language concepts with states, events, transitions and actions. Since this is not possible in C, the obvious workaround is to use external state machine modeling tools (such as Statemate[16] or visualSTATE[17]) and then generate the implementation. However, using an external tool leads to challenges with the integration of C code (for example, in the actions) and with tool integration and synchronization in general. An approach based on language engineering would embed first-class state machines directly into C code, while retaining the advantages of first-class representation:

```
statemachine SM {
  event E1
  state S1 {
    entry { // entry action for S1 }
    on E1 [guard for E1 in S1] -> S2
    exit { // exit action for S1 }
  }
```

---

[15] The approach can be extended to include entry and exit actions by using another array, in which the cells represent pointers to functions that contain the entry and exit action code. Guard conditions can be handled with yet another table that contains pointers to Boolean functions.

[16] http://www-03.ibm.com/software/products/us/en/ratistat

[17] http://www.iar.com/en/Products/IAR-visualSTATE

```
    state S2 {
      ...
    }
    ...
}
```

This representation is more concise and less error-prone, since the state machine itself is represented directly. Since it is embedded into C, the guards can be C expressions and the action code can be C statements. The IDE would provide type checking for the expression, as well as state machine-specific constraint checks and IDE support for the state machine syntax. The state machine can be translated to any of the above-mentioned low-level implementations. In addition, it can be translated to the input for symbolic model checkers for verification.

The last example is close to mbeddr's syntax for state machines. The details are discussed in Section 4.6.

2.4.3 *Example 3: Requirements Tracing*

Requirements tracing [Watkins & Neal, 1994; Jarke, 1998] refers to pointing from implementation artifacts (such as code) to requirements. Trace pointers are often typed to characterize the nature of the relationship (e.g., `implements`, `refines` or `tests`). By following these pointers from a particular piece of code, it becomes clear which requirement the piece of code fulfils. This is useful to find out why a particular piece of code is the way it is. By following the pointers in reverse order, developers and auditors can determine which code fragments are a consequence of a given requirement. This is useful to decide which parts of the system may have to be revisited when a requirement changes. Current C IDEs do not support tracing directly; instead, special comments or macros are used:

```
TRACE(REQ_CALIBRATION)
int calibrate( int measurement ) {
  return measurement * FACTOR + OFFSET;
}

int getValue() {
  int raw = readFromDriver(ADC1_ADDRESS);
  TRACE(REQ_CALIBRATION)
  return calibrate(raw);
}
```

The code above attaches a trace that points to the `REQ_CALIBRATION` requirement to the `calibrate` function; it also attaches a trace to the code that calls the function in the process of measuring a value. The approach has several problems. First, there is no IDE support (such as code completion) when entering the requirement IDs, and a separate consistency checker has to be used to ensure that only valid requirement IDs are used. A more serious problem is that it is not always clear to which program element a trace belongs. Writing the trace "over" the traced element works for coarse-grained elements, but not generally: for example, one cannot write a trace "over" a number literal in a complex expression. This problem gets worse when considering program evolution or refactorings: attention has to be paid to keeping the TRACE macros together with their traced element. It is impossible to detect an erroneously moved trace automatically.

A solution based on language engineering would add tracing as a cross-cutting aspect to a language, while keeping it generic enough to be attached to any program element (the specific implementation approach depends on the particular flavor of language engineering used). It is important to emphasize that the trace really is *attached*, so when the traced element is moved or refactored, the trace always moves with it. Code completion and referential integrity checking with requirements documents can be provided directly in the IDE. mbeddr's solution for tracing is discussed in Section 4.8.

2.4.4 *Kinds of Extensions*

The three examples above have been chosen specifically because they are quite different, to illustrate the ways in which languages may have to be extended to build meaningful domain-specific tools.

Units are a fine-grained extension: single literals may have to be annotated with units. They require deep integration with the existing grammar and type system. However, they do not affect code generation to C; they are just thrown away upon generation or compilation.

State machines are an example of a coarse-grained extension in which new, "big" things are added to a program. While this may sound simpler initially, coarse-grained extensions often embed other C concepts inside them. The expressions in guards or the statements in actions are examples. Also, state machines affect code generation: they have to be translated to existing idioms for state machines in C. In addition, the need for formal analysis requires the generation of additional code as an input to the model checker.

Requirements traces are yet another kind of extension. in that they are generic: they should be attachable to *any* program element expressed in *any* language. There is no deep semantic integration with the base language. However, IDE support should still be provided.

2.4.5 *Combining Extensions*

To make the problem of extending the input data to tools even harder, in many scenarios several of these extensions are used in the same program. The three example extensions, in fact, could be combined rather nicely. Below is a program that uses a mix of the extensions proposed above. It contains a state machine with physical units embedded in the guard conditions, and traces attached to transitions.

```
statemachine TrainDoorController {
  event DOOR_BUTTON;
```

```
  state DOORS_CLOSED {
    trace REQ_BUTTON_OPENS_DOORS_ONLY_OPEN_WHEN_STOPPED
    on DOOR_BUTTON [speed == 0 mps] -> DOORS_OPEN
  }
  state DOORS_OPEN {
    entry { openDoors(); }
    trace REQ_BUTTON_CLOSES_DOORS_WHEN_OPEN
    on DOOR_BUTTON [] -> DOORS_CLOSED
    exit { closeDoors(); }
  }
  ...
}
```

The need to be able to combine these extensions immediately rules out the possibility of using separate tools for each of them: it is very unlikely that existing state machine modeling tools will support physical units and requirements tracing. It also becomes clear that using naming conventions, macros, comments or external files does not scale regarding non-ambiguity, robustness, refactoring and tool support.

2.4.6 *Another Example: Requirements Engineering*

The examples of extensibility discussed above used a programming language as the data structure to be extended. However, the challenges illustrated above are just as relevant for other artifacts. Requirements engineering is an example. In most existing requirements engineering tools requirements are collections of prose paragraphs, often numbered, organized in a tree, and with relationships among them (`refines` or `preempts`). However, different organizations have to express different additional data for requirements. This ranges from various simple string attributes (who is responsible, in which milestone will it be implemented) through project management data (how much effort is allocated, which work packages are defined), through tables with specific data (prices) to embedded DSLs that express business rules formally (pricing rules, insurance calculation rules). A requirements engineering tool should be extensible, so that it can work with (and provide tool support for) all these different kinds of data. mbeddr's support for requirements engineering has these capabilities; they are discussed in Section 4.8.

2.5   GENERIC TOOLS, SPECIFIC LANGUAGES

The *Generic Tools, Specific Languages* approach uses language engineering to solve extensibility challenges like the ones discussed in the previous section (an overview of language engineering is provided in Section 7.5). It is defined as follows:

> **Definition:**   *Generic Tools, Specific Languages* is an approach for developing tools and applications in a way that supports easier and more meaningful adaptation to specific domains. To achieve this goal, *Ge-*

neric Tools, Specific Languages generalizes programming language IDEs to domains traditionally not addressed by languages and IDEs. At its core, *Generic Tools, Specific Languages* represents applications as documents/programs/models expressed with suitable languages. Application functionality is provided through an IDE that is aware of the languages and their semantics. The IDE provides editing support, and also directly integrates domain-specific analyses and execution services. Applications and their languages can be adapted to increasingly specific domains using language engineering; this includes developing incremental extensions to the existing languages or creating additional, tightly integrated languages. Language workbenches act as the foundation on which such applications are built.

The context in terms of tools and tool extension has been provided in Section 2.3; related work on the language engineering necessary for *Generic Tools, Specific Languages* and on language workbenches is discussed in Section 7.5. The rationale of the approach relies on the five ingredients discussed below. Where applicable, connections to data, control and presentation integration discussed in Section 2.3 are established.

Data Must be Extended, not Just Functionality   To develop meaningful domain-specific tools as adaptations of existing, generic tools, it is not enough to add new functionality exposed via buttons, views or new file formats (i.e., extending the tool). For many use cases it is essential to be able to extend existing data formats, as a means of providing the data on which new functionality relies. As demonstrated in the previous section, traditional data integration, in which the additional data is put into separate files, is not feasible for many kinds of extensions.

From Data Formats to Languages   The purpose of a data format is to define the structure with which a valid instance document has to conform, plus possibly additional consistency constraints (a data format is essentially a metamodel, which is why metamodel-based data integration is popular [Burmester et al., 2004; Amelunxen et al., 2008]). A data format also defines (explicitly or implicitly) what valid instance documents mean, i.e. it defines the semantics of the data format. This corresponds *exactly* to the abstract syntax and semantics of languages. The only thing languages add to this is a convenient concrete syntax[18]. By adding a concrete syntax to data formats, the discussion about data format extension is moved from data formats into the world of languages[19]. In this sense, language IDEs become data manipulation tools; *Generic Tools, Specific Languages* relies on using language technologies to create "user interfaces" for data (instead of windows, buttons and list views). Note that the challenge of control integration is addressed by providing an

---

[18] XML is not what I consider a *convenient* concrete syntax. It is more like a serialization format.

[19] Often, languages are much more strict about constraints, type systems or the semantics of instance documents, so when going from a data format to a language, it is likely that these aspects will have to be strengthened as well.

IDE for manipulating programs written in one or more extensible languages. Traditional control integration is not required[20].

Extensible Languages   Over the last few years the language engineering community has made a lot of progress in terms of language modularization, extension and composition (discussed in Section 7.5). Existing languages can be extended in a modular fashion, i.e., without invasively changing the base language; independently developed languages can be used together in a single program (i.e. extensions can be composed); and languages that have not been intended for composition at the time they were developed can nonetheless be used together in a single program (language embedding). This modularization, extension and composition comprises the abstract and concrete syntax, the type system, the execution semantics (realized through interpreters and transformations), as well as the IDE support. Using this approach, the *specific languages* in *Generic Tools, Specific Languages* can be realized: based on a set of generic base languages, tailored versions of the languages can be created for specific contexts. The units and state machines examples from the previous section are cases of language extension; the tracing example is a case of embedding.

Syntactic Diversity   If language technologies are used as a substitute for classical tools, languages should be able to use more diverse notations than just linear sequences of characters. Additional notations include tables, mathematical symbols (such as fraction bars, symbols like $\sum$ or $\int$ as well as matrices) and of course graphical diagrams, as well as free-form prose text and perhaps forms. Projectional editors are capable of supporting all of these in a tightly integrated form[21] (textual expressions in tables, mathematical symbols in program code or free-form prose text in C comments). In this way engineering environments can be built that use the wide range of notations expected by users, and known from special-purpose tools available today.

Language Workbenches   Language Workbenches are tools for efficiently developing and using languages (see Sections 6 and 7.5). They provide productive DSLs and APIs to express all aspects of language definitions (concrete and abstract syntax, type systems, semantics) as well as their IDEs (syntax coloring, code completion, go-to-definition, find-usages, refactoring, testing, debugging, searching or visualization). The leading language workbenches (such as MPS, Spoofax[22] or Rascal[23]) have evolved from focusing on the de-

---

[20] I do not suggest to replace database management systems with language workbenches – they don't scale that well, and this makes no sense. As will become clear in this thesis, the data I refer to here is more like metadata: data structure definitions, algorithms, (business) rules, and, in the end, program code or models.

[21] In MPS, graphical notations are still a work in progress, but it is clearly visible on the horizon. Also, the integration of these notational styles has been demonstrated by Intentional Software's Domain Workbench [Simonyi et al., 2006], another projectional editor.

[22] http://strategoxt.org/Spoofax

[23] http://www.rascal-mpl.org/

velopment of one language at a time towards developing sets of related languages: cross-language go-to-definition or find usages is supported, as is language modularization, extension and composition and multi-level transformation. Language workbenches also provide other generic facilities such as model search, visualization, version control integration with diff/merge or support for hyperlinking program output. Because all of these facilities are agnostic relative to the actual language, and can be customized for any given language, they provide a solid foundation for building engineering tools. By hosting the base languages and their extensions in a single language workbench, presentation integration is achieved. Language workbenches are the *generic tools* referred to in the title of this thesis.

By building engineering tools on top of language workbenches, language engineering facilities are also available *to the application developer*. So, in contrast to essentially all other tool development paradigms used today, third parties can use *the same* mechanisms for building their own extensions as were used to implement the basic set of languages provided by the engineering tool. Third parties are *not* at a disadvantage from having to use limited second-class tool or language extension constructs (such as UML profiles [Fuentes-Fernández & Vallecillo-Moreno, 2004] or internal DSLs in languages such as Xtend[24] or Scala[25]). This is the fundamental shift in the design of tools that lets anybody[26] customize tools with *specific languages*, suitable for their particular domain.

In spite of the existing research on language engineering, mbeddr is the first system in which language engineering is attempted at a large scale with a projectional editor. This leads to the following set of research questions.

2.6   RESEARCH QUESTIONS

The introduction pointed out that the validation of *Generic Tools, Specific Languages* rests on two pillars. The first pillar is that the approach actually results in tools that are useful to the end user in the particular domain. This aspect is evaluated for mbeddr in Chapter 5, based on the challenges for embedded software development introduced in Section 3.2. The second pillar evaluates the process of building mbeddr based on language engineering and language workbenches. Chapter 10 performs this task based on the research questions specified below.

Domain-Specific Extensibility   The limitations in the ability to adapt tools to particular domains leads to tools that are badly adapted to domains. This has been illustrated in Sections 2.4, 3.2 and 3.4 for embedded software. One question addressed by this thesis is whether the *Generic Tools, Specific Languages* approach leads to tools that do not have these problems.

---

[24] http://www.eclipse.org/xtend/

[25] http://www.scala-lang.org/

[26] *Anybody* refers to the fact that the tool is open enough for such customizations; developers who want to build customizations of course need certain skills. This is discussed in Chapter 10.

Language Modularity and Projectional Editing   To a degree, language modularity and composition is available with today's tools, as discussed in Chapter 7. A research question is whether language modularization, reuse in new contexts and the ability to combine independently developed extensions work in practice, and whether projectional editing is a suitable foundation.

Tool Scalability   The maturity and usability of MPS for application programmers is evaluated in Section 5.3.2. However, there is an open question about whether MPS also scales for the language developer in terms of handling the complexity associated with the large number of languages for implementing *Generic Tools, Specific Languages* in mbeddr, and whether the tool scales in terms of performance.

Implementation Efforts   Obviously, the *Generic Tools, Specific Languages* approach is only useful if the efforts required for building productive domain-specific tools is reasonable. The development of mbeddr provides a handle for judging these efforts.

Learning Curve   Language workbenches like MPS are sophisticated, multi-faceted tools. To be usable at scale, the effort of learning how to use them and, for example, building extensions for mbeddr, must be reasonable, i.e., at the same level as learning mainstream programming languages.

––––––––––––––––––

Summary — *The remainder of this thesis details* Generic Tools, Specific Languages *as well as mbeddr as an example of the approach. In particular, the next chapter introduces the context of mbeddr: the field of embedded software engineering and its current state of the art. It also outlines how mbeddr addresses important challenges in the field. Part II then looks at the development of embedded software with mbeddr, and Part III investigates the language engineering process used to create mbeddr.*

Application to Embedded Software Development

Abstract — *Embedded software is a fertile ground for the application of* Generic Tools, Specific Languages. *A lot of embedded software is written in C, which, while efficient, lacks robust mechanisms for building meaningful abstractions in a way that retains the efficiency required for embedded software and provided by C. Using modeling tools, on the other hand, often leads to problems with tool integration. This chapter motivates and introduces mbeddr, an extensible set of domain specific languages for embedded software engineering, which was built to validate the* Generic Tools, Specific Languages *approach.*

3.1 EMBEDDED SOFTWARE

mbeddr applies the *Generic Tools, Specific Languages* approach to embedded software development. Wikipedia defines the term *Embedded Software* as follows[1]:

> Embedded software is computer software written to control machines or devices that are not typically thought of as computers. It is typically specialized for the particular hardware that it runs on and has time and memory constraints. [..] Manufacturers 'build in' embedded software in the electronics of cars, telephones, modems, robots, appliances, toys, security systems, pacemakers, televisions and set-top boxes, and digital watches, for example. This software can be very simple, such as lighting controls running on an 8-bit microprocessor and a few kilobytes of memory, or can become very sophisticated in applications such as airplanes, missiles, and process control systems.

An introduction to embedded software is offered by Simon [1999] and Douglass [2010]. A thorough treatment of realtime embedded software is provided by Kopetz [2011].

The amount of software embedded in devices is growing and its value for businesses is increasing rapidly (see, for example, the German National Roadmap for Embedded Systems [Damm et al., 2010]). Developing this embedded software is challenging: in addition to increasingly more complex functional requirements, the software also has to fulfil strict operational requirements. These include reliability (a device may not be accessible for maintenance after deployment), safety (a failure may endanger life or property), efficiency (the resources available to the system may be limited) or realtime constraints (a system may have to run on a strict schedule prescribed by the

---

[1] http://en.wikipedia.org/wiki/Embedded_software

environment). The dependence on specific hardware platforms, the need for hardware/software co-development, product line engineering and the need to integrate mechanical and electrical engineers into the development process further complicates the situation.

3.2 CHALLENGES IN EMBEDDED SOFTWARE

This section investigates a few specific challenges in embedded software. They are the motivation for applying the *Generic Tools, Specific Languages* approach to embedded software. This specific set of challenges is derived from personal experiences and obvious shortcoming in existing tools. However, the challenges are in line with those reported by other authors from different communities (representative examples are Sztipanovits & Karsai [2001]; Lee [2000, 2008]; Broy [2006]; Kuhn et al. [2012]); specific connections are pointed out below. The usefulness of mbeddr is evaluated against these challenges in Section 5.

Abstraction Without Runtime Cost   Abstractions are generally accepted as essential for productively developing maintainable and high-quality software. Domain-specific abstractions provide more concise descriptions of the system under development. Examples in embedded software include dataflow blocks, state machines (see Section 2.4.2), or interfaces and components. On one hand, adequate abstractions have a higher expressive power that leads to programs that are shorter, easier to understand, maintain and analyze and can be better supported by the IDE. On the other hand, by restricting the freedom of programmers, domain-specific abstractions also enable constructive quality assurance. For embedded software, where runtime footprint and efficiency is a prime concern, abstraction mechanisms are needed that can be resolved before or during compilation, and not at runtime. Several publications point out the need to handle the increasing complexity of embedded software systems [Broy, 2006; Woodward & Mosterman, 2007]. Abstraction without runtime cost is a way of addressing these. Lee [2000] emphasizes concurrency, which also require adequate abstractions to keep the complexity under control. Liggesmeyer & Trapp [2009] suggest that model-driven development, which essentially enables meaningful, statically resolved abstractions, is the future of embedded software development.

C Considered Unsafe   A lot of embedded software is developed using C. While C is efficient and flexible, several of C's features are often considered unsafe. For example, unconstrained casting via `void` pointers, using `int`s as Booleans, the weak typing implied by `union`s or excessive use of macros can result in runtime errors that are hard to track down. Consequently, these unsafe features of C are prohibited in safety-critical domains. For example, standards for automotive software development such as MISRA [MISRA, 2004] limit C to a safer language subset. However, most C IDEs are not aware of these and other, organization-specific, restrictions, so they are enforced with separate checkers that are often not well integrated with the IDE. This makes it unnecessarily hard for developers to comply with these restrictions efficiently. An example of such a checker that analyzes memory safety, an issue that is arguably a consequence of the fact that C is inherently unsafe, is discussed by Dhurjati et al. [2003].

Program Annotations For reasons such as safety or efficiency, embedded systems often require additional data to be associated with program elements. Examples include physical units, coordinate systems, data encodings or value ranges for variables. As discussed in Section 2.4.1, these annotations are typically used by specific, often custom-built analysis or generation tools. Since C programs can only capture such data informally as comments, macros or `pragmas`, the C type system and IDE cannot check their correct use in C programs. They may also be stored separately (for example, in XML files) and linked back to the program using names or other weak links. Even with tool support that checks the consistency of these links and helps navigate between code and this additional data, the separation of core functionality and the additional data leads to unnecessary complexity and maintainability problems. Lee [2000] points out robustness as a challenge. Program annotations that support better type checking help with robustness. Broy [2006] points out quality assurance as another challenge, specifically in automotive software.

Static Checks and Verification Embedded systems often have to fulfil strict safety requirements. Industry standards for safety (such as ISO-26262, DO-178B or IEC-61508) require that for high safety certification levels various forms of static analyses are performed on the software, and more and more embedded software systems have to fulfil strict safety requirements [Liggesmeyer & Trapp, 2009]. The static analyses range from simple type checks to sophisticated property checks, for example by model checking [Ivanicic et al., 2005]. Since C is a very flexible and relatively weakly typed language, the more sophisticated analyses are very expensive. Using suitable domain-specific abstractions (such as the state machines shown in Section 2.4.2) leads to programs that can be analyzed much more easily. Static verification also becomes increasingly important in the context of multicore processors. These are increasingly used in embedded software [Levy & Conte, 2009], and the associated concurrent programming challenges have to be mastered. Formal verification techniques can help with proofing the correctness of concurrent programs, for example to detect deadlocks or race conditions [Engler & Ashcraft, 2003]. A related problem is the optimization of systems, for example in the context of deployment [Dearle et al., 2010]. There too it is essential that programs are described at an abstraction level that represents the to-be-optimized program elements as first-class concepts.

Process Support There are at least three cross-cutting and process-related concerns relevant to embedded software development. First, many certification standards (such as those mentioned above) require that code be explicitly linked to requirements such that full traceability is available (see Section 2.4.3). Today, requirements are often managed in external tools (such as

Excel, Clearcase[2] or DOORS[3]) and maintaining traceability to the code is a burden to the developers and often done in an ad hoc way, for example via comments, macros or `pragma`s. Fine-grained traceability is pointed out as a specific challenge by Kuhn et al. [2012].

Second, many embedded systems are developed as part of product lines with many distinct product variants, in which each variant consists of a subset of the (parts of) artifacts that comprise the product line. This variability is usually captured in constraints expressed over program parts such as statements, functions or states. Most existing tools come with their own variation mechanism, if variability is supported at all. Integration between program parts, the constraints and the variant configuration (for example via feature models [Beuche et al., 2004]) is often done through weak links, and with little awareness of the structure and semantics of the underlying language. For example, the C preprocessor, which is often used for this task, performs simple text replacement or removal controlled by the conditions in `#ifdef`s. As a consequence, variant management is a huge source of accidental complexity.

The third process-related concern is documentation. In most projects, various software architecture and design documents have to be created and kept in sync with the code. If they are created using Word or LaTeX, no actual connection exists between the documentation and the code. If parts of the code are renamed or otherwise changed, the documentation has to be kept in sync manually. This is tedious and error-prone. Better tool support is required.

There are additional challenges that are outside the implementation of an embedded software system. These include for example safety analysis with FMEA [Goddard, 1993, 2000] or FTA [Lee et al., 1985], the challenges associated with distributing the development of the systems between the OEM and one or more suppliers, and just scaling the development effort to large and distributed teams. These concerns are beyond the scope of this thesis.

The challenges outlined above lead to heavy reliance on tools in embedded software development:

- *Abstraction Without Runtime Cost* leads to the use of modeling tools and code generation. Since most systems require different abstractions for different parts of the system, a whole set of modeling tools is often used in the same project. Alternatively, adequate abstraction is sacrificed for runtime efficiency, leading to intricate low-level code that is hard to understand, maintain and check (see the next item).

- *C Considered Unsafe* leads to the integration of various additional code checkers or review tools into the process.

- *Program Annotations* are especially challenging, as illustrated in the previous chapter, since keeping this information external to the core system

---

[2] http://www-03.ibm.com/software/products/en/clearcase

[3] http://www-03.ibm.com/software/products/us/en/ratidoor

code makes it hard to keep in sync. All kinds of external synchronization tools are built.

- *Static Checks and Verifications* have two consequences for tooling. First, to perform meaningful verifications, the programs have to be expressed at the right abstraction level with the right abstractions. This leads to the proliferation of diverse modeling tools. Second, the actual analysis and verification tools have to be integrated into the tool chain as well, possibly including transformations to the required input formats.

- *Process Support* is hard because all three – requirements tracing, product line variability and documentation – are cross-cutting, which means that they affect many or all implementation artifacts – and consequently, all the tools used to develop these artifacts.

Many real-world systems require addressing several or all of these challenges. This leads to one of the following two approaches. The first alternative is that sets of specialized tools are used together. Often these tool chains are ad-hoc solutions that do not scale in terms of complexity or program size. In particular, the approach leads to significant challenges in integrating these tools and keeping the data synchronized. The study about the use of model-driven engineering tools [Whittle et al., 2013] cited earlier makes this point:

> The majority of our interviewees were very successful with MDE but all of them either built their own modeling tools, made heavy adaptations of off-the-shelf tools, or spent a lot of time finding ways to work around tools. The only accounts of easy-to-use, intuitive tools came from those who had developed tools themselves for bespoke purposes. Indeed, this suggests that current tools are a barrier to success rather than an enabler [..] Complexity problems are typically associated with off-the-shelf tools. Of particular note is accidental complexity – which can be introduced due to [..] [a] lack of flexibility to adapt the tools to a company's own context [..].

Another alternative is to use integrated engineering tools that address many or all of these challenges. However, this approach has significant problems as well: the tool may not be able to handle all the challenges, or it must be adapted to address additional, domain-specific concerns. Most of today's engineering tools are not extensible in this way, though. Again, citing from Whittle et al. [2013]:

> Our interviews point to a strong need for tailoring of some sort: either tailor the tool to the process, tailor the process to the tool, or build your own tool that naturally fits your own process. Based on our data, it seems that, on balance, it is currently much easier to do the latter. Some tool vendors actively prohibit tailoring to the process, but rather a process is imposed by the tool for business reasons.

The reasons for the limited support for extensibility is twofold. The first reason is mentioned in the quote above. There are often business reasons, in the sense that the tool vendor may not want the tools to be extensible, because it increases support cost or cannibalizes another tool sold by the vendor.

There is probably another reason, though: mainstream engineering tools are typically not built on a foundation that supports meaningful extension like contemporary language workbenches. Of course, this claim is hard to prove: commercial tool vendors do not publish their internal tool architecture. But there are indications: if engineering tools were built on top of a platform that supports meaningful extension, then some vendors would make this accessible to customers. However, as studies such as Whittle et al. [2013] as well as my own experience suggest, this is not the case with mainstream engineering tools. There is one exception: some more recent UML tools, such as MagicDraw[4], use the UML metamodel internally, resulting in reasonable support for UML profiles. However, since MagicDraw only supports (UML-like) graphical notations, it is not a general solution to the problem of extensible tools. Also, many of today's engineering tools have a long history, and their kernels were implemented well before language workbenches were scalable and mature.

Even though language engineering and language workbenches have been around for a long time (see Section 7.5), I am not aware of research that attempts building an engineering tool on top of a language workbench, exploiting the *Generic Tools, Specific Languages* approach. The contribution of this thesis is to evaluate whether this is possible, using embedded software as the example domain.

3.3 THE MBEDDR SOLUTION APPROACH

This thesis proposes applying the *Generic Tools, Specific Languages* approach, which exploits language engineering and language workbenches, instead of the existing approaches discussed in Section 3.4. mbeddr is an implementation of this approach based on JetBrains MPS. The remainder of this thesis describes mbeddr, an extensible set of languages for C-based embedded software development built on top of the JetBrains MPS language workbench. In particular, Section 5.2 investigates how mbeddr addresses the challenges for embedded software introduced at the beginning of this chapter (Section 3.2).

mbeddr provides a fully featured IDE for C and for arbitrary extensions of C as well as any other language developed in mbeddr. Figure 3.1 shows a screenshot. The system is structured into layers and concerns; Figure 3.2 provides an overview. This section only briefly introduces the various languages and extensions; much more detail is provided in Chapter 4.

Implementation Concern   The implementation concern addresses the development of applications based on C. On the core level, mbeddr comes with

---

[4] http://www.nomagic.com/products/magicdraw.html

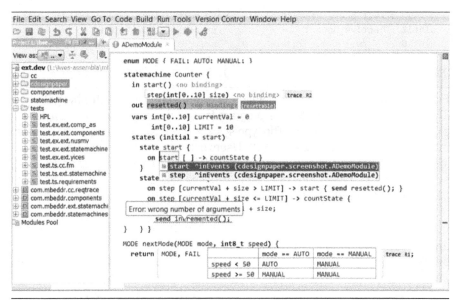

Figure 3.1 An mbeddr example program using five separate but integrated languages. It contains a module with an `enum`, a state machine (`Counter`) and a function (`nextMode`) that contains a decision table. Developers can write regular C code inside state machines and decision tables. The IDE provides code completion for all languages (see the `start`/`stop` suggestions) as well as static error validation (`Error...` hover). The green `trace` annotations are traces to requirements that can be attached to any program element. The red parts with the `{resettable}` next to them are presence conditions: the respective elements are only included in a program variant if the configuration feature `resettable` is selected.

User Extensions	to be defined by users									
Default Extensions	Test Support	Decision Tables							Glossaries	Use Cases & Scenarios
	Compo-nents	Physical Units	State Machines	State Machine Verification	Decision Tables	Contracts				
Core	C core			Model Checking	SMT Solving	Dataflow Analysis	Visual-ization	PLE Variability	Documen-tation	Requirements & Tracing
Platform	JetBrains MPS									
Backend Tool	C Compiler, Debugger and Importer			NuSMV	Yices	CBMC	PlantUML			
	Implementation Concern			Analysis Concern			Process Concern			

Figure 3.2 mbeddr is organized into three concerns and five layers. The concerns address C-based implementation, formal analysis as well as process. The five layers are the MPS platform, the mbeddr core facilities, default extensions as well as the ability for users to create their own extensions. Finally, a number of backend tools (primarily C compilers and verification tools) are integrated.

```
exported struct phase_readings_s {          void initialize(phase_readings_s pr) {
  uint32/W/ active_power;                      pr.active_power = 0 W;
  uint16/V/ V_rms;                             pr.V_rms = 0 V;
  uint16/A/ I_rms;                             pr.I_rms = 0 A;
};                                           }
```

Figure 3.3 mbeddr supports annotation of types and literals with physical units. The type system then checks the program for unit compatibility (for example, assigning V to A is a type error). The type system also calculates with units, so when multiplying V and A, this results in W. Users can define custom units (such as the V or A in the example above) in terms of predefined SI base units (for an example, see Section 4.3). Finally, unit definitions can also include value conversions (as in $°F \Leftrightarrow °C$), which can be used in C programs.

an implementation of C in MPS. There are a few minor differences to C99, and the preprocessor is not exposed to the user. On the default extensions layer, the implementation concern comes with C extensions for interfaces (Figure 3.4) and components (Figure 9.6), state machines (Figure 3.6) and physical units (Figure 3.3), among others. The user extensions layer is by definition empty; users can easily extend the C core as well as any of the default extensions. The implementation concern also ships with an extensible debugger that is able to debug on the level of the extensions, so the abstractions do not break down when debugging becomes necessary. Finally, mbeddr also supports importing existing header and implementation files, to support interoperability with legacy libraries or implementation code. At the foundation layer, the implementation concern relies on a C compiler, a C debugger and tools for importing existing C code into mbeddr. By default, mbeddr uses the gcc compiler, the gdb debugger and the Eclipse CDT for analyzing and importing textual C code.

```
exported c/s interface Orienter {
  int16 heading()
    post(0) result >= 0 && result <= 359
  void orientTowards(int16 heading, uint8 speed, DIRECTION dir)
    pre(0) heading >= 0 && heading <= 359
}
```

Figure 3.4 Client/server interfaces are sets of operations, which each have typed arguments and a return type (mbeddr also has sender/receiver interfaces which declare data items). Operations can specify contracts. These include pre-conditions (which must be true when the operation is called) and post-conditions (which must hold when the operation finishes; result is a keyword that represents the return value of the function). In addition, protocol state machines are also supported (not shown). These specify the valid call sequence of operations (for example, in a file system interface, open() must be called before read()). Contracts can be checked statically via bounded C-level model checking and at runtime.

34

```
exported component DLT645GetMeterConfigurationCommand extends nothing {
  provides IDLT645HostCommandHandler getMeterConfigurationCommandHandler

  boolean getMeterConfigurationCommandHandler_processCommand(
      Dlt645Message* request, Dlt645Message* response)
    <= op getMeterConfigurationCommandHandler.processCommand {

    uint8* tx8 = &response->payload.uint8[response->idx];

    tx8[0] = NUM_PHASES;
    tx8[1] = NEUTRAL_MONITORED;
    tx8[2] = PHASE_CORRECTION_SUPPORT | RTC_SUPPORT | CORRECTED_RTC_SUPPORT | TEMPERATURE_SUPPORT;
    tx8[3] = MEASURES_ACTIVE_POWER | MEASURES_APPARENT_POWER | MEASURES_VRMS | MEASURES_IRMS |
        MEASURES_POWER_FACTOR | MEASURES_MAINS_FREQUENCY | MEASURES_QUADRATURE_REACTIVE_POWER;
    tx8[4] = hex<00>;

    response->length += 5;
    return true;
  } runnable getMeterConfigurationCommandHandler_processCommand
} component DLT645GetMeterConfigurationCommand
```

Figure 3.5 Components are modular units of behavior. They expose their services
via provided interfaces (cf. Figure 3.4). They can also express required interfaces,
which means they can invoke operations on them. Components can be instantiated, and each required interface is connected to a provided interface of another
instance. Operations from provided interfaces are implemented via runnables. In
fact, runnables can be triggered by other events in addition to receiving calls on
provided interfaces, including a timer and during initialization. This trigger mechanism is extensible, so domain-specific triggers can be hooked in.

Analysis Concern   This concern adds static analyses to some of the default extensions provided by the implementation concern. The analysis itself
is performed by an existing external tool. However, mbeddr integrates the
tool tightly by (a) providing language abstractions to conveniently describe
behavior that can be analyzed, (b) translating this description to the input of
the analysis tool, (c) running the tool, and (d) lifting the output of the tool
back to the original abstraction level, to make it easier to understand for the
user. The integrated analyses are based on symbolic model checking, SMT
solving and C-level model checking. Specifically, the following analyses are
available[5].

State machines can be checked with a symbolic model checker. This ver-
ifies a set of default properties and optional user-defined properties. State
machines are checked for conformance to these properties. The implementation is based on the NuSMV[6] model checker. Decision tables (see the bottom of Figure 3.1 for an example) can be checked for completeness (all input

---

[5] The analysis tools themselves are implemented in a way that makes it relatively easy to use
them for checking other suitable behaviors. In essence, their input languages and the tooling to
invoke the tool are part of the mbeddr core. Other behavioral descriptions can be analyzed by
transforming them to these languages. This is why the analyses discussed above are considered
default extensions.

[6] http://nusmv.fbk.eu/

```
[verifiable]
statemachine Counter initial = initialState {
  var bounded_int[0..MAX] currentVal = 0
  var bounded_int[0..MAX] LIMIT = 10

  in start() <no binding>
  in step(bounded_int[0..10] size) <no binding>

  out someEvent(bounded_int[0..MAX] x, boolean b) => handle_someEvent
  out resetted() => resetted

  state initialState {
    on start [ ] -> countState { send someEvent(MAX, true && false || true); }
  }
  state countState {
    on step [currentVal + size > LIMIT] -> initialState { send resetted(); }
    on step [currentVal + size <= LIMIT] -> countState { currentVal = currentVal + size; }
    on start [ ] -> initialState {  }
  }
}
```

Figure 3.6 State machines define `in` events that can be triggered explicitly by C code or implicitly when they are bound to, for example, interrupts, as well as `out` events which can be bound to external code and fired from within a state machine. State machines also define states and transitions. States can be nested and have entry and exit actions. Transitions refer to an `in` event as a trigger, may have a guard condition (a Boolean C expression) and optionally contain a transition action. State machines can be executed by transforming them to C code, and can be statically checked using the integrated symbolic model checker.

value combinations are covered) and consistency (for each set of input values, only one result value is possible). The analysis is performed by the Yices SMT solver[7]. Feature model configurations are checked for consistency: feature models contain constraints that cannot be evaluated by "just looking"; the Yices SMT solver is used to check these constraints. Finally, interface contracts can be checked statically. As Figure 3.4 shows, interfaces can specify pre- and post-conditions (based on the design by contract approach [Meyer, 1992]) as well as protocol state machines that specify the valid invocation order of interface operations. These contracts can be checked for each implementing component via CBMC[8], a C-level model checker.

Process Concern   The process concern includes cross-cutting facilities that are useful when integrating mbeddr into the development process. They are generic in the sense that they can be integrated with arbitrary other languages, such as all the default and user-defined C extensions. mbeddr supports requirements engineering, product line variability and documentation.

The requirements engineering support provides a language for describing requirements. Each requirement has an ID, a short description, an optional

---

7 http://yices.csl.sri.com/
8 http://www.cprover.org/cbmc/

36

```
[#define LOW_THRESHOLD = 100;]-> implements LowThreshold
[#define HIGH_THRESHOLD = 200;]-> implements HighThreshold

uint32 limit(uint32 value) {                    -> implements LimitValuesToThresholds
  if (value > HIGH_THRESHOLD) {
    return HIGH_THRESHOLD;
  } else if ( value < LOW_THRESHOLD ) {
    return LOW_THRESHOLD;
  }
  return value;
} limit (function)
```

Figure 3.7 The green labels are requirements traces. These are essentially typed pointers to requirements. They can be attached to any program element expressed in any language, thereby enabling ubiquitous traceability. While the default target of a trace is a requirement, the facility is extensible to enable tracing to other artifacts, such as function models.

longer prose, a priority and any number of additional attributes. Require-ments can also be nested and express relationships to other requirements. Requirements traces [Jarke, 1998] can be attached to any program element expressed in any language (see Figure 3.7), supporting ubiquitous traceabil-ity. The requirements facility also supports reverse-tracing, so users can find out which parts of implementation artifacts depend on any particular require-ment. Importantly, the requirements tooling is extensible: arbitrary additional data, expressed in any language, can be added to a requirement. In this way, support for use cases, collaborations and scenarios has been added in a mod-ular way.

mbeddr's support for product line engineering can be split into two parts. First, there is a formalism for defining feature models and configurations based on these feature models. This represents a purely conceptual descrip-tion of variability, independent of any particular implementation. The second part maps the variability expressed in feature models to arbitrary implemen-tation artifacts by using presence conditions [Czarnecki & Antkiewicz, 2005]. These are Boolean expressions over features that determine how the program element they are attached to depends on the features selected for a given vari-ant. If the expression evaluates to false, the element they are attached to is removed during generation. As a consequence of MPS' projectional editor, the presence conditions can also be evaluated in the editor. This allows program variants to be viewed and edited. While presence conditions are static and work for any language, there is also C-specific support to evaluate variability at runtime.

Visualization provides a facility to render diagrams. The facility relies on PlantUML[9] as the backend, which supports most of UML's diagrams (an ex-ample is shown in Figure 3.8). The diagrams are shown directly inside the mbeddr IDE; by clicking on a node in the diagram, the respective source node

---

[9] http://plantuml.sourceforge.net/

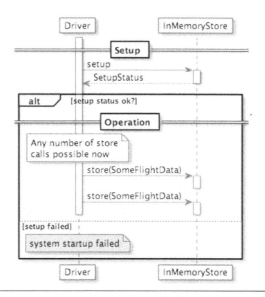

Figure 3.8 The visualizations based on PlantUML support class diagrams, sequence diagrams, state charts, activity diagrams and others. Any language concept can contribute a diagram, so the system is extensible.

in the MPS editor is selected, supporting navigability between diagram and code. Any program element can contribute visualizations, making the facility generically usable.

The documentation aspect supports writing prose documents as part of an mbeddr project, exportable as HTML or LaTeX. What makes this aspect worthwhile is that it supports close integration with program elements: program elements can be referenced (with real references that are renamed if the element itself is renamed) and program code can be embedded as text or as an image. The embedded code is updated whenever the document is regenerated, avoiding manual synchronization of the documentation. In the same way visualizations (as described in the previous paragraph) can be embedded, and also updated whenever the document is re-rendered to LaTeX or HTML.

3.4 THE STATE OF THE ART

This section discusses the state of the art for embedded software development tools and compares them – where applicable – to mbeddr. The section looks at industry mainstream approaches, the use of DSLs in embedded software, alternative ways of extending C and formal analyses.

3.4.1 *Mainstream Approaches*

Embedded systems are highly diverse, ranging from rather small systems such as refrigerators, vending machines or intelligent sensors through building automation to highly complex and distributed systems such as aerospace or automotive control systems. This diversity is also reflected in the constraints on their respective software development approaches and cost models. For example, flight control software is developed over many years, has a large budget, an expert team and emphasizes safety and reliability. The less sophisticated kinds of embedded systems mentioned above are developed in a few months, often with severe budget constraints, by smaller teams and often with less know-how about software engineering (many developers are electrical or mechanical engineers by training). The requirements for safety and reliability are much less pronounced. The tools and approaches used to develop these systems reflect these differences. The most important ones are discussed in this section.

Safety Tools   Highly safety-critical systems (those with a SIL-level 3 or 4 as defined in IEC 61504[10]) are often developed with tools such as SCADE[11]. These tools are certified, i.e., it is legally allowed to use such tool in the development of safety-critical software *without* manually reviewing and/or certifying the generated code. These tools are typically expensive and not extensible – it is currently beyond the state of the art to combine extensibility with the need for certification. Safety tools also support a number of artifacts beyond code, such as fault tree analysis (FTA), failure mode and effects analysis (FMEA), strict requirement tracing, safety case documentation and all kinds of advanced analyses based on these artifacts and the code.

mbeddr is not explicitly suited for developing safety-critical software: it does not yet generate MISRA-compliant code and it does not yet address the additional artifacts described above. However, by using the domain-specific abstractions, integrated formal verifications and cross-cutting requirements tracing, mbeddr is certainly better suited for safety-critical software than pure C. However, the qualification or certification of the system has to happen on the level of the generated C code.

Standard Architectures   Systems that are based on a standardized architecture or middleware, such as AUTOSAR[12] in the automotive domain, are often developed with tools that are specific to the standard (such as Artop[13] in the case of AUTOSAR). These tools directly support the abstractions relevant to the standard architecture. In the case of AUTOSAR, these abstractions include interfaces, components, descriptions of electronic control unit (ECU) hardware and the deployment of software components onto ECUs. Tools for standards such as AUTOSAR typically rely on code generation and middleware-specific frameworks and libraries for execution. Many standards like AUTOSAR address the overall system architecture and the deployment model. They make no assumptions about the actual implementation of components in terms of behavior or algorithms. This is because the abstractions

---

[10] http://www.61508.org/

[11] http://www.esterel-technologies.com/products/scade-suite/

[12] http://www.autosar.org/

[13] http://www.artop.org/

required to describe the implementation are more specific than just "automotive software". For example, a window lifting controller can be expressed as a simple state machine, whereas a radar that detects pedestrians requires sophisticated image processing algorithms. More specialized tools are used for these aspects, which then have to be integrated with AUTOSAR tools. Many of those tools use model-driven development techniques as well (see below).

mbeddr is not specific to any of these standards. However, as a consequence of the extensibility, standard-specific or architecture-specific abstractions can be added easily. For example, as part of the LW-ES research project, BMW Car IT is currently implementing an extension for the mbeddr components language to make it compatible with AUTOSAR, so that BMW can evaluate mbeddr. In addition, mbeddr can be adapted to more specific domains. While state machines for implementing the window lifter are already available, custom extensions such as vectors, matrices and their respective operators can be added to support image processing.

Model-Driven Development Model-driven development and automatic code generation[14] is particularly well-suited for systems that are highly structured in terms of a particular implementation paradigm in which developers can express application structures and behavior in terms of high-level abstractions related to the paradigm. As mentioned before, using higher-level abstractions leads to more concise programs and simplified fault detection using static analysis techniques. An example is the Simulink Design Verifier[15].

The most versatile and widespread approaches include state-based behavior (Figure 3.9) and dataflow block diagrams (see Figure 3.10). The former can be used to implement discrete behavior (as in the window lifter mentioned above), whereas the latter are particularly well suited for continuous systems (such as the control systems involved in engine control). Prominent examples of these kinds of tools are Statemate (mentioned earlier), ASCET-SD[16] or Matlab/Simulink[17].

Like many other tools discussed so far, the mainstream tools used in this way are not particularly extensible (for example, the community has been struggling to integrate Matlab/Simulink with tools for managing product line variability [Beuche & Weiland, 2009; Yoshimura et al., 2008; Kliemannel et al., 2010]). Developers are forced to cast their (potentially quite specific) requirements into the abstractions provided by the tool. For example, I have seen dataflow models with dozens or hundreds of "parallel running signals" because the modeling tool does not support the creation of "composite signals", or just completely different abstractions for implementing a particular kind of system.

---

[14] There is some confusion about terminology here. What is called *model-driven development* in the mainstream is often called *model-based development* or *auto-code generation* in embedded software. This thesis sticks to the mainstream terminology.

[15] http://www.mathworks.com/products/sldesignverifier

[16] http://www.etas.com/

[17] http://www.mathworks.com/products/simulink

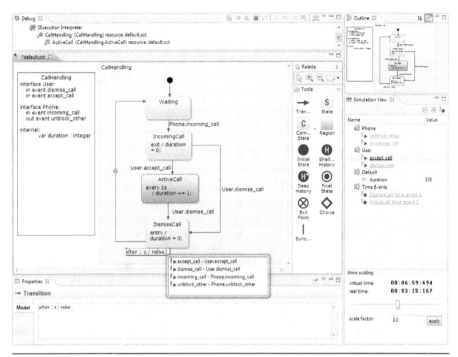

Figure 3.9 State-based systems use discrete state and the transitions between them as the core abstraction. Transitions are triggered by events. A state has entry and exit actions, and, optionally, transitions also have actions. Transitions can also have guard conditions, which are Boolean expressions that have to be true for a transition to fire as an event comes in. State machines are suitable for describing (potentially complex) discrete behavior, in particular if the state machine formalism supports hierarchical states. State machines can also be simulated and are straightforward to integrated into debuggers. Two major execution modes are used. The first one uses the events to trigger the state machine. The second one uses a timer to trigger the state machine at regular intervals, and it is then checked whether events are present in an event queue.

mbeddr can be seen as a flavor of model-driven development, in the sense that developers work at higher levels of abstraction and code generation is used to translate these abstractions to C code. Formal methods that exploit the abstractions for meaningful analyses are also supported. However, there are two important differences compared to mainstream model-driven development tools. First, mbeddr is fully open, so additional abstractions can be added at any time. Second, because everything is directly integrated with C, there is no particular challenge in integrating different independent extensions in terms of tooling. In some rare cases there may be semantic problems; this is an example of the well-known problem of feature interaction [Calder et al., 2003]. Currently mbeddr does not support graphical notations for state machines or dataflow, as a consequence of MPS' inability to work with graph-

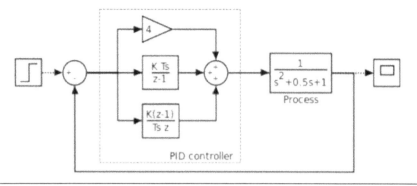

Figure 3.10 The dataflow paradigm is centered around data values "flowing" through a system. In dataflow block diagrams, data values flow from block to block; calculations or transformations are encapsulated in the blocks, and the lines represent dependencies – the output of one blocks "flows" into the input slot of another block. There are three different execution modes. The first one considers the data values as continuous signals. At the time when one of the inputs to a block changes, all output values are recalculated. The change triggers the recalculation, and the recalculation ripples through the graph. The second mode considers the data values as quantized, unique messages. A new output message is calculated only if a message is available for all inputs. The recalculation synchronizes on the availability of a message at each input, and upon recalculation, these messages are consumed. The third approach is time-triggered. Once again, the inputs are understood to be continuous signals, and a scheduler determines when a new calculation should be performed. The scheduler also makes sure that the calculation "ripples through from left to right" in the correct order. This model is typically used in embedded systems.

ical notations. However, MPS will get support for graphical notations in 2014, at which time these notations will be added to mbeddr.

Manually-Written C Code   According to a study by Ebert & Jones [2009], the state of the practice is that 80% of companies implement embedded software in C. In particular, the following kinds of systems are often implemented in C:

1. Systems that are not very safety-critical (SIL 1-2) are often implemented in C. Higher SIL-level systems are often implemented with SCADE (mentioned above) or with Ada, for which certified compilers exit. There are safer dialects of C, (basically restricted sub-languages), that make C more suitable for safety-critical systems. Examples include Cyclone [Jim et al., 2002] and the Misra C standard [MISRA, 2004].

2. As mentioned, most modeling tools address one particular behavioral paradigm, such as state-based or dataflow-oriented. When multiple paradigms must be integrated in a single system, using a set of modeling

tools in one project is often not an option because of the problems with tool integration. C is often used as the fallback, the lowest common denominator.

3. Systems that require a lot of low-level programming, such as device drivers, are particularly well-suited to implementation in C. With pointers, pointer arithmetic and direct access to memory-mapped devices or I/O ports, C is very well suited for these low-level tasks.

Summing up, C is good at expressing low-level algorithms and produces efficient binaries, but its limited support for defining custom abstractions can lead to code that is hard to understand, maintain and extend. So, while C actually is a good fit for the third case listed above, it is not such a good fit for the first, and in particular, the second case. Here, C is used mostly used because of a lack of alternatives.

mbeddr retains all the low-level capabilities of C (item 3), because all of C is available in mbeddr (unless parts of it are explicitly restricted in order to obtain a safer subset). As a consequence of mbeddr's extensibility, arbitrary domain-specific extensions can be created (supporting items 1 and 2) with very little effort (discussed in Section 10.1 and the rest of Chapter 10). These extensions include full IDE support, making them accessible to mainstream developers. The fact that extensions are *directly* integrated with C removes one of the biggest challenges in model-driven development, the Customization Cliff (introduced by Steve Cook[18]):

> Once you step outside of what is covered by your DSL, you plunge down a cliff onto the rocks of the low-level platform.

If DSLs are built as incremental, layered extensions of a base language, users can drop down to the next less-abstract language in the stack. In the worst case, they can always use the facilities of the base language *without* having to switch the tool and *without* facing challenges in integrating the DSL code and the base language code.

Manually-Written C++ Code   Based on private conversations of the author with developers industry (including from Bosch, BMW and Harmann Becker), complex embedded software that is not targeted to especially small target platforms is increasingly developed with C++. Examples include entertainment and navigation systems in cars. However, overall, C++ still plays a relatively limited role in embedded software development. This is due to three major reasons.

1. There is still the perception that C++ is "fat and slow". While this is not necessarily true today, it was true in the early days of C++ compilers, and these perceptions from the past still linger on. And in fact, when using C++, special attention has to be paid to the overhead incurred. For

---

[18] blogs.msdn.com/b/ stevecook/archive/ 2005/12/16/504609.aspx

example, polymorphic method calls do incur a (limited) performance penalty, and a degree of non-determinism in terms of execution speed. To do object-oriented programming well, dynamic memory allocation is useful, which is often at odds with the need to allocate all memory at system startup to avoid out-of-memory errors at runtime. And excessive use of templates, while useful in terms of execution speed, can lead to bloated program sizes. There are subsets of C++ (such as Embedded C++ [19]) that limit the overhead, but they are used relatively rarely, as Bjarne Stroustrup explains on his website[20].

2. For many target platforms, there are no C++ compilers, so C++ cannot be used at all. C++-specific libraries may also not exist, and using C++ with C libraries may not be very useful.

3. Many embedded software developers are (former) electrical or mechanical engineers, and they are not necessarily familiar with some of the advanced software engineering concepts supported by C++. They essentially develop "C in C++", which does not yield big benefits.

mbeddr currently does not support C++[21]. However, it supports many of the same software engineering concepts. For example, mbeddr's components support essentially what C++ classes are used for in embedded programming: a clear separation between interface and implementation, and the ability to have different implementations for the same interface. However, mbeddr supports this via translation to C source, so no C++ compilers are necessary for the target device. In addition, special care has been taken to not incur a performance overhead. For example, mbeddr components can be translated to support polymorphism (which incurs a limited runtime overhead), but a second translation option exist that does not support polymorphism (avoiding the overhead, but also limiting the flexibility of users). Another use case of C++ is to use template meta programming to create compile-time "language extensions". mbeddr supports developing language extensions natively, so there is no need to use templates for this purpose. In contrast to templates, mbeddr's language extensions provide much better IDE support and avoid the cryptic messages in the case of an error for which template meta programming is notorious.

3.4.2 *DSLs in Embedded Software*

It is obvious from the above discussions that domain-specific abstractions can be useful in embedded software. Studies such as those by Broy et al. [2011] and Liggesmeyer & Trapp [2009] show that DSLs substantially increase productivity in embedded software development. Empirical studies also found

---

[19] http://www.caravan.net/ec2plus/

[20] http://www.stroustrup.com/bs_faq.html#EC++

[21] A first prototype of C++ is currently being developed, tackling mainly the challenges of templates and operator overloading.

that there is a need for tools that are more specific for an application domain yet flexible enough to allow adaptation [Graaf et al., 2003; Liggesmeyer & Trapp, 2009]. And in fact, DSLs are increasingly used for embedded software [Axelsson et al., 2010; Hammond & Michaelson, 2003; Andalam et al., 2009]. Examples include Feldspar [Axelsson et al., 2010], a DSL for digital signal processing; Hume [Hammond & Michaelson, 2003], a DSL for real-time embedded systems, as well as the approach discussed by Gokhale et al. [2008], which uses DSLs for addressing quality of service concerns in middleware for distributed realtime systems. All these DSLs generate C code, but the DSL program is not syntactically integrated with C. This separation is useful if the the DSL code and the C code actually express separate concerns in the domain. However, it is likely that at least some of these DSLs should have been integrated syntactically with C, but were not, because of the technical difficulties of doing so.

mbeddr supports arbitrary degrees of syntactic integration with C. This includes external DSLs that have no syntactic integration and generate C code; DSLs which are syntactically separate, but *reference* C program elements; and DSLs which are syntactically embedded into C code, where the abstractions are typically generated down to C as well (a systematic discussion of language composition approaches can be found in Chapter 7). The last approach in particular is used extensively in mbeddr.

Syntactically extending C to adapt it to a particular problem domain is not a new idea. For example, Palopoli et al. [1999] present an extension of C for realtime applications, Boussinot [1991] proposes an extension for reactive systems, and Ben-Asher et al. [1996] present an extension for shared memory parallel systems. However, these are all *specific* extensions of C, typically created by invasively changing the C grammar. They also do not include IDE support for the extensions.

mbeddr is fundamentally different. While it builds heavily on domain-specific abstractions, it provides an *open framework* and tool for defining *modular*, incremental extensions of C, as well as the IDE. This is enabled by exploiting the underlying language workbench[22].

An extensible version of C has also been implemented in the Xoc extensible C compiler described by Cox et al. [2008], which supports arbitrary extensions. It uses a parser-based approach and source-to-source translation to transform modular C extensions into regular C code. In contrast to mbeddr, Cox' approach is limited by the fact that it uses a traditional, parser-based approach (only textual notations are supported, and the risk of ambiguities in present) and that it does not address IDE extension.

---

[22] The specific C extensions discussed above are all good examples of extensions that could be implemented as language extensions in mbeddr, if the need arises.

There are other ways of addition abstractions to C programs. The most wide-spread are libraries and macros. As discussed in this section, language extension is more powerful than these alternatives.

Libraries and Frameworks   Libraries rely on defining functions that can be called by the client program. This almost always incurs runtime overhead (some functions may be inlined, which reduces the performance hit but increases the program size). More advanced libraries and frameworks require further indirection through function pointers. While adding additional indirections is not always a problem, it can be in some time-critical scenarios. Language extensions can lead to low runtime overhead because they are statically translated to C and can make use of optimizations to generate efficient code (just like compilers). In addition, a library cannot extend the type system of C and extend the IDE in terms of custom constraints, syntax highlighting or refactorings. Language extension based on language workbenches can provide all of these. Finally, by making abstractions first-class by using language extension, the degrees of freedom available to users for implementing functionality can be restricted in accordance with the extension language definition. While this sounds like a drawback, it has important advantages with regard to the analyzability of the code. For example, it is relatively easy to translate a first-class representation of a state machine to the input of a symbolic model checker and run it in a relatively short time. Verifying a state machine implemented via `switch`-statements or cross-referencing arrays (as shown in Section 2.4.2) requires model checking on the C code level. This is much more expensive because of the much bigger state space of the C program. It is also harder to express domain-level properties, since they have to be expressed in terms of the low-level implementation, and it is hard to make sense of the output of the model checker in terms of the abstraction level of the state machines. In short, language extension can provide much better support for analyzing code than library-based extension. A final limitation of libraries is that the syntax cannot be adjusted. While other programming languages (such as Scala, Ruby or Xtend) allow programmers to design libraries that can use syntax that, for example, approximates the state machine syntax shown in Section 2.4.2, this is not feasible with C.

Macros   In contrast to function calls, macros are resolved statically by the preprocessor, which avoids runtime performance overhead, but may increase the size of the binary. Macros have many of the same disadvantages as libraries. The syntax can only be adapted in a very limited way; they essentially look like function calls. When defining macros, the static type checker and the IDE support cannot be adapted easily along the way. In addition, macros do not even perform a type check when they are called. The biggest problem with macros is, however, that they operate on the text level. Macros can perform any syntactic substitution, but there is no guarantee that the resulting C code is syntactically correct and can be compiled. Especially when several macros are used or macros calls are nested, it is easy to create C code that contains errors; some of them can be subtle, as a consequence of the mistaken use of parentheses (which means that although the code will compile, the result of the computation is wrong because of "different" operator precedence). Another problem is that many IDEs cannot deal well with macros, which leads to code that cannot be effectively navigated in the IDE. A similar problem exists with analysis tools.

In today's state of the art, macros are used extensively. For example, whole macro libraries have been developed, such as Protothreads [Dunkels et al., 2006] (which implements lightweight threads), SynchronousC [von Hanxleden, 2009] and PRET-C [S. Andalam, 2010] (both adding constructs for deterministic concurrency and preemption). These are all good candidates for abstractions that could be reified as language extensions based on mbeddr.

Using libraries or macros is by no means always bad, because language extension also has a significant drawback: building an extension requires language engineering skills; many application developers will not be able to do this. So language engineering should only be used in those cases where its advantages (flexible syntax, type system support, static translation, formal analysis) are useful. In other cases, in-program abstractions such as functions or components should be used.

3.4.4 *Formal Analyses*

An important part of mbeddr is the support for directly integrated formal analyses. The analyses operate on certain domain-specific extensions of C, which makes their implementation more efficient compared to analyses running on low-level C code. Execution of the analyses is directly integrated into the mbeddr IDE, and the results of the analyses are represented in terms of the abstraction level of the extension, not on the level of the analysis tool. This makes verification much more accessible to "normal" developers. This section compares this approach to other approaches in this space.

General Approach   Formal analysis techniques for general-purpose languages are supported by a range of tools. Some academic approaches are discussed by Karthik & Jayakumar [2005], Mine [2011] and Puccetti [2010]. Commercial tools include Polyspace [23], the Escher C Verifier[24], Klocwork[25] or Spec# [Naumann & Barnett, 2004]. However, experiences show that a substantial amount of code annotations are often needed to capture the constraints or domain-level semantics of the code and make meaningful analyses feasible. The reason is that when encoding domain-specific abstractions in general-purpose languages, much of the domain semantics is lost. Trying to analyze the code for properties relative to these domain semantics requires users to "add back in" the semantics that were lost when encoding the abstraction in

---

[23] http://www.mathworks.de/products/polyspace/

[24] http://www.eschertech.com/products/ecv.php

[25] http://www.klocwork.com/

the lower-level language. The following piece of code shows a `max` function with annotations to make it analyzable with the Frama-C[26] Jessie plugin (this example is taken from the Jessie user guide):

```
/*@ requires \valid(i) && \valid(j);
  @ requires r == \null || \valid(r);
  @ assigns *r;
  @ behavior zero:
  @ assumes r == \null;
  @ assigns \nothing;
  @ ensures \result == 1;
  @ behavior normal:
  @ assumes \valid(r);
  @ assigns *r;
  @ ensures *r == ((*i < *j) ? *j : *i);
  @ ensures \result == 0;
  @ */
int max(int* r, int* i, int* j) {
  if (!r) return 1;
  *r = (*i < *j) ? *j : *i;
  return 0;
}
```

Adding these annotations and constraints is tedious and error-prone. In the above example they are longer than the actual implementation and they are added in comments, so there is not even IDE support. The annotations are also often based on formalisms that are not necessarily simple for normal developers to use. Consequently, tools like the ones mentioned above are only used in highly safety-critical contexts, and only by specialists.

The obvious alternative, avoiding GPLs altogether and moving completely to DSLs like state machines, first-order logic or linear algebra, has proven to be impractical in many cases because their expressivity can be too limited for real- world problems, and because of the challenge of integrating the various formalisms and their tools in a single development project.

mbeddr provides a middle ground between these two alternatives. It simplifies some of the analyses provided by existing verification tools by expressing the behavior with extensions to C that embody relevant semantics directly, avoiding the need to reverse engineer the semantics for static analysis. For example, by expressing state-based behavior directly using state machines instead of a low-level C implementation, the state space relevant to a model checker can be reduced significantly, making model checking less costly. However, since the respective analyzable fragments are embedded into C, their semantic integration with the rest of the C-based system is not a problem. The same is true for tool integration, which is provided by the language workbench for all of the languages and extensions. The input to the analyzer is created by generating the respective formalism automatically.

---

[26] http://frama-c.com/jessie

However, this approach does not fundamentally solve the problem that some formalisms are restricted in terms of expressiveness for real-world problems. For example, to be able to run a symbolic model checker on a state machine, the state machine cannot embed arbitrary C statements in its actions, since these cannot be checked by a symbolic model checker. mbeddr addresses this challenge in the following way. State machines can be marked as `verifiable`, expressing the user's intent to verify it with a model checker. If a state machine is marked in this way, additional constraints prevent the use of problematic language features. For example, in the case of actions, users cannot embed C statements in the actions. Instead they can only fire *out events*, which can be bound to C functions or other pieces of executable code. Properties verified by the model checker can only refer to the occurrence of an out event, but cannot take into account the effects the code to which the event is bound may have on the overall system. While this limits the power of the approach, it also makes it practicable[27]. The overall approach relies on the concept that users have to make a conscious decision about whether they want verifiability or not. In the former case, they may have to live with a limited language, while in the latter case, they can use the full power of C or its extensions. This decision can be made separately for each (potentially verifiable) program part.

Jackson & Sztipanovits [2006] define a methodology for constructing programs that are analyzable. In the correct-by-construction methodology programs are continuously checked by using only polynomial time algorithms. In this manner the verification is done continuously and is an integral part of the development process. mbeddr's integration of verification tools can be seen as a pragmatic operationalization of the correct-by-construction approach in which the analyzable program fragments are incrementally extended by using suitable analyzable language extensions.

Usability of Formal Analyses   Today, formal analyses are only used by a small group of expert developers, usually in safety-critical contexts [Corbett et al., 2000]. This is true even though the approach scales to reasonable program sizes, and can also be beneficial to "normal developers". The major problem with formal analyses in practice is usability. The problem can be separated into three challenges (as discussed by Loer & Harrison [2002]). First, it is difficult to formalize the problem in the language of the verification tool (known as the model construction problem); second, it is difficult to formalize the properties to be verified, and, third, once the result is obtained (at the abstraction level of the verification tool) it is difficult to lift it and interpret it at the domain level. All these challenges are due to the gap between domain-specific abstractions and how they are reflected in programs on the one hand and the abstractions of the analysis tool on the other.

mbeddr addresses these problems by letting users use suitable domain-specific abstractions to write the code. For analysis, mbeddr automatically

---

[27] mbeddr also includes C-level model checkers that can address effects produced by arbitrary C code.

translates this domain-specific code into the input formalism of a verification tool. For some formalisms, default properties are automatically checked, so users do not have to write any properties at all (for example, in consistency checking for decision tables). For other verification techniques, users are able to specify custom properties in addition to the default properties. For state machines, mbeddr provides a high-level, user friendly language for specifying such properties based on the patterns discussed by Dwyer et al. [1999]. While this may remove some of the expressive power of the actual input language (LTL or CTL for model checking), it makes writing properties much easier for developers – a trade-off that works for mbeddr and its users. Finally, the results of running the verification tool are lifted back to the abstraction level of the original domain-specific description of the behavior. This makes the interpretation of the results much simpler.

The idea of integrating formal verification techniques into IDEs is not new. For example, there is significant work to integrate C model checkers into IDEs such as Eclipse or MS Visual Studio [Beyer et al., 2004; Fehnker et al., 2007; Ball et al., 2004]. In contrast to these approaches, mbeddr uses language engineering to embed higher-level, domain-specific descriptions of behaviors directly in the C code, which leads to the benefits discussed in the previous paragraph.

Specific Analyses   The analyses implemented by mbeddr have been well known in the literature for many years, and mbeddr's contribution is not the improvement of these verification techniques. Instead, its contribution is the integration of these analyses with language engineering technologies and the IDE. This way we hope to help achieve a wider application of formal methods with practitioners.

With regards to model-checking state machines, Clarke & Heinle [2000] present early work that translates a fragment of the StateCharts language into the input for the SMV model checker. Arcaini et al. present in detail properties of state machines that represent vulnerabilities and defects introduced by developers that can be automatically verified [Arcaini et al., 2010]. The properties are classified into minimality, completeness and consistency. mbeddr implements checks for these properties by default for each state machine.

With regards to verifying feature models, mbeddr's approach is similar to the one presented by Mendonça et al. [2009].

With regards to checking decision tables, Eles and Lawford propose an approach for defining and analyzing tabular expressions in Simulink similar to mbeddr's analysis of decision tables [Eles & Lawford, 2011]. In addition to using an SMT solver (as mbeddr does), they also use a theorem prover, mainly for dealing with non-linear expressions.

With regards to checking component contracts, there is significant related work on integrating C model checkers into development environments [Beyer et al., 2004; Ball et al., 2004]. There is also work on generating verification properties from higher-level models [Zalila et al., 2012] and to lift the analyses results from the code level back to the model level [Combemale et al.,

2011]. mbeddr is different, mainly in that instead of using separate models to generate verification properties, it uses language extensions as the source. This allows mbeddr to retain the benefits of generating verification conditions from higher-level abstractions, while still supporting tight integration of these abstractions with the rest of the code base. Using higher-level abstractions as the source for the analysis means that deriving the verification conditions is straightforward, and lifting the counter-example back to the higher abstraction level eliminates a significant amount of noise and thereby improves usability. The direct integration of the higher-level abstractions with the rest of the code base means that mbeddr avoids the semantic and tool integration issues that arise when (verifiable) parts of programs are expressed with different formalisms and/or tools than regular C code: in mbeddr, the extensions have clearly defined semantics in terms of C, and the tool integration is seamless.

3.4.5 *Process Aspects*

So far this section has looked at alternative approaches for the implementation and verification aspect of mbeddr. This subsection addresses process-related aspects: the documentation of software systems, the management of requirements and the realization of product line variability.

Documentation   Essentially all mainstream tools, including modeling tools, requirements management tools or other engineering tools, treat prose as an opaque sequence of characters. Direct integration with code, in the form of (deep) references or realtime embedding of code fragments, are typically not supported. An exception are Wiki-based tools, such as Fitnesse for acceptance testing[28]. There, executable test cases are embedded in Wiki code. A big limitation is that there is no IDE support for the (formal) test case description language embedded in the Wiki markup. One major engineering tool that treats prose text respectfully is Mathematica[29]. With its Computable Document Format (CDF) it supports mixing prose with mathematical expressions. It even supports sophisticated type setting and WYSIWYG. Complete books, such as the Mathematica book itself, are written with Mathematica. In contrast, mbeddr does not support WYSIWYG. However, mbeddr documents support integration with arbitrary MPS-based languages, whereas Mathematica supports integration only with its own (fixed) programming language.

Many programming languages have ways of embedding comments; some program elements, typically arguments to function-like constructs, can be referenced from within the comments: Java has JavaDoc, Scala has ScalaDoc and C has Doxygen[30]. Using tools, API reference documentation can be generated from the code comments. However, these tools are limited in that they use regular comments (based on proximity to the documented element), they require

---

[28] http://fitnesse.org/

[29] http://www.wolfram.com/mathematica/

[30] http://www.doxygen.org

special IDE support to synchronize the names of referenced elements and – in contrast to mbeddr – they are not extensible with regard to the kinds of program elements that can be referenced from within the comments. Also, while mbeddr supports documentation comments, it can also be used the other way round: instead of embedding comments in code, mbeddr supports writing documents that reference and embed code. This is important for higher-level design documents.

Another example of an extensible language that supports writing documents that are tightly integrated with code is Racket, with its Scribble [Flatt et al., 2009] language. Racket is a syntax-extensible version of Scheme, and this extensibility is exploited for Scribble. Following their paradigm of *documentation as code*, Scribble supports writing structured documentation (with LATEX-like syntax) as part of Racket. Scribble supports referencing program elements from prose, embedding scheme expressions (which are evaluated during document generation) and embedding prose into code (for JavaDoc-like comments). The main differences between mbeddr's approach and Racket Scribble is that Scribble is implemented as Racket macros, whereas mbeddr's facility is based on projectional editing. Consequently, the range of document styles and syntactic extensions is wider in mbeddr. Also, mbeddr directly supports embedding figures and visualizations.

An alternative way of writing documents that are integrated tightly with code that is often used in book publishing is custom tool chains, typically based on LATEX or Docbook[31]. Program files are referenced by name from within the documents, and custom scripts include the program code during output generation. mbeddr's approach is much more integrated, since, for example, even the references to program fragments are actual (checkable) references and not just names. The overall structure is more robust in terms of referential integrity.

The idea of more closely integrating code and text is not new. The most prominent example if the idea is probably Knuth's literate programming approach [Knuth, 1984], in which code fragments are embedded directly into documents; the code can be compiled and executed. While we have built a prototype with mbeddr that supports this approach, we have found referencing the code from documents (and generating it into the final output) more scalable and useful.

Requirements Engineering   The facilities for collecting prose requirements provided by mbeddr are not especially interesting. What is interesting is the ability to embed DSL programs into requirements, and ubiquitous traceability.

DSLs have traditionally not seen much use in requirements engineering; they are typically associated more with the implementation phase or with software architecture. However, as demonstrated by mbeddr, DSLs, and especially extensible DSLs, can be very useful in requirements engineering, because they support incrementally adding formal abstractions to prose requirements, thereby making requirements incrementally more processable. Other

---

[31] http://www.docbook.org/

tools, for example, itemis' Yakindu Requirements[32] also implement this idea: it also uses (mostly) textual DSLs plus visualization. In contrast to mbeddr, however, extensibility is more limited, since the underlying language workbench (Eclipse Xtext[33]) supports only limited forms of language extension.

Favaro et al. [2012] present an approach to requirements engineering that has some commonalities with mbeddr. Like mbeddr, they have the goal of introducing structured, model-based requirements. Their approach relies on the use of a Wiki enriched by semantic links, and they also provide a requirements browser inside the IDE (Eclipse) supporting some navigation capabilities from the requirement to the artifact (but not vice versa). They emphasize two points: a) the importance of having an adaptable mechanism for requirements, depending not only on the nature of the project, but also on the kind of the requirement, with a lighter process for "non-technical" requirements; b) the fact that requirements and implementation artifacts are intrinsically integrated. mbeddr realizes these two points. In addition, mbeddr provides specific IDE support for any particular kind of formal language embedded into the requirements.

Winkler and von Pilgrim perform a literature review on traceability in the context of model-driven software development [Winkler & Pilgrim, 2010]. They conclude that tracing is rarely used in practice, the most prominent reason being the lack of proper tool support. Lack of tool support is also identified as a major cost driver for traceability by Watkins & Neal [1994]. Today, traceability from code to requirements is mostly done with comments; in some cases specialized tools check the IDs of requirements in these comments for consistency with the requirements themselves. Most configuration management systems support traceability only on the artifact level, and not on the level of program elements inside these artifacts. Experience shows that this level of granularity is not enough [Kuhn et al., 2012]. Also, when several engineering tools are used in the same project, cross-tool traceability becomes an integration challenge. mbeddr's approach, which supports element-level traceability from any artifact to requirements or other specifications, provides a solution to this dilemma and could therefore contribute to helping practitioners in adopting requirements traceability, particularly in contexts where the process requires it.

Other tools, such as the above-mentioned Yakindu Requirements, support traceability for various kinds of artifacts, including Xtext files, genetic text files or EMF models. In contrast to mbeddr, the trace information itself is kept separate from both the source and the target model. Also, the solution is not fully generic, since adapters have to be built to enable Yakindu to interface with additional artifacts beyond those that are supported by default. mbeddr's approach is fully generic.

mbeddr does not address the question of finding out, maybe after the implementation has been finished, which program elements have to be traced to

---

[32] http://www.yakindu.de/requirements/

[33] http://eclipse.org/xtext

which requirements: tracing in mbeddr is still a manual process. Approaches to partially automate the process include the use of techniques from information retrieval [Hayes et al., 2003]; a collection of best practices is described by Cleland-Huang et al. [2007].

Variability Support For product line variability, mbeddr adopts industry best practices. Expressing variability with feature models is the state of the art. Overlaying feature-based variability over programs has been done before as well. The C preprocessor can be used to this effect using `#ifdefs`. The approach can also be used on models. For example, Czarnecki and his group have overlaid feature-based variability over UML diagrams [Czarnecki & Antkiewicz, 2005]. mbeddr's approach is different, in that feature-based variability can be overlaid over models and code in the same way – there is no difference between the two in the first place: both kinds of artifacts are expressed with MPS languages. Since presence condition expressions are also expressed with a formal language, the expressions can be formally checked and interpreted. The ability to show the program/model with feature clauses enabled or not, and to show (and edit) the model in a variant-specific way, is also radically different than mainstream tools. However, the idea is inspired by CIDE, a specific solution for C described by Kästner [2010]. However, mbeddr's approach is more general, since it works for any language within MPS. VML [Loughran et al., 2008] is another tool (based on Eclipse EMF) that can map configurative variability to arbitrary models. However, since source code (C, Java) is not represented with EMF in Eclipse, a special solution had to be created to "adapt" VML to source code.

Showing statically that every valid variant of the feature model will result in a structurally valid program has been done before by Czarnecki & Pietroszek [2006] for the case of UML models and OCL constraints. Also the tool developed by Czarnecki & Antkiewicz [2005] has static validation, to make sure that every variant of the UML model is structurally correct. Another approach to the same problem is described as part of the AHEAD methodology by Thaker et al. [2007].

The idea of using DSLs to describe variability in product lines is not new. Various authors have published about this (Batory et al. [2002]; Mernik et al. [2005]; Tolvanen & Kelly [2005]) and the approach is used in practice. mbeddr's approach is different, since the various DSLs can be mixed and integrated.

Summary — *This chapter provided an overview of mbeddr and its relationship to* Generic Tools, Specific Languages. *It also provided context by comparing mbeddr to the state of the art in embedded software development tools. More details about mbeddr's features are discussed next in Chapter 4. The experiences of application developers are discussed in Chapter 5.*

Part II

Using mbeddr for Embedded Software Engineering

An Overview of mbeddr's Features

Abstract — *mbeddr provides domain-specific abstractions that address the problems of embedded software engineering discussed in Chapter 3. This chapter gives an overview of mbeddr's key abstractions, including extensions for testing and reporting, physical units, interfaces and components, decision tables and state machines as well as languages to support software documentation, requirements engineering and product line variability. The overview is given from the perspective of an embedded software engineer using mbeddr to develop applications and uses simple examples.*

4.1   MBEDDR'S VERSION OF C

To be able to extend C with MPS' facilities, C itself has to be implemented in MPS first. This entails the definition of the language structure, syntax and type system. In the process, some aspects of C were changed. Some of these changes are a first step in providing a safer version of C. Other changes were implemented because the result is more convenient to the user, or because it simplified the implementation of the language in MPS. Table 4.1 shows an overview of these changes. Out of eight changes total, four address improved robustness and analyzability, two improve application developer usability and three are to simplify the implementation in MPS. Some of the important changes to regular C are discussed below.

Modules   mbeddr C provides *modules*. A module contains the top level C constructs such as `structs`, functions or global variables. These module contents can be `exported`. Modules can import other modules, in which case they can access the exported contents of the imported modules. While header files are generated when the mbeddr C code is exported to text for compilation, mbeddr does not expose them to the user: modules provide a more convenient means of modularizing programs and controlling which elements are visible globally. The following piece of code shows an example module written in mbeddr. Except for the `module` itself and the `exported` keyword, it looks like regular C code.

```
module PlainCDemo {

  #constant uint16 MAX_POS = 100;

  exported struct Position {
    uint16 x;
    uint16 y;
  };
```

```
int8 add(int8 x, int8 y) { return x + y; }

void normalizePosition(Position* p) {
  if (p->x > MAX_POS) { p->x = MAX_POS; }
  if (p->y > MAX_POS) { p->y = MAX_POS; }
}

exported int32 main(int32 argc, string[] argv) {
  int8 x = add(10, 2);
  Position p = {(uint16) x, (uint16) add(20, 22)};
  normalizePosition(&p);
  return 0;
}
}
```

Preprocessor mbeddr C does not support the preprocessor. Empirical studies such as Ernst et al. [2002] show that it is often used to emulate missing features of C in an ad-hoc way, leading to problems with maintainability and analyzability. Instead, mbeddr C provides first-class support for the most important use cases of the preprocessor. Examples include the modules mentioned above (replacing headers and #include) as well as the support for variability discussed in Section 4.9 (replacing #ifdefs). Global constants are available directly, and macro functions are better replaced with language extensions, since these include type checks and IDE support. Removing the preprocessor and providing specific support for its important use cases goes a long way in creating more maintainable and more analyzable programs (cf. the challenge of *Static Checks and Verification*).

Difference	Reason
No preprocessor	Robustness
Native Booleans (and a cast operator for legacy interop)	Robustness
enums are not ints (special operators for next/previous)	Robustness
C99 integral types required	Robustness
Modules instead of headers	App dev convenience
hex<..>, oct<..>, bin<..> instead of 0x.. and 0..	Simplified implementation
Type annotation on type (int[] a instead of int a[])	Simplified implementation
Cleaned-up syntax for function types and function pointers	App dev convenience, simplified implementation

Table 4.1 Changes in mbeddr C compared to regular C. Out of eight changes, four are for reasons of improved robustness and analyzability, two are for application developer convenience and three are to simplify the implementation in MPS.

Types   mbeddr supports more specific types compared to C. For example, it introduces a separate `boolean` type, and does not interpret integers as Booleans by default (a cast operator is available to deal with legacy code). To avoid cross-platform compatibility problems, mbeddr requires the use of size-qualified types (such as `int8` or `uint32`) instead of platform-dependent types (such as `int` or `long long`).

Type decorations, such as array brackets or the pointer asterisk, must be specified on the type, not on the identifier (`int[] a;` instead of `int a[];`). This has been done for reasons of consistency and to simplify the implementation in MPS: it is the property of a type to be an array or a pointer, not the property of an identifier. Identifiers are just names.

Function Pointers   mbeddr supports a more readable version of C's function pointer syntax. The code below uses a `typedef` to define a new type that represents functions that take a `Trackpoint*` as an argument and also return a `Trackpoint*` (`Trackpoint` is a struct defined elsewhere). The `nullify` function conforms to this signature, which is why a reference to this function can be assigned to the variable `processor`. The `:` operator represents function references, mbeddr's version of function pointers (the numbers behind the `assert` statements used to identify a particular `assert` in log messages; they are automatically projected and read-only).

```
typedef (Trackpoint*)=>(Trackpoint*) as DataProcessorType;
DataProcessorType processor;

Trackpoint* process_nullifyAlt(Trackpoint* tp) {
  tp->alt = 0;
  return tp;
}

test case testProcessing {
  Trackpoint tp = {x = 0, y = 0, alt = 100 };
  processor = :process_nullifyAlt;
  Trackpoint* res = processor(&tp);
  assert(1) res->alt == 0;
}
```

mbeddr also supports lambdas, which are essentially anonymous functions. The following test case assigns a lambda to the `processor` variable and then invokes it.

```
test case testLambdaProcessing {
  Trackpoint tp = {x = 0, y = 0, alt = 50 };
  processor = [p| p->alt = 100; p; ];
  assert(0) processor(tp)->alt == 100;
}
```

Build Process   The customary way to build C-based software is to use `make` files. However, on some embedded platforms, non-standard `make` files are used, or the C code has to be built with custom build systems. mbeddr provides `BuildConfigurations` to abstract over the actual build system. The following piece of code represents the build configuration for a Hello, World program.

```
Build System:
  desktop
    compiler: gcc
    compiler options: -std=c99
    debug options: -g

Configuration Items
  reporting: printf

Binaries
  executable HelloWorld isTest: false {
    included modules
      HelloWorld
  }
```

A build configuration first defines the build system. By default, it is `desktop`, which means that the regular `make` file format is used, and `gcc` is used for compilation. A suitable `Makefile` is generated. By plugging in other build systems, arbitrary other files can be generated to control the build process.

The configuration items control how various C extensions are translated back to C. At least the `reporting` configuration is needed for Hello World, since it controls how the actual output of the "Hello, World" message is translated. The following code shows the `HelloWorld` module which defines a message that is then reported from within the `main` function (reporting is discussed in the next section). This `HelloWorld` module is included in the executable in the build configuration shown above.

```
module HelloWorld {
  messagelist messages {
    INFO helloWorld() active: Hello, World
  }
  exported int32 main(int32 argc, string[] argv) {
    report(0) messages.helloWorld();
    return 0;
  }
}
```

4.2 TESTING AND REPORTING

The ability to test code is essential for developing robust software. This is especially true for embedded software, where reliability is usually an important

60

concern[1]. Also, some target devices do not support debugging, so extensive testing is the only way to find and fix bugs.

However, testing embedded software is not always easy. Automated testing on the target device can be hard because of the challenge of reporting back success or failure (an example of the challenge of observability [Binder, 2000]). Not all devices have screens or other output facilities that can be readily used, so sometimes test results or debug messages are reported over a serial line, or stored in an error storage area and read back later. Running the tests on a PC is also not always feasible, because code may depend on specific characteristics of the target device such as timing, memory structure or I/O devices. mbeddr addresses the former problem with a platform-independent error-reporting facility. The latter problem can be addressed to some degree with suitable custom language extensions (such as the registers discussed in Section 10.1).

Addressed Challenges   Support for testing does not directly address any of the challenges outlined in Section 3.2, but it is closely related to *Static Checks and Verification*.

4.2.1 *Language Extensions*

Reporting   As shown in the Hello, World example in the previous section, messages can be output via the reporting framework. Users define messages, and `report` statements can then be used to output an instance of the message. Messages have a severity level (`INFO`, `WARN`, `ERROR`), an ID and a textual description. In addition, messages may have arguments.

`report` statements are translated during generation according to the build configuration (`reporting` item). The default is `printf`, which means that a `report` statement is translated to console output. Alternative transformations can, for example, write into an error store, a common approach in embedded software. Since the `report` statements are transformed during generation, the generator can automatically add the location of the `report` statement in the code to the error message, making it simpler to relate the error report to the cause. The following example code reports an error if a queue approaches three-quarters full:

```
void addToQueue(Trackpoint* tp) {
  report(0) messages.queueGettingFull()
            on pos >= QUEUE_SIZE * 3/4;
  pos++;
  if ( pos >= QUEUE_SIZE ) pos = 0;
  queue[pos] = tp;
}
```

---

[1] As a consequence, coverage measurement for test cases is useful. While we have not implemented this for mbeddr, we have implemented it for the commercial ACCEnT product which builds on top of mbeddr.

Notice how the check for a three-quarters full queue is part of the `report` statement, and not implemented as a surrounding `if`. This is because report messages can be disabled (selectively or globally), in which case no output message is generated because the `report` statement is removed from the code. In this case it is also important that no overhead is incurred from checking the condition associated with a report message. By making the condition part of the `report` statement, the check that triggers a message can be disabled/removed along with the `report` statement and the message.

Unit Tests   The previous section showed that mbeddr comes with a top level `test case` construct. Inside these test cases, a number of special language constructs, such as `assert` and `fail`, are available. An `assert` statement uses reporting to report an error if a test fails[2].

Executing Tests   The `test` expression is used for executing sets of test cases. It is typically used in the `main` function of a test program in the following way:

```
exported int32 main(int32 argc, string[] argv) {
  return test testAddToQueue, testQueueFilling;
}
```

The `test` expression invokes all the tests passed as arguments. The test cases themselves are translated in such a way that they return the number of failed assertions. The `test` expression sums up these return values of all invoked tests. In other words, `test` evaluates to the sum of failed assertions in all invoked test cases. By returning this number to the operating system (as the return value of `main`), a script or `make` file is informed of failing tests.

Failed tests, and in particular failed assertions, lead to a message on the console[3]. The message contains the qualified name of the failed test and assertion, and also the hyperlinked node ID of the failed assertion. Clicking on the link in the MPS console view selects the failed assertion in the editor directly. By linking the assertions to test specifications or requirements via traces (discussed in Section 4.8), full traceability from the failed test to the original requirement can be established.

4.2.2 *Extensibility*

Some of mbeddr's C extensions come with their own test support. For example, components support mocks and stubs (Section 4.4), and a special syntax is available for testing state machines (Section 4.6).

4.3 PHYSICAL UNITS

Embedded software is typically part of a hardware system. Consequently, the software often deals with values obtained from the real world through sen-

---

[2] We decided to not use CUnit (`http://cunit.sourceforge.net/`) to keep the footprint low and to be able to optimize the tests statically.

[3] This is only true for the default `printf` reporting mode.

62

```
                   -1
derived unit mps = m * s  for speed
convertible unit kmh for speed
conversion kmh -> mps = val * 0.27

#constant MAX_SPEED = convert[100 kmh -> mps];

int8/mps/ calculateSpeed(int8/m/ length, int8/s/ time) {
  int8/mps/ s = length / time;
  if (s > MAX_SPEED) {
    s = MAX_SPEED;
  } if
  return s;
} calculateSpeed (function)
```

Figure 4.1 The units extension ships with the SI base units. Users can define derived units (such as the mps in the example) as well as convertible units that require a numeric conversion for mapping back to SI units. Type checks ensure that the values associated with unit literals use the correct unit and perform unit computations (as in $speed = \frac{length}{time}$). Errors are reported if incompatible units are used together, as in the case where length and time were added.

sors. These values usually represent a physical property of the environment, and as such have a unit associated with them. Programming languages do not directly support units, which can lead to program errors. This challenge has been discussed in the introduction (Section 2.4.1), and the study by Kuhn et al. [2012] describes missing support for units as a major problem with today's modeling tools. The crash of NASA's Mars Climate Orbiter was caused by unit conversion errors[4].

To address this problem, mbeddr provides first-class support for physical units as a modular extension. The extension supports type checking expressions for unit compatibility, computations with units (dividing m by s results in m/s), as well as value conversions (as in °C and °F). Figure 4.1 shows the use of units in mbeddr.

Addressed Challenges   The units are an example of the *Program Annotations* challenge. They also provide *Abstraction without Runtime Cost.*

4.3.1   Language Extensions

Annotating Units   The Trackpoint data structure introduced earlier represents trackpoints of a recorded flight[5]. As such, the various members of the

---

[4] http://mars.jpl.nasa.gov/msp98/news/mco990930.html

[5] This example is loosely modeled after a system that records the flight path of airplanes as a sequence of Trackpoints for later evaluation. Such a system is used, for example, in gliding as part of the OLC competition (http://www.onlinecontest.org/).

`struct` represent physical quantities and should be annotated with physical units. Units are part of types and can be added to any numeric type.

```
struct Trackpoint {
    int8 id;              // sequence ID of the trackpoint
    int8/s/   timestamp;  // timestamp as taken from GPS time
    int8/m/   x;          // longitude, simplified as a number
    int8/m/   y;          // latitude, simplified as a number
    int8/m/   alt;        // altitude as of the GPS
    int8/mps/ speed;      // current speed, if available
};
```

`s` and `m` are SI base units[6], so they are available by default. The `mps` (meters per second) unit used for the `speed` member is not an SI base unit, and hence has to be defined before it can be used. Unit declarations are module contents, so they can be defined in any implementation module:

```
derived unit mps = m s    for velocity
```
⁻¹

To prevent type-checking errors, the correct units now have to be used when assigning values to the members of the `Trackpoint` struct. Similarly, the assertions in the introductory tests have to use units:

```
Trackpoint tp = { id = 1, timestamp = 0 s,
                  x = 0 m, y = 0 m, alt = 100 m };
assert(0) tp.id == 1 && tp.alt == 100 m;
assert(1) tp.id == 1 && tp.alt == 0 m;
```

Unit Computations and Checks   The type system calculates resulting units based on the units used in expressions. For example, the following program fragment will result in an error, because of the attempt to add `m` and `mps`. Trying to add `tp.x` and `tp.y` will work – both are meters.

```
int8 someInt = tp.x + tp.speed; // error, adding m and mps
```

mbeddr also computes resulting units if quantities of different units are multiplied or divided. For example, the following code is valid:

```
int8/mps/ speed = (tp2.x - tp1.x) /
                  (tp2.timestamp - tp1.timestamp);
```

Value Conversions   The examples so far have only dealt with unit checking and the computation of resulting units, and not with value conversions, as in dealing with $°C$ and $°F$. Convertible units can be used for this purpose[7]:

```
convertible unit degC for temperature
convertible unit degF for temperature
conversion degC -> degF = val * 9 / 5 + 32
conversion degF -> degC = (val - 32) * 5 / 9
```

---

[6] http://en.wikipedia.org/wiki/SI_base_unit

[7] Note that mbeddr can actually use the $°C$ and $°F$ notation. However, I was unable to use it in the LaTeX `lstlisting` environment, hence `degC` and `degf`.

The following function takes a temperature in °C and stores it in a database:

```
void storeTemperature(int8/degC/ temp) {
  // store temp in some data store
}
```

If this function were to be called with an argument in °F, a type error would be reported. To fix the error, a conversion has to be triggered:

```
int8/degF/ aTempInF = 100 degF;
storeTemperature(convert[aTempInF -> degC]);
```

The convert expression does not explicitly refer to the conversion rule; the system finds an appropriate one automatically if one is in scope. However, the user has to explicitly request a conversion (using the convert expression) – conversions are never performed automatically. This is because they incur runtime overhead and may lead to overflows in the underlying variables. By requiring users to use the convert expression explicitly, the user is made aware of the potential risks.

4.3.2 Extensibility

Physical units are essentially just a tag on a type, plus rules that determine how these tags influence type compatibility. Other such tags, beyond those based on SI base units, can be useful. Examples include currencies (where assigning or adding USD to EUR should be prevented) or coordinate systems (where local coordinates cannot be used when global coordinates are expected). Both of these extensions have been prototyped; the underlying framework is flexible enough to be able to work with non-SI units.

4.4 COMPONENTS

Program modularization is essential to managing complexity. It helps tackle big problems by breaking them down into a set of smaller problems. Modularization is also the basis for reuse, since a well-defined module can be reused in different contexts. To make this possible, a module must clearly specify its interface – otherwise it is unclear how other modules should interact with it. In addition, once an interface is defined, the inner workings of a module can be hidden from, and hence changed without affecting, client code. Ideally, it should be possible to plug in different implementations behind the same interface. This helps with testing, because mocks and stubs can be used in place of the real implementation with no change in the interface.

C has only very limited support for modularizing programs. Functions are modules, in the sense that their signature is a (weak) interface specification, and they can be reused in different contexts. Defining modules that contain several (cooperating) functions is much harder; header files can be used for this purpose to some extent. They support the provision of several implementations for the same set of functions defined in a header file by linking different `.c` files that implement the functions in the header. A similar effect can be achieved with `#ifdefs`. However, all of this relies on the preprocessor, and the approach is brittle[8]. An alternative implementation relies on function pointers, as well as arrays or structs that contain collections of related function pointers. However, maintaining all these function pointers consistently is tedious and error-prone.

Component-based software development [Brown, 1996; Clements, 1995] takes the approach further. Depending on the specific formalism, components have very rich descriptions of their interfaces, such as pre- and post-conditions (inspired by Design By Contract [Meyer, 1998]) or protocol state machines (as used in SDL[9]). Hierarchical decomposition, in which one component is structured into connected instances of other components, is also widely supported (for example, in UML [Bock, 2004]).

mbeddr supports components with rich interfaces, including pre- and post-conditions and protocol state machines, compile-time and runtime polymorphism, and component instantiation, as well as hierarchical decomposition[10].

Addressed Challenges   Components are an example of *Abstraction without Runtime Cost*. As a consequence of the better modularizability of the code and improved testability, they also contribute to addressing the challenge that C *is Considered Unsafe*. Finally, components are an important building block for product line engineering, so they are also a part of mbeddr's *Process Support*.

4.4.1 Language Extensions

Client-Server Interfaces   mbeddr supports client-server interfaces, which support remote procedure call-style interaction, as well as sender-receiver interfaces, which represent replicated data. This section focuses on client-server interfaces. The following interface defines an operation[11] that processes `Trackpoints`. Operations are similar to C function prototypes regarding the types that can be used in the arguments or the return type:

```
module Components imports DataStructures {
  exported cs interface TrackpointProcessor {
    Trackpoint* process(Trackpoint* p);
  }
}
```

To enhance the semantic richness of the interface, pre- and post-conditions can be added. By default, these are checked at runtime, and a report message is output if one of them fails. However, static checking is also supported, as described in Section 4.4:

---

[8] In C++, classes are available. Classes are modules in the sense of the above description. However, the discussion in this section is restricted to C.

[9] http://sdl-forum.org/SDL/

[10] In terms of the low-level implementation, mbeddr relies on structs with function pointers, as mentioned above.

[11] An interface can of course have any number of operations.

```
Trackpoint* process(Trackpoint* p)
  pre(0)  p != null
  pre(1)  p->id != 0
  pre(2)  p->timestamp != 0 s
  post(3) result->id != 0
```

The contract is specified on the *interface*, but it is checked for each *component* that implements the interface. There is no way for an implementation to prevent the checks of its provided interfaces from being executed.

A Simple Component   Components provide and require ports, and each port is associated with an interface. A *provided* port offers the services defined by the interface to other components; this is similar to the concept of implementing interfaces in Java. A *required* port expresses a component's need to access the specified interface on another component, a concept roughly comparable to dependency injection [Fowler, 2004]. The following trivial component provides the `TrackpointProcessor` interface. A component that implements an interface through a provided port has to implement the operations defined by this interface; the IDE reports an error if this is not the case, and a quick fix allows users to automatically implement all provided operations. To implement an operation, a component defines a runnable[12], which is essentially a method. In the example below, the `Nuller` component provides the `processor` port with the `Trackpoint` interface. The implementation of `process` sets the altitude to `0m` (hence the component's name `Nuller`):

```
exported component Nuller extends nothing {
  provides TrackpointProcessor processor
  Trackpoint* process(Trackpoint* p) <- op processor.process {
    p->alt = 0 m;
    return p;
  }
}
```

Runnables are activated by triggers. The `op` trigger executes a runnable when an operation is invoked on a provided port. Other triggers include `on init`, which essentially makes a runnable a constructor, and `timed`, which executes the runnable on a schedule. The mechanism is extensible; for example, the examples on component language extensibility below show a runnable triggered by an interrupt. In the example, the `process` runnable is triggered by an incoming invocation of the `process` operation on the `processor` port.

Instances   To test the component, an instance of `Nuller` has to be created first. In contrast to classes in object-oriented programming, component instances are intended to be instantiated during the initialization phase of the program, and often reside on the stack as global variables. This is to avoid out-of-memory errors as the program executes, a condition that is hard to deal with in embedded software. Instance configurations are used to define

---

[12] The notion of *runnables* is inspired by the AUTOSAR standard.

and connect instances. Instance configurations can also host adapters, which make a provided port of a component instance (`Nuller.processor`) available to a regular C program under the specified name (`n`):

```
instances nullerInstances {
  instance Nuller nuller
  adapt n -> nuller.processor
}
```

The next step is writing a test case that accesses the `n` adapter – and through it, the `processor` port of the `Nuller` component instance `nuller`. The code creates a new `Trackpoint`, using `0` as the `id` – intended to trigger a contract violation of `pre(1) p->id != 0`. The code also initializes the instance configuration (which allocates memory and initializes internal fields):

```
exported test case testNuller {
  initialize nullerInstances;
  Trackpoint tp = { id = 0 };
  n.process(&tp);
}
```

Running the test case results in a runtime contract failure that is reported – by default – on the console.

Advanced Contracts A new interface, `TrackpointStore`, declares an API for working with a queue of `Trackpoint`s (to keep the example simple, the implementation actually just stores one element):

```
exported cs interface TrackpointStore {
  void store(Trackpoint* tp)
  Trackpoint* get()
  Trackpoint* take()
  boolean isEmpty()
}
```

There are several semantic constraints that apply to this interface: it should not be possible to `get` or `take` trackpoints from the store if it is empty, and no additional trackpoints should be stored if it is full. These constraints can be expressed as pre- and post-conditions. Note in the code below how the `isEmpty` operation is marked as `query` so that it can be used in pre- and post-conditions, and the `old` keyword is used to access values of `query` operations from *before* the execution of the operation:

```
exported cs interface TrackpointStore {
  void store(Trackpoint* tp)
    pre(0) isEmpty()
    pre(1) tp != null
    post(2) !isEmpty()
    post(3) size() == old(size()) + 1
  Trackpoint* get()
    pre(0) !isEmpty()
    post(1) result != null
```

```
    post(2) size() == old(size())
  Trackpoint* take()
    pre(0) !isEmpty()
    post(1) result != null
    post(2) isEmpty()
    post(3) size() == old(size()) - 1
  query int8 size()
  query boolean isEmpty()
}
```

These pre- and post-conditions mostly express a valid sequence of the operation calls: store has to be called before get is allowed, etc. Alternatively, this
can be expressed directly with protocols:

```
exported cs interface TrackpointStore2 {
  // store goes from the initial state to a new state nonEmpty
  void store(Trackpoint* tp)
    protocol init(0) -> new nonEmpty(1)

  // get expects the state to be nonEmpty, and remains there
  Trackpoint* get()
    protocol nonEmpty -> nonEmpty

  // take expects to be nonEmpty and then becomes empty
  // if there was one element in it, it remains in
  // nonEmpty otherwise
  Trackpoint* take()
    post(0) result != null
    protocol nonEmpty [size() == 1] -> init(0)
    protocol nonEmpty [size() > 1] -> nonEmpty

  // isEmpty and size have no effect on the protocol state
  query boolean isEmpty()
  query int8 size()
}
```

Stateful Collaborating Components The component above was stateless
and did not collaborate with any other component. In realistic cases, this
is different: component instances will encapsulate data, represented as *fields*,
and will have required ports to use services provided by other component instances. The code below shows a component that implements the Trackpoint-
Store interface to store a single trackpoint. There is a field Trackpoint*
storedTP; that represents component state. There is also an on-init runnable
that acts as a constructor:

```
exported component InMemoryStorage {
  provides TrackpointStore store
  Trackpoint* storedTP;

  void init() <- on init { storedTP = null; }
```

```
    void store(Trackpoint* tp) <- op store.store { storedTP = tp; }

    Trackpoint* get() <- op store.get { return storedTP; }

    Trackpoint* take() <- op store.take {
      Trackpoint* temp = storedTP;
      storedTP = null;
      return temp;
    }

    boolean isEmpty() <- op store.isEmpty { return storedTP == null; }

    int8 size() <- op store.size { return storedTP == null ? 0 : 1; }
  }
```

To illustrate the use of required ports, the `Interpolator` component shown below implements the `TrackpointProcessor` interface in a way that uses the `TrackpointStore` interface:

```
exported component Interpolator extends nothing {
  provides TrackpointProcessor processor
  requires TrackpointStore store

  init int8 dividend;
  Trackpoint* process(Trackpoint* p) <- op processor.process {
    if (store.isEmpty()) {
      store.store(p);
      return p;
    } else {
      Trackpoint* old = store.take();
      p->speed = (p->speed + old->speed) / dividend;
      store.store(p);
      return p;
    }
} } }
```

This component expresses that it requires a `TrackpointStore` interface connected to its `store` port. Any component that implements the `TrackpointStore` interface can be used to fulfil this requirement (see below). The example also shows how to call operations on required ports using the dot notation familiar from object-oriented programming (`store.store(p);`). The component also uses an `init` field. This is a regular field from the perspective of the component (i.e., it can be accessed from within the implementation), but it is special in that a value for it has to be supplied when the component is instantiated. Instances of the two components can now be defined and connected:

```
instances interpolatorInstances {
  instance InMemoryStorage store
  instance Interpolator ip(dividend = 2)
  connect ip.store to store.store
  adapt ip -> ip.processor
}
```

Notice how a value for the init field `dividend` is passed in as part of the definition of an instance of `Interpolator`. The `connect` statement is used to connect the required port `store` of the `ip` instance to the `store` provided port of the `store` instance. If required ports are not connected, an error will be reported on the `ip` instance (there are also `optional` required ports which may remain unconnected). Another test case can now be written like this:

```
test case testInterpolator {
  initialize interpolatorInstances;
  Trackpoint p1 = { id = 1, timestamp = 1 s, speed = 10 mps };
  Trackpoint p2 = { id = 2, timestamp = 2 s, speed = 20 mps };

  ip.process(&p1);
  assert(0) p1.speed == 10 mps;
  ip.process(&p2);
  assert(1) p2.speed == 15 mps;
}
```

Visualization   Components and interfaces can be rendered as a diagram to show their dependencies (Figure 4.2). A similar diagram can be rendered for the instances and their connectors.

Static Wiring   By default, calls on required ports (and adapters) are transformed to C in a way that supports polymorphism: different implementations can be used for the same interface *in the same program*; the decision as to which generated function to call is made at runtime. To make this possible, the generated code uses an indirection via a function pointer. This indirection implies a runtime performance overhead. To avoid this overhead, a second transformation mode is available. It can only be used if, for any given interfaces, only *one* implementation is used throughout a program. In this case, calls to the function generated from this single implementation are generated when the operation is called; the indirection and the performance overhead is avoided.

Composite Components   Composite components represent hierarchical decomposition of systems. A composite component contains connected instances of other components. It can also delegate some of the ports of internal instances to its own boundary. Composite components can be instantiated like any other component. The following is part of a composite component from the Smartmeter project[13].

```
composite component EnergyDataDisplayStack {
  requires IEnergyDataProvider energyDataProvider
  requires IRTC rtc
  requires ITickerPool tickerPool
  provides ITask updateTask
```

---

[13] The Smartmeter project is a commercial project that develops the implementation of a smart meter based on mbeddr.

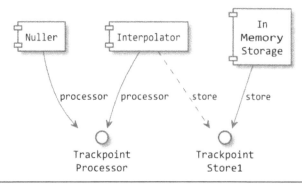

Figure 4.2 A visualization of components and interfaces, as well as their dependencies. Solid lines represent provided ports, dotted lines represent required ports. Diagrams like this one can be rendered automatically for every module that contains components and interfaces.

```
void setup() <= on init { initialize internal instances; }

internal instances() {
  instance EnergyDataDisplayImpl display
  delegate energyDataProvider to display.energyDataProvider
  delegate rtc to display.rtc
  ...

  instance LCDLineImpl lcdLine(conf = &LCD_LINE_CONFIG)
  connect display.energyDataLCDLine to lcdLine.lcdLine

  instance LCDLineOutputterImpl output
  connect output.lcdLine to lcdLine.lcdLine
  connect display.energyDataLCDLineOutputter
          to output.lcdLineOutputter

.. } }
```

Composite components are a means of reusing more complex structures built from components. Another means for reusing some of the runnables is to have one component `extend` another one, just like class inheritance in object-oriented programming.

Sender-Receiver Interfaces   Sender-receiver interfaces are essentially structs, i.e. they are a set of typed and named data items. A component that provides a sender-receiver interface owns the data storage for these items and can update their values. A component that requires a sender-receiver interface can read the data values. Sender-receiver interfaces are a structured approach for shared memory, a pattern frequently used in embedded systems.

Mocks   Mocks are parts of programs that simulate the behavior of another part, specifically for a given scenario or test case. Mocks are well known from object-oriented programming [Thomas & Hunt, 2002]; mbeddr adopts them for testing components. The crucial point about mocks is that they implement each operation *invocation* separately (the steps in the code below), whereas a regular component or a stub just describes each operation with *one* implementation. This makes a mock implementation much simpler *for a given scenario* – it does not have to replicate the algorithmic implementation of the real component. In this way mocks improve the controllability [Binder, 2000] of the system. Mocks also enhance the observability [Binder, 2000] of the system, since they support asserting behavior "from the inside" of the mocked component.

For example, to test whether the Interpolator works correctly with the TrackpointStore interface, a mock can be used. The testInterpolator test introduced above expects the following: when process is called first, the store is still empty, so the interpolator stores a new trackpoint. When process is called again, the test expects the interpolator to call take and then store. In both cases, isEmpty must be called first. This behavior can be tested explicitly via a mock:

```
mock component StorageMock report messages: true {
  provides TrackpointStore1 store
  Trackpoint* lastTP;
  total number of calls is 5
  sequence {
    step 0: store.isEmpty return true;
    step 1: store.store {
        assert 0: parameter tp: tp != null
      }
      do { lastTP = tp; }
    step 2: store.isEmpty return false;
    step 3: store.take return null;
    step 4: store.store
  }
}
```

This mock component expects five invocations in total. In particular, it expects a sequence of calls, in which the first one must be a call to isEmpty; the mock returns true. The next expectations is a call to store, and for the sake of the example, the mock checks that tp is not null. It also stores the tp parameter in a field lastTP so it can be can returned later. The next expectation is another isEmpty query, which now returns false. Next, a call to take is expected, and then another call to store. Notice the returning of null from take: this violates the post-condition! However, pre- and post-conditions are *not* checked in mock components, because their checking may interfere with test cases that test erroneous behavior and the system's reactions to it. Two more ingredients are required to use the mock in a test. The first one is the instances and the wiring. Notice the connection of the interpolator and the mock:

```
instances interpolatorInstancesWithMock {
  instance StorageMock storeMock
  instance Interpolator ip(dividend = 2)
  connect ip.store to storeMock.store
  adapt ipMock -> ip.processor
}
```

The second ingredient is the test case itself. Obviously, it has to fail if the mock saw something other than what it expected on its port. This is achieved by using the `validatemock` statement in the test:

```
exported test case testInterpolatorWithMock {
  initialize interpolatorInstancesWithMock;
  Trackpoint p1 = { id = 1, timestamp = 1 s, speed = 10 mps };
  Trackpoint p2 = { id = 2, timestamp = 2 s, speed = 20 mps };
  ipMock.process(&p1);
  ipMock.process(&p2);
  validatemock (0) interpolatorInstancesWithMock:storeMock;
}
```

The component language provides more support specifically for testing. For example, test cases can call runnables in components without them being exposed via a provided port. This avoids the need to create interfaces and ports just for testing, which would expose behavior that should not be exposed.

4.4.2 Verification

As mentioned earlier, the contracts specified on interfaces are checked at runtime for every implementing component. A message is reported if a contract fails. In addition, it is possible to check the correctness of contracts statically. The verification uses CBMC[14], a bounded model checker for C. Since the verification can take some time, it is not part of the regular type checks; instead, it can be run in the IDE on demand or during the nightly build from the console.

Bounded model checking essentially "simulates" a program by exploring its state space [Clarke et al., 2004]. The state space of a C program can be huge, so to make model checking feasible a number of configuration parameters have to be set. These are available as part of the `verifiable` annotation. Parameters include the entry point of the verification (the point from which the simulated program execution starts) and the loop unwinding length (how many iterations through a loop should be successfully tried until the loop is assumed to "always work"). It takes some experimentation to find values for these parameters that result in a sufficiently detailed analysis while still running the analysis in a reasonable time.

As an example, the `InMemoryStorage` component introduced earlier is verified. Since it implements the `TrackpointStore` interface, it has to respect the contracts prescribed by this interface. Among other things, the contract specifies that, after an invocation of `store`, the `isEmpty` method must be false:

---

[14] http://www.cprover.org/cbmc/

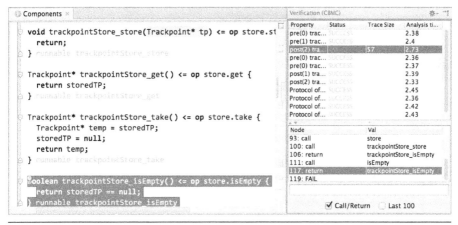

Figure 4.3 After changing the implementation of `trackpointStore_store` to *not* store a trackpoint, the post-condition that checks that the store is not empty after calling `store` fails. Running the verification, the table on the top right shows which pre- and post-conditions hold and which failed. When clicking on a failed one, the table on the bottom right shows an example program flow that leads to the failure.

```
exported cs interface TrackpointStore1 {
  void store(Trackpoint* tp)
    post(2) !isEmpty()
  ...
}
```

Assuming `isEmpty` is implemented correctly, a failure of this post-condition can be provoked by changing the implementation of the `store` operation to *not* store the argument (see the top of the code in Figure 4.3; it just returns). If the verification is run, it creates the output shown in the right part of Figure 4.3.

4.4.3 Extensibility

Like any language implemented in MPS, the components extension is inherently extensible. The following three aspects are worth highlighting:

Component Contents   The contents of a component are generic, in the sense that every language concept that implements `IComponentContent` can be plugged in. Using this mechanism, state machines can live inside components. This is discussed in some detail in Section 4.6.

Triggers   By default, runnables can be triggered `on init`, when an operation is invoked on a provided port, or when a value required via a sender-receiver interface changes. However, additional triggers can be plugged in by extending the abstract concept `RunnableTrigger`. For example, in the Smartmeter project, we have implemented an `interrupt` trigger:

```
component TemperatureProviderImpl {
  provides ITemperatureProvider temperatureProvider

  uint16/raw_C/ temperature = 0 raw_C;
  ...
  void interruptHandler() <= interrupt {
    if ((ADC10MCTL0 & hex<0F>) == ADC10INCH_10) {
      uint16/raw_C/ corrected = introduceunit[ADC10MEM0 -> raw_C];
      temperature = temperature - (temperature >> 3) + corrected;
    }
    // ClearADC10IFGbyreadingADC10MEM0
    ADC10IFG = hex<00>;
  }
}
```

This trigger specifies that *some* interrupt triggers this runnable; it is not yet specified *which* interrupt. The actual interrupt is specified for each instance. This is important, since the various instances of a single component may be triggered by different interrupts:

```
instances instances {
  instance TemperatureProviderImpl tp
  bind ADC10 -> tp.interruptHandler
  ...
}
```

Interrupts themselves are first-class entities, because they are used in other contexts as well. They can be declared as module contents:

```
// Temperature
exported interrupt ADC10
```

Different Generators   New generators can be plugged in to generate different code from programs using the components language. As part of the LW-ES research project, BMW has built a generator that generates code that is compliant with the AUTOSAR API. Among other things, this generator addresses the way components invoke operations on required calls: they have to call AUTOSAR API functions to allow communication over a distributed system.

In addition, an XML file has to be generated that defines the structure of a component, to enable integration and deployment tools to make use of the component. However, to be able to generate this XML file, additional information is needed. This information is supplied via annotations (explained in Section 7.4.5), which are additional "pieces of code" that can be attached to program elements without that element's concept having to know about it: annotations can be attached *after the fact*. In this way *different* generators can add *different* additional data to the same program elements.

```
exported component Judge extends nothing {
  provides FlightJudger judger
  int16 points = 0;
  void judger_reset() <= op judger.reset {
    points = 0;
  } runnable judger_reset
  void judger_addTrackpoint(Trackpoint* tp) <= op judger.addTrackpoint {
    points += 0
  } runnable judger_addTrackpoint
  int16 judger_getResult() <= op judger.getResult {
    return points;
  } runnable judger_getResult
} component Judge
```

points += 0	tp->alt <= 2000 m	tp->alt >= 2000 m
tp->speed < 150 mps	0	10
tp->speed >= 150 mps	5	20

Figure 4.4 A decision table represents a two-level decision process. It is an expression and hence can be embedded everywhere where expressions are expected, for example, in components. In turn, decision tables can use arbitrary embedded expressions, such as literals with units.

4.5   DECISION TABLES

Decision tables represent two-level decisions. The row and column headers contain Boolean expressions, the remaining cells contain expressions of other types. The semantics is that if a row header r and a column header c are true, then the value of the whole expression table is the value at the cell r, c. While decision tables are a relatively simple extension, they are very useful in practice for multi-step decisions because of the very intuitive notation and their inherent verifiability.

Addressed Challenges   Decision tables, particularly due to the static verifications they support, address the challenge of *Static Checks and Verification*.

4.5.1   *Language Extensions*

mbeddr decision tables are translated to nested **if** statements. The table is evaluated column headers first; row headers are only evaluated if a particular column header matches. Decision tables are expressions; this means that they *always* have to evaluate to a value. Since the conditions in the table may all be false for a given set of input values, a default value has to be specified. Figure 4.4 shows an example decision table.

The following piece of code shows a test case for the component with the decision table from Figure 4.4. Among other things, it makes use of a convenient form of the **for** statement that works on ranges. The limits of the range can be exclusive or inclusive, represented with open or closed brackets, respectively. The example iterates from 0 to 4, since 5 is excluded. The `introduceunit` construct can be used to "sneak" a unit into a regular value. This is useful for interacting with non-unit-aware (library) code:

```
instances instancesJudging {
  instance Judge theJudge
  adapt j -> theJudge.judger
}

exported test case testJudging {
  initialize instancesJudging;
  // j is the adapter to the judger port
  // of the theJudge component instance
  j.reset();
  Trackpoint[5] points;
  for (i in [0..5[) {
    points[i].id = i;
    points[i].alt = introduceunit[1850 + 100 * i -> m];
    points[i].speed = 130 mps + 10 mps * i;
    j.addTrackpoint(&points[i]);
  }
  assert(0) j.getResult() == 0 + 0 + 20 + 20 + 20;
}
```

Realistic decision tables usually have intricate combinations of conditions, and it is easy to overlook inconsistencies. As usual, testing has the coverage problem, and it is easy not to test a specific corner case. Verification can be used to good effect.

4.5.2 Verification

To enable verification of a decision table, it must be marked as `verifiable`. This annotation introduces additional type checks that report errors if the table uses expressions that cannot be verified with the underlying Yices SMT solver. An example of an unverifiable expression is a non-linear expression (such as `tp->alt * tp->alt > 2000 m2`).

The verification checks decision tables for completeness and consistency. A *complete* table covers all possible combinations of inputs. Consequently, the default value is optional for `verifiable` decision tables. A *consistent* table is free from overlap: every combination of input values leads to a unique decision. Running the verification on the example table in Figure 4.4 reports the following result:

```
SUCCESS: Table complete.
FAIL: cells (1, 1) and (1, 2) are inconsistent.
  tp.id: 0
  tp.timestamp: 0
  tp.x: 0
  tp.y: 0
  tp.speed: 0
  tp.alt: 2000
...
```

Completeness of the table can be successfully verified, but the result also reports failures because the cells (1,1) and (1,2) are inconsistent. If the verifier finds an error, it communicates this to the user by presenting a counter example. In this case the problem is related to the altitude being 2000 m: in this case it is not decidable which alternative should be used. The problem can be fixed for example by changing `tp->alt <= 2000` m to `tp->alt < 2000` m (the <= was replaced with a <). Running the verification again results in success.

4.5.3 Extensibility

Decision tables are not extensible per se, but they can be combined with other extensions. For example, the table in Figure 4.4 is embedded in a component, and the table itself uses physical units in the conditions.

4.6 STATE MACHINES

Next to components and physical units, state machines [Harel, 1987] are one of the main C extensions available in mbeddr. State machines are ubiquitous in embedded software development [Samek, 2002] for implementing discrete behavior. Section 2.4.2 discussed some typical C-based implementation approaches. All of them are low-level, tedious, error-prone and not very suitable for analysis, so there is clearly a need for first-class support.

The core abstractions in state machines are states, events and transitions. A state machine is said to be "in" a state at any time, and one state is marked as the initial state. Transitions move the system from one state to another as a reaction to an external event. Different states react to the same event differently, i.e., they have different transitions for the same event. In this way the behavior exhibited by a state machine depends on the state it is in. In addition to being triggered by an event, a transition can also have a guard condition, which is a Boolean expression that has to be true for the transition to fire. This way, more fine-grained decisions can be made as to the behavior of the state machine when a given event is received. The guards may refer to event parameters, to local variables owned by the state machine, or to values provided by external interfaces (such as I/O devices). Optionally, state machines may be hierarchical [Yannakakis, 2000] (where a state can contain a another state machine), can express parallel states (where the system is in more than one state at the some time) or include the notion of history [Börger et al., 2000] (as a way of supporting reeneterability).

State machines must interact with their environment. One means of interaction is for the environment to supply the events that trigger transitions. In addition, the reaction of a state machine to an event may have an affect on the environment as well. To do so, states can have entry actions and exit actions, and transitions may have transition actions.

There are two main execution paradigms for state machines: event-driven and time-triggered. For event-driven state machines, an incoming event triggers a reaction of a state machine. In time-triggered state machines a scheduler executes a state machine regularly. The events are taken from a queue, or the values of variables are checked as part of guard conditions.

Different implementations of the state machine paradigm support different subsets of the features discussed so far. mbeddr's state machines can be hierarchical and support entry, exit and transition actions. In this sense they are similar to UML state machines [Booch et al., 1998]. They differ from UML in that they do not support parallel states or history[15], and additionally contain local variables. By default, mbeddr uses the event-driven execution paradigm, but the time-triggered one can be implemented as well. Since MPS does not yet support graphical notations, mbeddr uses a textual notation[16]. However, graphical visualizations can be rendered automatically.

Even though protocols for interfaces (see Section 4.4) are also state machines, the two extensions are not related, since they have very little in common. The state machines discussed here are much richer, whereas the protocol state machines for components directly integrate with the interfaces and operations, in particular in the generated low-level C code.

Addressed Challenges   State machines are an example of *Abstraction without Runtime Cost*. The support for model checking addresses the challenge of *Static Checks and Verification*.

4.6.1   Language Extensions

As an example, this section illustrates a state machine that judges flights.[17] The idea is that the state machine receives sequences of trackpoints (via an event) and then awards points for the flight represented by this sequence of trackpoints. Here are some of the requirements for how points are awarded:

- 100 points once a flight lifts off
- 10 points for each trackpoint where the plane flies more than 100 m/s,
- 20 points for each trackpoint where the plane flies more than 200 m/s,
- 100 points for a successful landing
- -1 points for each trackpoint where the plane is on the ground, rolling (one should land in as short a distance as possible)

Implementing a State Machine   State machines are module contents: They can be entered along with functions, global variables or struct declarations. The airplane will be in various states, such as on the ground, flying, landing (and still rolling), landed, or crashed. The state machine will have the following states:

---

[15] There is no particular reason why mbeddr's state machines could not support these features. They just have not been needed yet, which is why they are not yet available.

[16] When MPS supports graphical notations in 2014, support for graphical state machines will be added.

[17] As mentioned earlier, this example is inspired by the gliding OLC, which records cross-country flights and then awards points for distance and speed flown.

```
statemachine FlightAnalyzer initial = beforeFlight {
  state beforeFlight {  }
  state airborne {  }
  state landing {  }
  state landed {  }
  state crashed {  }
}
```

The state machine has two events: `next`, which represents the next trackpoint submitted for evaluation, and `reset`, which resets the judgement process. Events can use arbitrary C types as arguments: a `Trackpoint*` is used in the example. To accumulate the judgement result, a local variable `points` is added:

```
statemachine FlightAnalyzer initial = beforeFlight {
  in next(Trackpoint* tp)
  in reset()
  var int16 points = 0
  // states from above
}
```

Whenever the state machine enters `beforeFlight`, i.e., when it starts and after it is reset, the `points` have to be set to zero. This can be achieved using an entry action. In addition, every other state must react to the `reset` event by transitioning back to `beforeFlight`:

```
state beforeFlight {
  entry { points = 0; }
}
state airborne {
  on reset [ ] -> beforeFlight
}
state landing {
  on reset [ ] -> beforeFlight
}
state landed {
  on reset [ ] -> beforeFlight
}
```

The various judgement rules mentioned above can be implemented as transitions. As soon as a trackpoint's altitude is greater than zero, the state machine transitions to the `airborne` state, and 100 points are added (`TAKEOFF` is a global constant representing `100`). While `airborne`, it depends on various combinations of speed and altitude whether a landing, a crash, high speed or very high speed is detected. The landing process is handled similarly.

```
state beforeFlight {
  entry { points = 0; }
  on next [tp->alt > 0 m] -> airborne
  exit { points += TAKEOFF; }
}
state airborne {
```

```
    on next [tp->alt == 0 m && tp->speed == 0 mps] -> crashed
    on next [tp->alt == 0 m && tp->speed > 0 mps] -> landing
    on next [tp->speed > 200 mps]
        -> airborne { points += VERY_HIGH_SPEED; }
    on next [tp->speed > 100 mps]
        -> airborne { points += HIGH_SPEED; }
    on reset [ ] -> beforeFlight
  }
  state landing {
    on next [tp->speed == 0 mps] -> landed
    on next [ ] -> landing { points--; }
    on reset [ ] -> beforeFlight
  }
  state landed {
    entry { points += LANDING; }
    on reset [ ] -> beforeFlight
  }
```

Interacting with Other Code – Inbound   State machines are types and must be instantiated to be used; any number of instances of a state machine can be created. State machines must also be initialized explicitly: this sets the current state to the initial state and initializes all local variables:

```
test case testFlightAnalyzer {
  FlightAnalyzer f;
  sminit(f);
}
```

To interact with a state machine, its events have to be triggered. The `smtrigger` statement is available to do this: it expects the target state machine instance and an event, with its parameters, as arguments (in the code below, `makeTP` is a helper function that allocates a new `Trackpoint` on the heap and returns its address):

```
smtrigger(f, next(makeTP(0, 20)));
```

To check whether the state machine behaves correctly, assertions must be added to the test case:

```
test case testFlightAnalyzer {
  FlightAnalyzer f;
  sminit(f);
  assert(0) smIsInState(f, beforeFlight);
  smtrigger(f, next(makeTP(100, 100)));
  assert(3) smIsInState(f, airborne) && f.points == TAKEOFF;
  ...
}
```

Special support is available for testing the transition behavior of state machines. This checks whether the state machine transitions to the desired state if a specific event is triggered. Below is an example of the `test statemachine` statement, which can only be used inside test cases:

```
test statemachine f {
  next(makeTP(200, 100)) -> airborne
  next(makeTP(300, 150)) -> airborne
  next(makeTP(0, 90)) -> landing
  next(makeTP(0, 0)) -> landed
}
```

Interacting with Other Code – Outbound   A state machine can have arbitrary C code in its entry, exit and transition actions. However, sometimes it has to interact with code that has already been written and resides outside the state machine. Interacting with external code can be done in two ways. The first one just calls a function from an action:

```
statemachine FlightAnalyzer initial = beforeFlight {
  ...
  state crashed {
    entry { raiseAlarm(); }
  }
}
...
void raiseAlarm() {}
```

Another alternative, which is more suitable for formal analysis (as discussed below) involves *out events*. From the entry action, an out event is sent, which has been defined earlier:

```
statemachine FlightAnalyzer initial = beforeFlight {
  out crashNotification()
  ...
  state crashed {
    entry { send crashNotification(); }
  }
}
```

Sending an event in this way has no effect, but it specifies that a particular event happens at this point. Model checkers can verify that this event occurs independently of what the event does. What remains to be done is to bind this event to application code. This can be done by adding a binding to the out event declaration:

```
out crashNotification() => raiseAlarm
```

The effect is the best of both worlds: the generated code calls the `raiseAlarm` function, but on the state machine level the implementation is abstracted from the intent, improving the structure of the state machine and making it verifiable.

Hierarchical State Machines   A problem with the above implementation of the state machine is that the `reset` events have to be handled similarly in each of the states. To avoid this repetition, hierarchical state machines can be used, in which a composite state can contain a sub-state machine, and the transitions declared on the composite state apply to all states in the sub-state machine:

```
composite state airborne initial = flying {
  on reset [ ] -> beforeFlight { points = 0; }
  on next [tp->alt == 0 m && tp->speed == 0 mps] -> crashed
  state flying {
    on next [tp->alt == 0 m && tp->speed > 0 mps] -> landing
    on next [tp->speed > 200 mps]
        -> flying { points += VERY_HIGH_SPEED; }
    on next [tp->speed > 100 mps]
        -> flying { points += HIGH_SPEED; }
  }
  state landing {
    on next [tp->speed == 0 mps] -> landed
    on next [ ] -> landing { points--; }
  }
  state landed {
    entry { points += LANDING; }
} }
```

State Machines as Tables   State machines can also be edited as tables (see Figure 4.5). The notation shows the in events as column headers and the states as row headers. The remaining cells contain the transitions. This provides a very useful overview, even though the actions are not shown for brevity. A third projection shows states as row headers and column headers, with the transitions in the content cells. This way, developers can quickly see which states are connected by which transitions.

Visualization   Like many other program elements in mbeddr, state machines can be visualized, Figure 4.6 shows an example. Various visualizations are available, for example with and without guard conditions (these can be long and disturb the layout algorithm).

```
exported statemachine FlightAnalyzer initial = beforeFlight {
                       next(Trackpoint* tp)                                    reset()
  beforeFlight [tp->alt == 0 m] -> airborne
  airborne     [tp->alt == 0 m && tp->speed == 0 mps] -> crashed    [ ] -> beforeFlight
               [tp->alt == 0 m && tp->speed > 0 mps] -> landing
               [tp->speed > 200 mps && tp->alt == 0 m] -> airborne
               [tp->speed > 100 mps && tp->speed <= 200 mps &&
                   tp->alt == 0 m] -> airborne
  landing      [tp->speed == 0 mps] -> landed                       [ ] -> beforeFlight
               [tp->speed > 0 mps] -> landing
  landed                                                            [ ] -> beforeFlight
  crashed
}
```

Figure 4.5 The table projection for state machines emphasizes the relationships between states and in events. The example above shows the non-hierarchical version of the `FlightAnalyzer` state machine discussed earlier in this section.

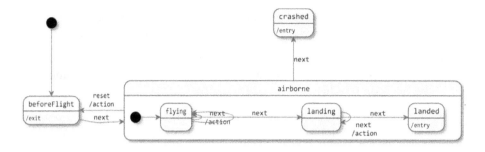

Figure 4.6 Visualization like this one can be created on the fly from every state machine. Users can click on states and transitions to select them in the editor.

4.6.2 Verification

Like decision tables, state machines can be verified. While in decision tables the verification is based on SMT solving, the state machine verification uses model checking [Clarke, 1997].

To verify a state machine, it must be marked as `verifiable`. Verifiable state machines are restricted in some ways, to make them checkable. For example, it is not possible to assign to the same variable more than once during one transition, taking into account all exit and entry actions, and action code cannot use arbitrary C statements. In particular, outbound integration with code must happen via out events (as discussed above) and the model checker will only check the *occurrence* of events, not their *effects*.

Model checking requires the specification of a set of properties which the state machine must conform to. Such properties are expressed in temporal logic [Clarke et al., 1986], which can quantify over a set of executions. Depending on the model checker used, such properties must be specified in one of various specification languages (LTL, CTL or CTL+). However, to hide some of the complexity of these specification from the application developer, mbeddr supports a set of higher-level property specifications based on the patterns introduced by Dwyer et al. [1999]. Examples include `P is true globally`, `P is false After Q Until R`, or `P is true Between Q and R`, where `P`, `Q` and `R` are Boolean expressions over states and local variables.

Based on the properties, the model checker then checks for each property whether it holds *in all cases*. If it does not, the result of the model checker is a counter example, i.e., one possible execution of the state machine that leads to a situation in which the property does not hold. In mbeddr, every state machine is checked for a number of properties *automatically*, so users do not have to specify them. Additional properties can be specified using the above-mentioned patterns. The automatic checks include the following:

- Is every state reachable, i.e. is there *some* sequence of events in the state machine that leads into each state. If not, the state is dead.

- Is every transition potentially executable, i.e. is there *some* sequence of events that fires each transition. If not, the transition could be removed.

- Are all transitions deterministic, i.e. is it always clear which transition must fire. If not, more than one transition could fire at a given time, and the decision of which one to fire is unclear[18].

- The state machines language supports bounded integers (i.e. integers that specify a value range). For each variable that uses a bounded integer type, the verifier checks that the variable actually stays within the specified bounds.

Verifying the `FlightAnalyzer` state machine leads to errors. The results claims that the `landing` state has non-deterministic transitions. The counter example is this:

```
State beforeFlight
in_event: next    next(0, -32768)
State beforeFlight
in_event: next    next(1, -32768)
State airborne
in_event: next    next(0, 101)
State landing
in_event: next    next(0, 0)
State landed
in_event: next    next(0, -32768)
```

In this example, in the `landing` state, the `next(0, 0)` event is fired and results in non-determinism (cf. the code for the `landing` state above). The first transition fires if `speed == 0`, which is the case for `next(0, 0)`. The second one fires in any case. Of course what the developer wanted to express is that the second one should only fire *otherwise*. In the generated C code it happens to work correctly because of the ordering of the transitions. But in general, the situation is ambiguous: `next(0, 0)` potentially fires both. The problem can be fixed by adding another guard condition:

```
state landing {
  on next [tp->speed == 0 mps] -> landed
  on next [tp->speed != 0 mps ] -> landing { points--; }
  on reset [ ] -> beforeFlight
}
```

Running the checker again reveals similar problems with the airborne state. After fixing these and other similar ambiguities, notice that the guard conditions can become long and hard to read:

```
state airborne {
  on next [tp->alt == 0 m && tp->speed == 0 mps] -> crashed
  on next [tp->alt == 0 m && tp->speed > 0 mps] -> landing
```

---

[18] In the mbeddr implementation based on a `switch` statement, the first of these transitions will fire. However, one should not rely on this fact and the verifier marks it as a problem.

```
    on next [tp->speed > 200 mps && tp->alt > 0 m]
        -> airborne { points += VERY_HIGH_SPEED; }
    on next [tp->speed > 100 mps && tp->speed <= 200 mps
            && tp->alt > 0 m]
        -> airborne { points += HIGH_SPEED; }
    on reset [ ] -> beforeFlight
}
```

This problem can be solved with macros. A macro is essentially a function that encapsulates complex expressions. If a macro needs to access event arguments, the macro has to be defined specifically for an event; in the code below, the two macros are defined for the next event. The code below also shows how ranges can be used to make the checks more concise.

```
statemachine FlightAnalyzer initial = beforeFlight {
    macro onTheGround(next)= tp->alt == 0 m
    macro inTheAir(next)= tp->alt > 0 m

    ...

    state airborne {
        on next [onTheGround && tp->speed == 0 mps] -> crashed
        on next [onTheGround && tp->speed > 0 mps] -> landing
        on next [tp->speed > 200 mps && inTheAir]
            -> airborne { points += VERY_HIGH_SPEED; }
        on next [tp->speed in ]100 mps, 200 mps] && inTheAir]
            -> airborne { points += HIGH_SPEED; }
        on reset [ ] -> beforeFlight
    }
}
```

4.6.3 Extensibility

Components   State machines cannot only be used as top-level elements in modules, they can also be embedded in components. In this case they can call required port operations from within guards, and out events can be bound to component runnables. It is also possible to bind an in event to a provided operation. This means that when the operation is called, this automatically triggers the respective event for the state machine. No adapter code has to be written.

Interrupt Triggers   Another extension that has been developed is a binding of in events to interrupts. In this case, it is assumed that a state machine has only one instance, and the interrupts specified for the in events are to affect this single instance. The instance is specified using the interrupt-driven instance field.

```
ProtocolSM protocol;

interrupt-driven instance protocol
statemachine ProtocolSM initial = stby {
    in msgReceived() interrupt 12
```

```
  var int8 sessionID = 0
  state stby {
    on msgReceived [ ] -> receiving {
      sessionID = someMemoryAccessAPI()[0];
    }
  }
  state receiving {
    ...
  }
}
```

As in the case of interrupt-triggered component runnables, the generators automatically create the interrupt handler code that feeds events into the state machine if an interrupt is received.

4.7 DOCUMENTATION

Even though developers and engineers would love to get rid of prose as part of the development process and represent everything with machine-processable languages and formalisms, prose plays an important role. Relevant examples include requirements engineering, comments, and design documents:

In *requirements engineering*, prose is the starting point for all subsequent formalizations. Classical requirements engineering uses prose in Word documents or Doors[19] databases, together with tables, figures and the occasional formula.

During the implementation phase, developers have to write *comments* in the code. These comments must be associated with program elements expressed in various languages. Comments also refer to code, and it is hard to keep these code references in sync with the actual code as it evolves. An example is comment that documents a function: the text in the comment typically makes reference to the arguments of the function.

Depending on the process, various *design documents* must created during or after the implementation. These are different from code comments in that they look at the bigger picture and "tell a story". In contrast to comments, they are not inlined into the code, they are separate documents. Nonetheless they are tightly integrated with the code, for example by referring to important program elements, or by embedding code fragments to explain a specific point. Today, such documents are usually written using LATEX, DocBook or Word – and synchronized manually with the implementation code.

To address all of these problems, mbeddr provides a set of languages for handling prose text, closely integrated with program code in various ways. Comments and design documents are discussed in this section; requirements engineering is discussed in Section 4.8.

Addressed Challenges The documentation support addresses the documentation aspect of the *Process Support* challenge.

---

[19] http://www-03.ibm.com/software/products/us/en/ratidoor/

The MPS language workbench on which mbeddr is built is a projectional editor. As mentioned, this has important advantages with regard to the extensibility of languages. However, it also means that the editor is a little more rigid than a regular text editor. In particular, until recently, MPS did not support multiline strings with the familiar editing experience of pressing `Enter` to create a line break, pressing ↑ to move the cursor to the line above the current one, or of deleting a few words on a line to "pull up" the text from the next line. However, the `mps-multiline`[20] MPS plugin, developed by Sascha Lisson, has enabled this behavior. In addition, an additional plugin, `mps-richtext`[21] enables embedding of program nodes into this multiline prose. At any location in multiline text a user can press `Ctrl-Space` and select a language concept from the code completion menu[22]. An instance of this concept is then inserted at the current location[23]. The program node "flows" with the rest of the text during edit operations. However, even though these program elements are part of a prose paragraph, they can still take part in constraints, type checks or refactorings – they are real program elements, and not just text. This enables tight and tool-supportable integration of prose and code.

Code Comments   In classical development or engineering tools, a comment is just a specially marked piece of text in the program code that is ignored by the parser or the tool in general. As part of this text, the names of program elements, such as module names or function arguments, are mentioned. This approach has two problems. First, the association of the comment to the commented element is only by proximity and convention[24] – usually the comment is above the element it is associated with. Second, references to other program elements are by name only – if the name changes, the reference becomes invalid, even though this is typically not checked by the tool. mbeddr improves on both counts.

First a comment is not just associated by proximity with the commented program node, it is actually *attached* to it. Structurally the comment is a child of the commented node, even though the editor shows it on top (Figure 4.7). If the element is moved, copied, cut, pasted or deleted, the comment always moves with the commented element.

Second, comments can contain embedded nodes (as discussed above) that refer to other program elements. For example, the comment on the state machine in Figure 4.7 references two of the states in the state machine. Some of

---

[20] `http://github.com/slisson/mps-multiline`

[21] `http://github.com/slisson/mps-richtext`

[22] Other editing gestures can also be used to insert nodes. For example, an existing regular text word can be selected, and, using a quick fix, it can wrapped with an `emph(...)` node, to mark the word as *emphasized*.

[23] To be able to use a language concept in prose text, it has to implement the `IWord` interface. The details of how this works are described in Section 8.17.

[24] This is true only in textual editors – graphical modeling tools usually do not have this problem.

```
// ┌ This state machine implements a way to grade ┐
   │ flights. It has separate states for the       │
   │ important flight phases, such as              │
   └ @child(beforeFlight) or @child(airborne).    ┘
statemachine FlightAnalyzer initial = beforeFlight {
  in next(Trackpoint* tp) <no binding>
  readable var int16 points = 0
  state beforeFlight {
    on next [tp->alt > 0 m] -> airborne
    exit { points += TAKEOFF; }
  } state beforeFlight
```

Figure 4.7 A state machine with a comment attached to it. The text in the comments references two of the states of the state machine.

```
mbeddr supports physical units. For example,
\code(struct) members can have physical units
in addition to their types. An example is
the @cc(Trackpoint/) in the @cm(DataStructures)
module. Here is the \code(struct):
```

Figure 4.8 This piece of document code uses \code tags to format parts of the text in code font. It also references C program elements (using the cm and cc tags). The references are actual, refactoring-safe references. In the generated output, these references are also formatted in code font.

the words that can be used in comments can be used in any comment (such as those that reference other modules or functions), whereas others are restricted to comments for specific language concepts (the references to states can only be used in a comment that is somewhere on or below a state machine).

Design Documents   mbeddr supports a documentation language. Like any other language for writing documents (such as LATEX or Docbook), it supports nested sections, text paragraphs and embedded images. Special IWords are used to mark parts of texts as emphasized, code-formatted or bold. Documents expressed in this language live inside MPS models, which means that they can be versioned together with any other MPS-based artifacts. The language comes with generators to LATEX and HTML; new ones (for example, to DocBook) can be added.

The documentation language also integrates with mbeddr languages, i.e. C, existing C extensions or any other language developed on top of MPS. The simplest case is a reference to a program element (Figure 4.8).

Code can also be embedded into documents. In the document source, the to-be-embedded piece of code is referenced. When the document is generated to LATEX or HTML, the actual source code is embedded either as text or as a screenshot of the editor in MPS. The latter is relevant because MPS supports non-textual notations such as tables, which cannot be sensibly embedded as text. Since the code is only embedded when the document is generated, the code is always automatically consistent with the actual implementation.

A language concept that implements the `IVisualizable` interface can contribute visualizations: the context menu for instances of the element has a *Visualize* item that users can select to render the diagram in the IDE. Examples of such visualizations are state machines (Section 4.6) and components (Section 4.4). The documentation language supports embedding these visualizations. As in the case of embedding code, the document source references a visualizable element. During output generation, the diagram is rendered and embedded in the output.

4.7.2 Extensibility

A hallmark of mbeddr is that everything can be extended by application developers, without invasively changing the extended languages. The prose-oriented languages can be extended as well. Here are a few examples:

Macro-Style Extensions Macro-style extension, in which a high-level abstraction is automatically expanded into a set of lower-level abstractions, can be used, both on the level of words and on the level of paragraphs in documents. For example, we have built a simple text-expander extension, where, for example, `\WRM` can be expanded into `With regards, Markus`.

Glossaries An obvious extension is support for glossaries. A glossary defines terms, which can be referenced from other term definitions, from regular text paragraphs or even requirements or code comments. Such term definitions are subconcepts of `AbstractParagraph`, so they can be plugged into regular documents. Figure 4.9 shows an example of a term definition.

The term definition in Figure 4.9 also shows how other terms are referenced using the `[Term|Text]` notation (such references, like others, are generated to hyperlinks when outputting HTML). The first argument is a (refactoring-safe) reference to the target term. The optional second argument is the text that should be used when generating the output code; by default, the text of the referenced term is generated into the output. Terms can also express relationships to other terms using the `->(...)` notation (this concept can only be used within term definitions). In this way a dependency graph is created between the terms in the glossary. A visualization is available that renders a diagram of this graph.

```
term:  Vehicle
A vehicle is ->(a special kind of [Car| ]).
A car typically has four [Wheel|Wheels].
```

Figure 4.9 A modular extension of the documentation language that supports the definition of glossary terms and the relationships between them. Terms can be referenced from any other prose, for example from comments or requirements.

```
The Drake equation calculates the number of
civilizations $N$ in the galaxy. As input,
it uses the average rate of star formation
$SF$, the fraction of those stars that have
planets $fp$ and the average number of
plane┌──────────────────────────────────────┐port life
     │ Error: type int8 is not a subtype of boolean │
$ne$. └──────────────────────────────────────┘s can be
calculated with $N   =   SF * fp * ne$.
```

Figure 4.10 An example in which variable declarations and equations are integrated directly with prose. Since the expressions are real C expressions, they are type checked. To make this possible, the variables have types; these are specified in the properties view, which is not shown in the figure. To provoke the type error shown above, the type of the N variable has been changed to `boolean`.

Formulas   Another extension adds variable definitions and formulas to prose paragraphs (Figure 4.10). When exported, they use the math mode of the respective target formalism. However, the variables are actual referenceable symbols and the equations are C expressions. As a consequence, the C type checker performs a type check for the equations (see the red underline under N in Figure 4.10). An interpreter for C expressions, which is available in mbeddr, can be plugged in to evaluate the formulas. This way, live test cases could be integrated directly with prose.

Going Meta   As demonstrated above, programs can be written in arbitrary languages, and can be integrated (by reference or by embedding) with documents written in the documentation language. However, sometimes the *language definitions themselves* need to be documented, to explain how to develop languages in MPS/mbeddr. To make this possible, a modular extension of the documentation language can be used to reference or embed language implementation artifacts. Similarly, documentation language documents can be embedded as well, to write documents that explain how to use the documentation language.

Cross-Cutting Concerns   mbeddr supports two cross-cutting concerns that can be applied to any language: requirements traces and variability. Since the documentation language is *just another language,* it can be used together with these cross cutting languages:

First, requirements traces (discussed in Section 4.8) can be attached to parts of documents such as sections, figures or paragraphs. In this way requirements traceability can extend into, for example, software design documents. This is an important feature in safety-critical contexts.

Second, to express product line variability (discussed in Section 4.9), a presence condition can be attached to document nodes such as paragraphs or sections. A presence condition is a Boolean expression over the features in a feature model. If the expression evaluates to false during output generation, the respective node is deleted. This way, documents such as user guides, configuration handbooks or software design documents can be made variant-aware in the same way as any other product line implementation artifact.

4.8 REQUIREMENTS

Collecting, organizing and managing requirements is mandatory for life-critical systems, and essential for mission-critical ones, and can be very useful in the development of other kinds of systems. Still, it is a cumbersome activity which either is relentlessly executed with major effort (typically if the customer or a certification standard/agency requires it) or is mainly overlooked, leading to poorly structured and maintained requirements.

A problem with the traditional way of collecting and maintaining requirements is the inadequacy of the supporting tools (see, for example, the study by Winkler & Pilgrim [2010]). In some fields, such as aerospace, automotive or telecoms, requirements are often collected and managed using MS Office documents or tools such as IBM Doors, which basically gather paragraphs of text with no or very limited structure. The relation between requirements and other artifacts such as implementation code or tests is collected in yet other documents, or with comments in the code, requiring manual synchronization between the requirements and these artifacts. It is not surprising that, when possible, practitioners try to escape this situation by either using simpler approaches for requirements elucidation (such as user stories[25]) or completely avoiding it. While agile approaches to requirements engineering limit the burden of managing them, they often do not provide a maintenance strategy for requirements; instead they are considered transient artifacts. This is not acceptable in many domains, where standards require a more structured approach to requirements management.

mbeddr's requirements language improves this situation in several ways. First, requirements are stored in the same way as any other mbeddr program – in XML files that can be versioned. Second, the requirements language is extensible, so domain-specific extensions can be plugged in seamlessly. Finally, mbeddr provides a tracing framework that can be used together with arbitrary mbeddr programs, expressed in any language.

Addressed Challenges   The requirements and tracing support addresses the respective aspect of the *Process Support* challenge.

4.8.1   *Languages and Language Extensions*

Requirements Versioned with Code   Traditionally, requirements are stored in a tool-specific database. Implementation artifacts are instead typically stored in version control systems (VCS) such as git, SVN or ClearCase. This situation leads to synchronization problems when trying to keep requirements in sync with the implementation. The natural solution would be to store

---

[25] http://en.wikipedia.org/wiki/User_story

```
Requirements FlightJudgementRules        show traces false
                                          filters
                                          imports ArchitecturalComponents
```

```
PointsForTakeoff /functional (0): Once a flight lifts off, you get 100 points
    Contains 1 data items and 0 child requirements

PointsFactor /functional (0): The factor of points
    Contains 1 data items and 0 child requirements

InFlightPoints /functional (0): Points you get for each trackpoint
    Contains 5 data items and 2 child requirements

Landing /functional (0): Stuff Relating to Landing
    Contains 1 data items and 2 child requirements
```

Figure 4.11 Requirements in mbeddr are arranged as a tree. The colored dots on the left reflect the trace status of a requirement (not traced, traced, traced with kind "implements", traced with kind "tested").

requirements and implementation artifacts in the same VCS. Since most of today's VCSs work with an update-and-merge strategy (as opposed to pessimistic locking), the requirements tool would need to support diff/merge for requirements as well.

In mbeddr, requirements are collected with a dedicated *requirements* language. Each requirement has an ID, a short summary, an optional longer prose description, a priority and any number of additional attributes. Requirements can also be nested. Figure 4.11 shows an example. The prose uses the same text editing facilities as discussed in Section 4.7. This makes it possible to conveniently edit larger pieces of prose, and, importantly, references to other requirements, use cases, actors or scenarios can be embedded in the prose in a refactoring-safe manner[26]; they are automatically kept in sync if the target is renamed or moved, and the IDE reports an error if the target is deleted. Together with explicit requirements dependencies expressed in the additional attributes section of a requirement (conflicts with, alternative to), these references can be used to build a rich requirements dependency graph, which can also be visualized (Figure 4.12).

Importantly, since mbeddr is based on MPS, and MPS comes with generic XML-based storage, all requirements are stored in XML files, along with any other implementation artifacts. This makes integrated versioning and branching simple. MPS also supports diff and merge for any arbitrary language based on the projected concrete syntax of each particular language, so support for diffing and merging requirements is available for free.

mbeddr's requirements tooling also has an importer to import requirements via XML or CSV files. In this way data migration from traditional requirements management tools is supported.

---

[26] Current mainstream requirements management tools such as Doors do not support this.

Traceability into Code The simplest kind of integration between implementation or design artifacts and requirements is tracing, where a program element has a pointer to one or more requirements. Such a trace pointer essentially expresses that this particular element is somehow related to a set of requirements. By using different trace kinds, the nature of "somehow related" can be qualified. Trace kinds typically include `implements` or `tests`.

Figure 4.13 shows a piece of mbeddr program code. The root element is a `module`, and it has an annotation that specifies a list of visible requirements modules. Traces can trace to any requirement in any of the referenced requirements modules, and traces can be added to any program element. There are four important characteristics of this approach:

1. The requirements trace is not just a comment. It is a well-typed program element that can be used for all kinds of analyses. For example, it is possible to select the requirement, open the Find Usages dialog, and obtain all program elements that have traces attached to the current requirement. The color coding in Figure 4.11 also exploits this information.

2. The trace is not an independent program element that is just "geographically close" to the program element it traces. Instead, the trace is a child element of the traced element. This means that, if the element is moved, copied, cut or pasted, the trace moves with it.

3. Since MPS is a projectional editor, the program can also be shown *without* the traces if the user so desires. The traces are still there and can be turned back on again at any time.

4. The tracing facility is *completely independent* of the traced language. Program elements defined in any (MPS-based) language can be traced. Users can define new languages, and the tracing mechanism will work with the new language automatically.

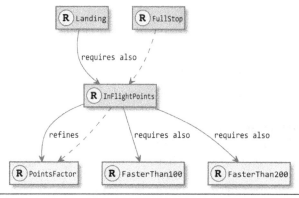

Figure 4.12 The requirements dependency graph for the `InFlightPoints` shows the downstream requirements it references (lower set of boxes, green) and the upstream requirements that depend on it (upper set of boxes, blue).

```
requirements modules: FlightJudgementRules
module StateMachines imports DataStructures, stdlib_stub, stdio_stub {

  [#define TAKEOFF = 100;]-> implements PointsForTakeoff
  [#define HIGH_SPEED = 10;]-> implements FasterThan100
  [#define VERY_HIGH_SPEED = 20;]-> implements FasterThan200

  statemachine FlightAnalyzer initial = beforeFlight {
    in next(Trackpoint* tp) <no binding>
    in reset() <no binding>
```

Figure 4.13 A C module with a set of constants that each have a trace to a single requirement. The tracing facility in mbeddr can add traces to any program element expressed in any language.

```
• scenario StoreFlight (0): A flight is stored in the store
  scenario StoreFlight
    Driver {
      == Setup ==
      -> InMemoryStore.setup(): SetupStatus
      alt setup status ok? {
        == Operation ==
        # Any number of store calls possible now
        -> InMemoryStore.store(SomeFlightData)
        -> InMemoryStore.store(SomeFlightData)
      else in case setup failed {
        ! system startup failed
} } }
```

Figure 4.14 An example scenario that describes interactions between collaborating components (and external actors).

While the tracing framework cannot remove the burden on users to manually establish and maintain the traces according to the actual relationship between the code and the requirements, the approach does solve all technical challenges in providing universally-applicable tracing support. However, the fact that referential integrity is automatically checked and arbitrary analyses can be built on top of the program/requirement/trace data can be used to ease the work of the developer: requirements and traces are "real code", and not just second-class metadata.

Use Cases, Actors and Scenarios   Many projects start out by collecting requirements in prose, for example in the way discussed above. However, when using prose only it is very hard to keep the overall system consistent – after all, there is no type checker or compiler for prose. One problem in this context is the definition of (functional) components, their responsibilities and their collaborations with other components, which express the high-level, functional structuring of the system under construction. One way to get to such components is to play through collaboration scenarios. These scenarios help understand which data a components owns, which services it offers, which other components it collaborates with, and which services one component uses from another component as part of such collaborations. However, if all of this is done only with pen and paper (CRC cards[27]), it can be tough to keep things consistent (this is the prose-only problem in a different guise). At some point, (somewhat) more formal descriptions have to be used.

In mbeddr, this is realized as follows. Since MPS supports arbitrary language extension and composition, it is possible to define additional DSLs that can be plugged into a requirement. To express the functional architecture, we have defined a DSL that has three top-level concepts: `actor` (an actor outside the system boundary), `component` (a functional building block of the system) and `scenario` (an example collaboration scenario between actors and components, not unlike sequence diagrams). The code below shows an example of a functional component. It lives inside a requirement, even though the original requirements language was not invasively changed.

```
component InMemoryStore {
  collaborates with FlightDataProvider:
  owns flights: Flight
  capability store(Flight): status
  capability setup(): status
}
```

Figure 4.14 shows a scenario, expressed with a textual language. Using this language, scenarios that are consistent with the definitions of the actors and components involved can be defined: if component A uses a capability from ("calls an operation on") a component B, and B is not defined as a collaborator of A, this results in an error in the IDE. A quick fix can then add B as a collaborator for A. Similarly, one can only use capabilities that are actually defined on the components. Finally, arguments to capabilities can only be taken from the data that is owned by the client component, or has been received via another capability call during that same scenario. As a consequence, after defining a set of scenarios, the components accumulate the data, capabilities and collaborators that are necessary to execute the scenarios: a functional architecture arises, "enforced" by the underlying language and its constraints. Scenarios are reminiscent of sequence diagrams, so they can also be visualized in this way (see Figure 4.15).

Requirements Reports The documents discussed in Section 4.7 cannot just be written manually, they can also be generated from other artifacts. For example, mbeddr's requirements language supports generating requirements reports from requirements modules. A report contains the requirements themselves, the custom attributes (via specific transformations) and trace information. This feature is implemented by transforming requirements collections to documents, then using the generators that come with the documentation language to generate the PDFs.

---

[27] http://en.wikipedia.org/wiki/CRC_Cards

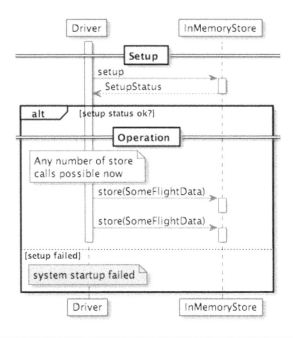

Figure 4.15 A scenario that describes example interactions between collaborating components (and external actors).

4.8.2 *Extensibility*

Use Cases, Scenarios and Actors   The language for expressing the functional architecture does not have expressions, sophisticated data types or a type checker. At this level of abstraction, these would be distractions – the goal of this language is the allocation of data, responsibilities and collaborations to the high-level functional building blocks of an application.

However, the language is extensible: new entities in addition to components or actors can be defined; components can have additional contents in addition to data items and capabilities, and scenarios can contain additional steps in addition to capability calls, headings, or alternatives. For example, a component may contain a wireframe mockup (which would have to be drawn outside of MPS) to represent UI aspects. It is also possible to add additional properties and then check constraints based on them. For example, components could be allocated to layers, and constraints could be used to check whether collaborations and capability calls respect layer constraints (for example, one can call from the `business` layer into the `persistence` layer, but not vice versa). These additional data and constraints can be added without invasively changing the basic scenario language, and can also be added *after* the initial set of components and scenarios have been defined, supporting incremental refinement of the language as understanding of the system grows. For example, systems engineers may first define the components and the scenarios. Then, in a second step, software architects may add the layer markup

- **functional PointsFactor (0):** The factor of points
  `constant int8 BASE_POINTS = 10`

- **functional InFlightPoints (0):** Points you get for each trackpoint

```
calculation PointForATrackpoint (int8): Points for each Trackpoints
     params int16 alt: current altitude of the trackpoint
            int16 speed: current speed of the trackpoint
```

= BASE_POINTS * 0	alt > 2000	alt > 1000
speed > 180	30	15
speed > 130	10	20

```
tests: PointForATrackpoint(500, 100) == 0
       PointForATrackpoint(500, 1200) == 0
```
Error: failed; expected 110, but was 100
```
       PointForATrackpoint(1100, 140) == 200
       PointForATrackpoint(2100, 140) == 110
```

Figure 4.16 A calculation is a function embedded into a requirement. They include test cases that allow "business people" to play with the calculations. An interpreter evaluates tests directly in the IDE for quick turnaround.

and the associated constraints, and then, if some of the constraints fail, split up or reallocate components to make them fit with the layer structure. Refactorings can be added to provide IDE support for such changes.

Formal Business Logic in Requirements The language for use cases, scenarios and actors addresses the challenge of becoming "more formal" with the goal of narrowing down the functional architecture of a system. Another way of getting incrementally closer to the implementation is to embed important parts of the business logic into requirements, and then use those in the implementation code.

Figure 4.16 shows two requirements. The first one defines a constant BASE_POINTS with the type int8 and the value 10. The second requirement defines a calculation PointsForATrackpoint. A calculation has a name, a list of parameters, and a result expression, which, in this case, uses a decision table. The calculation also references the BASE_POINTS constant. Using constants and calculations, business users can formally specify some important business data and rules, while not having to deal with the actual implementation of the overall system. To help with getting these data and rules correct, calculations also include test cases. These are evaluated directly in the IDE, using an interpreter: users can "play" with the calculations directly.

If the constants and calculations that business users specify in the requirements were *only* used in requirements, this would be only partially useful. In the end, these calculations should make their way into the code directly, without manual re-coding. Figure 4.17 shows a component, expressed in mbeddr's component extension. Inside the component, a calculation (the green code) is invoked using function call syntax. When this code is translated to C, the expression in the calculation is translated into C and inlined.

```
exported component Judge2 extends nothing {
  provides FlightJudger judger
  int16 points = 0;
  void judger_reset() ← op judger.reset {
    points = 0;
  }
  void judger_addTrackpoint(Trackpoint* tp) ← op judger.addTrackpoint {
    points += PointForATrackpoint(stripunit(tp->alt), stripunit(tp->speed));
  }
  int16 judger_getResult() ← op judger.getResult {
    return points;
} }
```

Figure 4.17 Implementation code can directly call calculation functions defined in requirements. In this case, a calculation is called from a component, expressed in the mbeddr components C extension.

The constant and the calculation are just examples of possible plug-in languages in mbeddr's requirements system. Any DSL, using a wide range of business user-friendly notations, can be plugged in and made available to C-based implementations.

Tracing into Other Artifacts   In many projects, requirements are not the last step before coding, and the functional architecture discussed in the previous section is too simplistic to describe the functionality of the system. Instead, other artifacts are developed, including system engineering models, functional models or physical models. Often these models are built with tools such as Matlab/Simulink[28] or Modelica[29], or use formalisms such as EAST-ADL[30], SysML[31] or UML. It is usually not possible to derive software artifacts from such models automatically, since they are too abstract. However, as software artifacts are developed, it is necessary to relate the software artifacts to these models.

To make this possible, mbeddr's tracing framework is extensible: other artifacts can be used as trace targets as well, as long as the respective language constructs implement an mbeddr-provided interface. In this way arbitrary descriptions or models, such as system models, functional models or component models, can be traced to. By adding an import facility, models created with the above-mentioned engineering tools can be integrated reasonably well with mbeddr-based artifacts. For example, we are currently implementing an importer for Matlab/Simulink models to support tracing to Simulink blocks from mbeddr program nodes. An alternative approach would be to keep the trace targets outside of mbeddr, for example in models created with SysML

---

[28] http://www.mathworks.com

[29] https://www.modelica.org

[30] http://www.east-adl.info/

[31] http://www.sysml.org/

or UML modeling tools, or in enterprise systems that manage these artifacts. In this case, the trace in mbeddr would be stored as some kind of ID or URL. By customizing code completion and constraint checking, the APIs of external tools or systems can be used to enforce consistency.

4.9 PRODUCT LINE VARIABILITY

The goal of product line engineering (PLE) is to efficiently manage a range of products (also often called variants in the context of PLE) by factoring out commonalities such that definitions of products can be reduced to a specification of their variable aspects. One way of achieving this is the expression of product configurations on a higher level of abstraction than the actual implementation. An automated mapping transforms the configuration to the implementation. Traditionally this higher level of abstraction is realized with feature models [Beuche et al., 2004] or similar configuration formalisms such as orthogonal variability models [Roos-Frantz, 2009] or decision models [Dhungana et al., 2007]. A feature model defines the set of valid configurations for a product in a product line by capturing all variation points (i.e. features), as well as the constraints between them.

Feature models are an efficient formalism for *configuration*, i.e. for *selecting* a valid combination of features from the feature model (this is in contrast to customization with DSLs; the difference is discussed by Voelter & Visser [2011]). The set of products that can be defined by feature selection is fixed and finite: each valid combination of selected features constitutes a product. This means that all valid products have to be "designed into" the feature model, encoded in the features and the constraints among them.

To actually implement a software product line, the variability expressed in feature models must be mapped to implementation artifacts. This can be done at runtime by querying which features are selected and then changing program execution, for example, with an `if` statement, or during generation. In the latter case, the program is configured based on the feature configuration, and then the configured model is processed as before via transformation, generation or interpretation. There are two different kinds of variability: in *negative* variability, DSL program elements can be annotated with *presence conditions*, Boolean expressions over the features of a feature model. When the DSL program is mapped to the solution space, a model transformation removes all those elements whose presence condition is false based on the current feature configuration. In the case of *positive* variability, a set of pre-built model fragments is created. The feature configuration selects a subset of them. The fragments are then merged using some DSL-specific or generic merge operator, resulting in a superimposed model representing the variant.

mbeddr supports a textual notation for feature models, and currently supports negative variability. Runtime variability is supported for C (and its extensions), whereas static variability is supported for any language.

Addressed Challenges The variability support addresses the respective aspect of the *Process Support* challenge.

Feature Models   mbeddr makes a clear distinction between the high-level description of variability and the mapping of the variability to artifacts. Feature modes are used for the specification of variability. In mbeddr, feature models use a textual notation, along with a graphical visualization. Below is a simple feature model that expresses variability over how flights are processed:

```
feature model FlightProcessor
  processing ? {
    nullify
    normalizeSpeed xor {
      maxCustom [int16/mps/ maxSpeed]
      max100
    }
  }
```

Every feature model has a root feature (`processing` in the example above). Features have child features, and the parent feature defines the constraints between the child features. By default, children are optional (marked by the `?` in the parent), which means that each of the children may be in the system or not, with no further constraints among them. `normalizeSpeed` has two children, `maxCustom` and `max100`. They are `xor`, so exactly one of them must be in a configuration if their parent feature is in the configuration. In addition to `?` and `xor`, child features can be mandatory (marked as `!`) or n-of-m (marked as `or`). Additional constraints that do not respect the tree structure can also be defined. For example, a feature may specify a `conflicts with` or `requires also` relationship to other features anywhere in the tree. Finally, features may have attributes. For example, `maxCustom` has an attribute `int16/mps/ maxSpeed`. Each valid configuration of this feature model must assign a value to each attribute of a selected feature.

Configuration   A configuration is an instance of a feature model in which some of the features are selected, and attributes have values. A configuration has to be valid with regards to the constraints defined in its feature model: for example, a configuration for `FlightProcessor` cannot have `maxCustom` and `max100` selected at the same time, since those two features are mutually exclusive (`xor`). Here is the simplest possible configuration which has no feature except the mandatory root feature:

```
configuration model cfgDoNothing configures FlightProcessor
  processing { }
```

Another valid configuration includes the `maxCustom` feature. Note that if `max100` were added as well, an error would be reported – the two are mutually exclusive.

```
configuration model cfgNullifyMaxAt200 configures FlightProcessor
  processing {
    nullify
```

```
    normalizeSpeed {
      maxCustom [maxSpeed = 200 mps]
    }
  }
```

Runtime Variability   As mentioned above, runtime variability means that a configuration is evaluated *at runtime*. Decisions about program execution are made based on this evaluation. To make this possible, the configuration has to be available as the program runs. The following program shows how to do this in mbeddr:

```
module RuntimeVariability imports FunctionPointers {
  feature model @ runtime for FlightProcessor;
  exported test case testRuntimeVar {...}
}
```

The `feature model @ runtime` creates a C data structure that can hold instances of the `FlightProcessor` feature model[32]. Users can now write variability-aware code. Below is a function that processes trackpoints depending on the configuration. Two things are worth mentioning: the first is the argument of type type `fmconfig<FlightProcessor>`. It represents a specific configuration for the `FlightProcessor` feature model (valid values are `cfgDoNothing`, `cfgNullifyOnly`, and `cfgNullifyMaxAt200`). The second important thing is the `variant` statement, whch is used to make parts of the procedural code dependent on the set of selected features:

```
Trackpoint processTrackpoint(fmconfig<FlightProcessor> cfg,
                             Trackpoint tp) {
  Trackpoint result;
  variant<cfg> {
    case (nullify && maxCustom) {
      result = process_nullifyAlt(tp);
      if (tp.speed > maxCustom.maxSpeed) {
        result.speed = maxCustom.maxSpeed;
      }
    }
    case (nullify && max100) {
      result = process_nullifyAlt(tp);
      if (tp.speed > 100 mps) {
        result.speed = 100 mps;
      }
    }
    case (nullify) { result = process_nullifyAlt(tp); }
    default { result = process_doNothing(tp); }
  }
  return result;
}
```

---

[32] Currently this data structure is a struct, with a Boolean member for each feature.

The `variant` construct is a new statement, so this only works for C, not for other languages. Currently mbeddr support only this form of runtime variability, but feature-dependent expressions or feature-dependent states (in state machines) would also be feasible, of course.

Assertions can now be added to the test case, calling the `processTrackpoint` function with several configuration models. Below is an example test case; it first creates a variable of type `fmconfig<FlightProcessor>` that holds a configuration (the same type as in the argument to `processTrackpoint`). It then uses the `store config` statement to store a configuration (`cfgDoNothing`) into the `cfg` variable. Finally it calls `processTrackpoint` with the configuration and the trackpoint and asserts the result:

```
exported test case testRuntimeVar {

  Trackpoint tp = {...};
  fmconfig<FlightProcessor> cfg;

  store config<FlightProcessor, cfgDoNothing> into cfg;
  Trackpoint res1 = processTrackpoint(cfg, tp);
  assert(0) res1.alt == 50 m;
  assert(1) res1.speed == 220 mps;

  store config<FlightProcessor, cfgNullifyOnly> into cfg;
  Trackpoint res2 = processTrackpoint(cfg, tp);
  assert(2) res2.alt == 0 m;
  assert(3) res2.speed == 220 mps;

  store config<FlightProcessor, cfgNullifyMaxAt200> into cfg;
  Trackpoint res3 = processTrackpoint(cfg, tp);
  assert(4) res3.alt == 0 m;
  assert(5) res3.speed == 200 mps;
}
```

In an actual system, `cfg` would probably be a global variable, so it can be accessed from everywhere. During program startup, a specific configuration would be stored in it, for example, after being read from a file.

Static Variability   In static variability, a variant of the program is constructed before execution. In mbeddr, the variant is created during generation. Static variability relies on the same variability specification (using feature models) as the runtime variability discussed above. As an example, a new implementation module with a test case in it is created, and the test is called from `Main`. A function sets the altitude of the trackpoint to zero:

```
module StaticVariability imports DataStructures {

  Trackpoint* process_trackpoint(Trackpoint* t) {
    t->alt = 0 m;
    return t;
  }
```

```
┌─────────────────────────────────────────┐
│Variability from FM: FlightProcessor      │
│Rendering Mode: product line              │
└─────────────────────────────────────────┘
module StaticVariability imports DataStructures {
  Trackpoint* process_trackpoint(Trackpoint* t) {
    {nullify}
    t->alt = 0 m;
    return t;
  } process_trackpoint (function)

  exported test case testStaticVariability {
    Trackpoint tp = {
      id = 1
      alt = 2000 m
      speed = 150 mps
    };
    {!nullify}
    assert(0) process_trackpoint(&tp)->alt == 2000 m;
    {nullify}
    assert(1) process_trackpoint(&tp)->alt == 0 m;
  } testStaticVariability(test case)
}
```

Figure 4.18 A program with static presence conditions attached to some program elements. Presence conditions can be attached to any program element, independent of the language. The color of a presence condition is derived from the expression itself, so different parts of the program that depend on the same presence conditions have the same color (an idea inspired by Kästner [2007]). By evaluating presence conditions in the projection rules, programs can be shown and edited as a specific variant.

```
exported test case testStaticVariability {
  Trackpoint tp = { id = 1, alt = 2000 m, speed = 150 mps };
  assert(1) process_trackpoint(&tp)->alt == 0 m;
} }
```

The nullification in the function should only happen if the `nullify` feature is selected in a particular configuration. To achieve this, two steps have to be performed. First, a dependency to a feature model has to be attached to the implementation module. Second, the `t->alt = 0 m;` statement has to be annotated with a presence condition. A presence condition is essentially a Boolean expression over features in a feature model. If that expression is `false` for a given configuration, the annotated element will be removed during generation. A presence condition is also added to the assertion in the test case. Figure 4.18 shows the program with the presence conditions.

To actually create the variant model during generation, a new configuration item has to be added in the build configuration.

```
variability mappings {
  fm FlightProcessor -> cfgNullifyOnly
}
```

This specifies that the `cfgNullifyOnly` configuration should be used during build. By changing this mapping, different variants of the system can be built.

4.9.2 Verification

As described by Batory [2005] and Czarnecki & Wasowski [2007], a particular advantage of feature models is that a straightforward mapping to logic exists. Using SAT solvers, it is possible to check, for example, whether a feature model has valid configurations at all, whether a particular configuration is valid, or to automatically complete partial configurations. This has been shown to work for realistically-sized feature models [Mendonça et al., 2009]. Pure::variants[33] maps feature models to Prolog to achieve a similar goal, as does the GEMS-based tool described by White et al. [2010].

mbeddr currently supports checking feature models for consistency, i.e., making sure that the additional constraints do not contradict each other. It also supports checking that a configuration conforms to the feature model.

Future checks will involve checking that presence conditions are plausible. A presence condition is not plausible if the combination of features expressed in the condition (for example, `f1 && f2`) can never happen (for example, because `f1` and `f2` are mutually exclusive). A final planned verification will make sure that artifacts remain structurally correct for any of the variants it can form according to the presence conditions and the associated feature model.

4.9.3 Extensibility

Features can have attributes, such as the `int16/mps/ maxSpeed` attribute on the `maxCustom` feature. This attribute uses a primitive type. However, arbitrary types can be used here, even types whose values are described with their own DSL. As a consequence of MPS' language composition facilities, the complexity and notation for the DSL can be arbitrary.

The approach described above uses feature models to vary artifacts expressed with languages. In some sense, the backbone of the system is the program, and this program is varied with a feature model. Attributes that use DSLs as their types invert this relationship, at least for parts of the system: the feature model is the master (describing a product line of systems), and the embedded DSL program fragments specify details for some of the features.

4.10 MISCELLANEOUS

This section discusses a number of additional mbeddr features that are very important for productive work, but are not directly related to the languages and language extensions supported by mbeddr. The topics are only introduced briefly; they are explained in more detail in the mbeddr user guide.

---

[33] http://pure-systems.com

106

As discussed in the introduction about language workbenches, one particular advantage of these tools is that they provide editor support for all languages built with the workbench, even in the face of modular language extension. This editor support includes syntax coloring, code completion, go-to-reference and highlighting for constraint and type system errors. However, many of the languages provide additional editor facilities such as the following:

- Quick fixes are on-the-fly program transformations. Quick fixes (also called intentions in MPS) can be accessed using the `Alt-Enter` menu. In mbeddr they are used extensively. Examples include marking module contents as exported, creating empty connectors for required ports in components, or for adding all transitively dependent modules to the build configuration.

- Automatic synchronization refers to the case in which one part A of a program depends completely and deterministically on another part B of the program. In this case, A can automatically be synchronized with B. For example, a component runnable must have the same signature as the operation it is triggered by. Automatic synchronization automatically ensures this.

- Most language workbenches support Find Usages on a program element, which finds all other program elements that refer to the selected one. For mbeddr, this functionality has been customized in many places to specifically find certain references. Examples include finding runnables that implement interface operations, finding provided and required ports for interfaces and finding requirements traces for requirements.

- A problem in projectional editors such as MPS is that one cannot create references to a program element that does not exist (yet). This means that, for example, an operation has to be created *before* a call to this operation can be written. This prevents top-down programming. mbeddr supports the on-demand creation of reference targets based on a quick fix in many cases. Examples include function calls (creating the function), transitions (creating the target state) or capability calls in requirements/scenarios (creating the called capability).

- Refactoring [Fowler & Beck, 1999] refers to improving the structure of a program without changing its semantics. In mbeddr several refactorings are available. Examples include Introduce Local Variable (which factors an expression into a new local variable), Extract Into New Module (which moves a set of selected module contents into a new module and imports it from the current one), or Wrap Into Composite State (which takes a set of selected states in a state machine and wraps them into a composite state).

```
                           ┌──────────────────────────┐
                           │ Warning: Unused parameter │
                           └──────────────────────────┘
int8 add(int8 x, int y) {
    return x;
}
```

Figure 4.19 Dataflow checks detect problems with the dataflow, such as the un-
used arguments shown here. The resulting errors or warnings are highlighted directly in the IDE, like any other error.

4.10.2 Dataflow Checking

mbeddr supports several kinds of program checks. Simple constraints check
name uniqueness, consistency of the build configuration, or ensure that every
interface operation has an associated runnable in a component. mbeddr also
supports type checks, which ensure that expressions, operation calls or assignments are type-compatible. A third kind of check concerns the dataflow
of the program[34]. Dataflow checks ensure, for example, that every argument
of a function is used (Figure 4.19), that every path through a function returns
a value or detects unnecessary `ifs`, because the value of the condition expression is constant `true` or `false`.

The dataflow checking facility builds on top of MPS' dataflow checking
framework, but it is specifically built to be extensible, like any other mbeddr
aspect. This allows the dataflow specifications for components or state machines to be plugged in.

4.10.3 Debugging

mbeddr supports debugging[35] at the level of the language extensions. So
when stepping through state machines or components, the step-in, step-over
or step-out granularity corresponds to the domain-specific code as seen in
MPS, not to the low-level implementation in the generated C code.

The same is true for the Watch window: this shows the symbols that are
relevant to the domain-specific abstractions (for example, component fields
and the connection targets of required ports of a component instance) as opposed symbols that are necessary for the implementation (such as the struct
that maintains a component's internal state). The Watch expressions also take
into account the mbeddr type. For example, Boolean values are represented as
`true` and `false`, even though their C-level representation is an integer. Similarly, a literal that uses a physical unit will be shown with the unit in the
Watch window.

---

[34] Dataflow checking has been implemented by Malte Jannasch as part of his Master's thesis.

[35] The debugger has been implemented by Domenik Paveltic as part of his Master's thesis; he
continues working on it as part of his PhD.

4.10.4 *Importer*

To develop realistic systems, it must be possible to work with existing code. There are two major scenarios: library access and legacy code import.

Library Access   In this scenario, only a header file must be imported, so mbeddr code can refer to its referenceable contents. mbeddr supports *external modules* for this purpose. An external module declares referenceable C constructs such as functions, constants or structs, and acts as a proxy for the real, textual header file. In addition, an external module may optionally specify a library (.a or .o file) that must be linked to the resulting executable:

```
external module stdio_stub resources header: <stdio.h> {
  void printf(const char* format, ...);
}
```

If a regular mbeddr module M uses an external module (such as the one shown above), the external module is imported in M. This allows code in M to reference the external module's contents (in the example, code in M could call printf). However, in the C code generated from M the *original* header will be included (stdio.h); no code is ever generated from an external module. This simplifies the task of importing headers, because only those parts of a header file that can be referenced from mbeddr code have to be imported. The implementation of macros, inline functions or the values of constants need not be imported.

   External headers can be created manually, which is feasible for small header files. Alternatively, an importer is available. However, C's preprocessor sometimes makes importing header files a challenge – see the next paragraph.

Importing Legacy Code   Parsing C code and building the respective mbeddr program tree would not be a problem if it were not for the preprocessor. Many C grammars are available to parse C programs. mbeddr integrates the Eclipse CDT C parser[36], which even performs name resolution and typing. The resulting AST can be transformed to mbeddr relatively easily.

   What makes importing C code hard is the preprocessor: it operates on the text level and can produce unparseable C code. In addition, the preprocessor is used to express product line variability [Tomassetti & Ratiu, 2013], which, ideally, should be retained and mapped to mbeddr's variability support. Such an importer is currently being built for mbeddr, but it is not yet finished.

4.10.5 *Version Control*

MPS stores all programs, including those written with mbeddr languages in XML files. These files can be managed with any of the existing file-based version control systems. In particular, we have used Subversion[37] and Git[38].

---

[36] http://www.eclipse.org/cdt/

[37] http://subversion.tigris.org/

[38] http://git-scm.com/

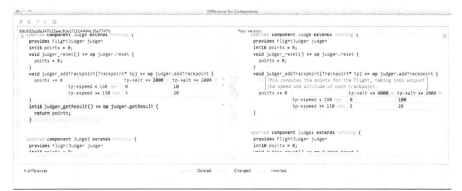

Figure 4.20 This dialog shows the diff between the local version and the latest version from git before a commit. The local version has changed two of the values in the decision table, has added a comment and has removed one runnable.

However, since the storage is XML-based, diff/merge requires special support from MPS: it is not feasible to diff/merge MPS files on the level of XML. However, as Figure 4.20 shows, MPS provides a diff/merge facility on the level of the projected syntax. This works automatically for any language. MPS also supports other version control operations directly from within the IDE. Examples include commit, revert or show history.

4.10.6   Command-Line Build

To be able to build mbeddr programs on a continuous integration (CI) server, it is necessary that the generation to C can be executed from the command line. MPS ships with an Apache Ant[39] task that can be used for this purpose. Ant is the lowest common denominator for build tools in the Java world – it can easily be integrated into newer or more sophisticated build systems such as Maven[40], and it can be called from all CI servers.

mbeddr comes with a wizard that can be used to generate the ant build file for an mbeddr project. This simplifies the task of setting up the `build.xml` correctly for a particular project.

Summary — *mbeddr has started out as a set of C extensions (state machines, interfaces and components, units). However, as this chapter has shown, the approach can be generalized to other aspects of embedded software engineering such as requirements, documentation or product line variability. Chapter 8 illustrates how these languages are built. The next chapter looks at the experience with mbeddr so far and validates it from the perspective of the application developer. A validation of mbeddr as an example of* Generic Tools, Specific Languages, *from the perspective of the language engineer, is provided in Chapter 10.*

---

[39] http://ant.apache.org/

[40] http://maven.apache.org/

Validation I: An Application Developer's Perspective

Abstract — *The* Generic Tools, Specific Languages *approach is only worthwhile if it leads to useful tools that address the challenges of embedded software development discussed in Chapter 3. In addition it should not introduce its own problems in terms of scalability, usability, learnability, infrastructure integration and interoperability with existing textual code. This chapter evaluates the use of mbeddr in embedded software development based on a number of applications developed with mbeddr: a smart meter, an AUTOSAR component, an ASIC tester, a Lego Mindstorms robot, a pacemaker and a synthesizer. The experience from these projects confirms our expectation of mbeddr's usefulness for embedded software development.*

5.1   EXAMPLE SYSTEMS AND THEIR USE OF MBEDDR

To validate the usefulness of mbeddr, this section relies heavily on experiences from a number of development projects run with mbeddr[1]. The projects range from demo applications to real-world development projects:

Smartmeter: The Smartmeter project is the first commercial use of mbeddr, and targets the development of the software for a 3-phase smart meter. A smart meter is an electrical meter that continuously records the consumption of electric power in a home and sends the data back to the utility company for monitoring and billing. The software comprises ca. 40,000 lines[2] of mbeddr code, has several time-sensitive parts that require a low-overhead implementation, and will have to be certified by the future operator. This leads to an emphasis on performance, testing, formal analyses and requirements tracing. The software exploits existing code supplied by the hardware vendor in the form of header files, libraries and code snippets, even though most of the system has since been rewritten. While the project is still going on, some experience can already be reported and some conclusions drawn. Smartmeter is proprietary, commercial software developed by itemis France, so the code is not available. ◄

Park-o-Matic: As part of the LW-ES project, BMW Car IT[3] has developed an AUTOSAR component based on mbeddr. This component, called Park-o-Matic in this thesis[4], coordinates various sensors when assisting

---

[1] Separate documents for some of these can be found at http://mbeddr.com/learn.html

[2] Section 5.3.1 discusses how this is measured in MPS' non-textual editor.

[3] http://www.bmw-carit.com/

[4] This is not the real name; I was not allowed to use the real name in the thesis.

a driver to park their car. It is fundamentally a state-based system. As part of this project, AUTOSAR-specific generators had to be built for the mbeddr components language. AUTOSAR defines the notion of software components that are close to mbeddr's components (because mbeddr's components were consciously modeled on AUTOSAR). However, the current mbeddr generators map the components to plain C. In the case of AUTOSAR, components have to integrate with the runtime environment (RTE), which means, for example, that calls on a required port have to be translated to AUTOSAR-specific macro calls. In addition, an XML file has to be generated that describes the software component, so that it can be integrated with others by an integration tool. The Park-o-Matic code is owned by BMW Car IT and is not available. ◄

ASIC Testing: Developed by Modellwerkstatt[5], an ASIC (Application-Specific Integrated Circuit[6]) is an electronic chip designed for a particular purpose. One of Modellwerkstatt's customers ordered a quite complex ASIC design, providing various I/O functions such as analog/digital conversion, filters and counters. The ASIC is used in an I/O module for control systems. One of the most important features the I/O module provides is an extensive self-test of the ASIC, which consists of approximately 60 cycles of the following procedure: reset chip, configure functionality, write value to output, read value from input and compare it to expected value. The original developers of the ASIC came up with an Excel spreadsheet that described the tests. Each row described one cycle with all configuration details; write values and expected read values were stored in the columns. What was needed next was a translation of the Excel file into C, which is executable by the target device. The respective generator was developed with mbeddr. The ASIC testing code is owned by Modellwerkstatt/Bachmann Electronic and is not available. ◄

Lego Mindstorms: This set of extensions for programming Lego Mindstorms[7] robots is the first significant demonstration project built with mbeddr. Mindstorm robots can be programmed with various tools and languages, among them C. There is also an implementation of the OSEK[8] operating system called Lejos OSEK[9]. We have developed several robots (and their respective software) based on a common set of C extensions on top of Lejos OSEK. OSEK is also used outside of Lego Mindstorms for real-world embedded applications, so this system is relevant beyond Lego. The system was developed by the mbeddr team. It has not been maintained and cannot be used with the current version of mbeddr; however, a few code examples are included in this chapter and as well as in Chapter 10. ◄

---

[5] http://www.modellwerkstatt.org/

[6] https://en.wikipedia.org/wiki/Application-specific_integrated_circuit

[7] http://mindstorms.lego.com/

[8] http://en.wikipedia.org/wiki/OSEK

[9] http://lejos-osek.sourceforge.net/

	Smart	Park	ASIC	Pace	Synth	Lego
Testing	•	•		•	•	
Physical units	•	•		•		
Components	•	•		•	•	•
Decision tables	•	•				
State machines	•	•		•		•
Documentation	•					
Requirements/Tracing	•	•		•		
Product lines	•					•
Analysis/Verification	•	○		•		
Language extensions	•			•		•
New generator		•				
Generation target only			•			

Table 5.1 This table shows which mbeddr extensions were used in which system. See the text below for details.

Pacemaker: This system addresses mbeddr's contribution to the Pacemaker Challenge[10], an international, academic challenge addressing the development and verification of safety-critical software, exemplified by a pacemaker. This system emphasizes code quality, verification techniques and systematic management of requirements. However, performance is also important, since the software must run on the very limited resources provided by the microcontroller in a pacemaker. This project was developed by Zaur Molotnikov at fortiss; the code can be downloaded from github[11]. ◀

Synthesizer: Aykut Kilic, a colleague at itemis, has developed a music synthesizer based on mbeddr. The system connects to an external keyboard and uses its input to synthesize sounds. The actual creation of the waveform happens with mbeddr code. While the system is relatively simple, it is quite time-critical: it is a soft realtime system – the sampling rate is 44.1kHz and control rate is around 800Hz. This system serves as a demonstration of mbeddr's capability to create efficient, low-level software. It also illustrates interfacing to external hardware. The code is available as MPS sources at github[12]; a textual read-only version is also available[13]. ◀

Table 5.1 shows how mbeddr's extensions were used in the various systems. The ASIC Testing system is an outlier: it uses none of mbeddr's extensions. The reason is that in this case separate DSLs were developed (reusing C's ex-

---

[10] http://sqrl.mcmaster.ca/pacemaker.htm

[11] https://github.com/qutorial/PaceMakerMPSModelling

[12] https://github.com/aykutkilic/aynth

[13] https://github.com/aykutkilic/aynth/blob/master/aynth.core/src_mbd/modulators.mbd

pression language) that used mbeddr's version of C as a generation target. It is also obvious that the Smartmeter system is the most exhaustive of the systems: it uses essentially all of mbeddr's extensions. As expected, the components extension is used most. It provides a well-structured and generic way to structure applications, and this is useful for most systems. The product line support is used only in the Smartmeter – it is the only system that exists in more than one variant. Analysis and verification was used successfully in two systems, and attempted – unsuccessfully – in one: the Park-o-Matic. Details are explained below. The reason that the documentation language is only used in one system is the usual one: documentation is schedule to be done at the end, then time runs out. Since the Smartmeter is an actual product, not documenting it is not an option. Another use case for the documentation language is the mbeddr user guide itself, which is currently being ported from LATEXto the documentation language to simplify maintenance. Three systems have built custom language extensions, and one project has built new generators for an existing language. These are discussed and evaluated in Chapter 10.1.

5.2   ADDRESSING THE CHALLENGES

This section revisits the challenges from Section 3.2 to show how mbeddr's features address these challenges. The challenges include abstraction without runtime cost (Section 5.2.1), C considered unsafe (Section 5.2.2), program annotations (Section 5.2.3), static checks and verification (Section 5.2.4) and process support (Section 5.2.5).

5.2.1   *Abstraction without Runtime Cost*

Chapter 4 discusses the abstractions provided by mbeddr for embedded software development. This section investigates whether and how these have been used in the example systems.

> **Smartmeter:** Smartmeter uses mbeddr's C extensions extensively. It uses mbeddr's components to encapsulate the hardware-dependent parts of the system. By exchanging the hardware-dependent components with stubs and mocks, integration tests can be run on a PC without using the actual target device. As a side effect, the software can be debugged on a normal PC, using mbeddr's debugger. While this does not cover all potential test and debugging scenarios, a significant share of the application logic can be handled this way. The smart meter communicates with its environment via several different protocols. So far, one of these protocols has been refactored to use a state machine. This has proved to be much more readable than the original C code. Table 5.2 provides an overview. In particular, interfaces and components are used heavily to modularize the system and make it testable. 54 test cases and 1,415 assertions are used. Physical units are used heavily as well, with 102 unit declarations and 155 conversion rules. The Smartmeter team reports significant benefits in terms of code quality and robustness. The developers involved

in the project had been thinking in terms of interfaces and components before; mbeddr allows them to express these notions directly in code. ◄

Area	Language Concept	No. of Instances
Components	Components	99
	Ports	335
	Runnables ("functions" in components)	368
	Interfaces	54
	Operations ("methods" in interfaces)	118
	Component instances	168
	Connectors (connecting ports of instances)	238
C Top Level	Modules	219
	Module dependencies	976
	Struct declarations	94
	Struct members	458
	Enum declarations	168
	Enum literals	1,708
	Constants	7,600
Testing	Tests	58
	Assertions	1,415
	Mock components	5
	Mock steps	22
Units	Unit declarations	102
	Conversion rules	155
State Machines	State machines	2
	States	17

Table 5.2 Numbers of instances of important concepts in the Smartmeter project.

Park-o-Matic: The core of Park-o-Matic is a big state machine which coordinates various sensors and actuators used during the parking process. The interfaces to the sensors and actuators are implemented as components, and the state machine lives in yet another component. By stubbing and mocking the sensor and actuator components, testing of the overall system was simplified. ◄

Lego Mindstorms: mbeddr's components have been used to wrap low-level Lego APIs into higher-level units that reflect the structure of the underlying robot, and hence makes implementing the application logic that controls the robot much simpler. For example, a interface `DriveTrain` supports a high-level API for driving the robots. It uses pre- and postconditions as well as a protocol state machine to define the semantics of the interface.

```
exported cs interface DriveTrain {
  void driveForwardFor(uint8 speed, uint32 ms)
    pre(0) speed <= 100
    post(1) currentSpeed() == 0
    protocol init(0) -> init(0)
  void driveBackwardFor(uint8 speed, uint32 ms)
```

```
    pre(0) speed <= 100
    post(1) currentSpeed() == 0
    protocol init(0) -> init(0)
  void driveContinouslyForward(uint8 speed)
    pre(0) speed <= 100
    post(1) currentSpeed() == speed
    protocol init(0) -> new forward(1)
  void driveContinouslyBackward(uint8 speed)
    pre(0) speed <= 100
    post(1) currentSpeed() == speed
    protocol init(0) -> new backward(2)
  query uint8 currentSpeed()
  void stop()
    post(0) currentSpeed() == 0
    protocol *(-1) -> init(0)   // the asterisk means 'any state'
  void turnLeft(uint8 turnDeltaSpeed)
    protocol init(0) -> init(0)
  void turnRight(uint8 turnDeltaSpeed)
    protocol init(0) -> init(0)
}
```

As a consequence of the separation between specification (interface) and
implementation (component), testing of line-following algorithms was
simplified. For example, since the motors are encapsulated into inter-
faces/components, mock implementations can be provided to simulate
the robot without using the Mindstorms hardware and API. Other components such as the `Orienter` use the motor components and provide a
high-level approach to orienting the robot based on the compass sensor.
The compass sensor itself requires a non-trivial sequence of operations to
retrieve an actual heading. This is encapsulated in the component.

```
void orienter_orientTowards(int16 heading, uint8 speed, DIR dir)
      <- op orienter.orientTowards {
  int16 currentDir = compass.heading();
  if ( dir == COUNTERCLOCKWISE ) {
    motorLeft.set_speed(-1 * ((int8) speed));
    motorRight.set_speed(((int8) speed));
  } else {
    motorLeft.set_speed(((int8) speed));
    motorRight.set_speed(-1 * ((int8) speed));
  }
  while ( !(currentDir in [heading - 4 .. heading + 4]) )
    currentDir = compass.heading();
  motorLeft.stop();
  motorRight.stop();
}
```

The top-level behavior of a line-follower robot was implemented as a state
machine. The state machine calls the above- mentioned components to
cause the necessary changes in direction or speed.

While this system was developed specifically for demo purposes early in the mbeddr project, it did confirm the right direction for mbeddr. The developers who built the Lego system were not proficient in C or embedded software, but could nonetheless quickly write robust code for NXT OSEK.

Synthesizer: The synthesizer is essentially a pipes and filters architecture [Buschmann et al., 1996a]. The first element in the chain creates a waveform (sine, sawtooth or other) and the subsequent filters act as processors that modify or distort the waveform in some way to create the unique sounds associated with synthesizers. The various filters were implemented as components. A single interface acts as the pipe, so that the implementing components could be chained arbitrarily. The following shows the outline of a simple example:

```
ringbuffer[int32, 10] Wavebuffer;

sr interface  IWave {
    Wavebuffer wave;
}

component Oscillator {
    provides IWave out;
}

component RingModulator {
    requires IWave in [2]
}

instances example {
    instance Oscillator osc1
    instance Oscillator osc2
    instance RingModulator mod
    connect osc1.out -> mod.in[0]
    connect osc2.out -> mod.in[1]
}
```

The synthesizer implementation exploits mbeddr's polymorphic interfaces and the ability to flexibly change the connections between components, in order to change the setup of the pipeline and hence change the sound produced. Components provide additional interfaces to pass control parameters to the processors (for example, to control the frequency of the waveform created, or the amount of distortion introduced by a specific filter). These interfaces are connected to external controls (knobs and sliders) used by the musician to change the sound.

Pacemaker: The default extensions have proven useful in the development of the pacemaker. The pacemaker uses mbeddr's components to encapsulate the hardware-dependent parts. Furthermore, the pulse generator system is divided into subsystems according to the disease these subsystems treat. The pacemaker logic for treating diseases is implemented as a state machine. This makes the implementation easier to validate and verify (discussed in Section 5.2.4. Requirements tracing simplifies the validation activities. ◄

A fundamental problem with higher-level abstractions is that in the event of an error, unacceptable performance or resource consumption, a user may have to deal with the underlying low-level implementation. However, the user may not understand this implementation, because they did not write the code (or the generator) and had previously just relied on the higher-level abstraction. This problem exists for macros, libraries and also for mbeddr's language extensions. mbeddr tries to limit this problem as far as possible: every valid extension-level program leads to a valid C program. This is ensured by automated unit tests and (initially maybe overly-) strict type system rules and constraints.

> **Smartmeter:** As the largest system built with mbeddr so far, the developers found a few bugs in the generators, which led to buggy generated code, even though the mbeddr-level program was valid. However, these problems were few and far between. It can be concluded from this experience that the existing language extensions are reasonably mature. ◄

mbeddr also provides an extensible debugger that lets users debug programs at the extension level. mbeddr also has a tool to find the source of a log statement on the extension level based on the log output.

Generating code from higher-level abstractions may introduce performance and resource consumption overhead. For embedded software, it is unacceptable for abstractions to incur significant overhead, although it is not clearly defined what "significant" means. However, a threshold is clearly reached when a new target platform is required to run the software, "just because" better abstractions have been used to develop it. The reason is that for many embedded systems, the unit cost (of the final product) is the primary cost driver. A larger hardware platform drives unit cost up, since it has to be deployed in every unit built and sold. As part of mbeddr development, we have not performed a systematic study of the overhead incurred by the mbeddr extensions, but preliminary conclusions can be drawn from the existing systems:

> **Smartmeter:** The Smartmeter code runs on the intended target device. This means that the overall size of the system (in terms of program size and RAM use) is low enough to work on the hardware that had been planned for use with the native C version. As explained above, this is an important criterion.
>
> Some of the extensions specifically built for in Smartmeter (registers and interrupts, discussed in Section 10.1) have no runtime footprint at all; they are mapped to plain C without any specific overhead. This is important because the realtime core that measures voltage and current in sync with the 50 or 60 Hz cycle supply is critical in that absolutely no overhead must be incurred there: "missing a cycle" can lead to faulty

measurements, incorrect billing, and ultimately legal consequences. In fact, the accuracy of the Smartmeter had been increased significantly, a direct consequence of better performance in the core measurement component. This, in turn, is a consequence of better testing and an overall cleaner architecture. ◄

Synthesizer: The task of a synthesizer is to create waveforms and process them with various processors and filters. The input that decides which frequency to produce and which processors to apply is provided by an external MIDI keyboard. All of this requires a reasonably fast system. mbeddr's components are used extensively, but still the performance is satisfactory: according to the developer, the system runs robustly. ◄

Pacemaker: The Pacemaker challenge requires the code to run on a quite limited target platform, the PIC18[14]). The C code is compiled with a proprietary C compiler. The overhead of the implementation code generated from the mbeddr abstractions is small enough for the code to be run on this platform in terms of performance, program size and RAM use. ◄

mbeddr's extensions can be partitioned into three groups. The first group has no consequences for the generated C code at all – the extensions are related to metadata (requirements tracing) or type checks (units). During generation, the extension code is removed from the program.

The second group consists of extensions that are trivially generated to C, and use at most function calls as indirections. The resulting code is similar in size and performance to reasonably well-structured manually written code. State machines (generated to functions with `switch` statements), unit value conversions (which inline the conversion expression) or unit tests (which become `void` functions) are examples of this group.

The third group of extensions incurs additional overhead, even though mbeddr is designed to keep it minimal. Here are some examples. The runtime checking of contracts is performed with an `if` statements that check the pre- and post-conditions, as well as assignments to and checks of variables that keep track of the protocol state. The following piece of C code is generated from a pre-condition that asserts that the argument p is not `null`; the overhead is the fact that the precondition leads to the `if` check:

```
struct void Nuller_processor_process(struct Trackpoint* p, ... ) {
  if ( !((p != 0)) ) {
    pre_1731059994647781332__1731059994647782993:
    // report error
  }
  // implementation
}
```

Another example is polymorphism for component interfaces, which use an indirection through a function pointer when an operation is called on a required port. The following is the code generated from a component runnable

---

[14] http://en.wikipedia.org/wiki/PIC_microcontroller

that, in the first line of the implementation, invokes the `save` method on a `store` required port:

```
struct void Interpolator_processor_process(
            struct DataStructures_Trackpoint* p,
            void* ___instance) {
   struct compdata_Interpolator* ___castedInstance =
       ((struct Components_compdata_Interpolator*)(___instance));
   (*___castedInstance->portops_store->save)
       (p, ___castedInstance->port_store);
   ...
}
```

Every component runnable gets an additional argument, the data for the current instance, ___instance. For technical reasons it is passed as a `void` pointer, and then downcast to the correct concrete type in the first line of every runnable. The second line in the code above is the actual call; the call is performed via a function pointer `save` (the name of the called operation) in the `portops` struct for the `store` required port. While the accesses to the members in the struct has no overhead because the addresses can be calculated by the compiler, the call through the function pointer is less efficient than a direct function call.

In this third group of extensions there is no way of implementing the feature in C without overhead. The user guide points this out to users, who have to make a conscious decision about whether the overhead is worth the benefits in flexibility or maintainability. However, in some cases mbeddr provides different transformation options that make different trade-offs with regards to runtime overhead. For example, if in a given executable an interface is only provided by one component, and hence no runtime polymorphism is required, the components can be connected statically, and the indirection through function pointers is not necessary. This leads to better performance, but also limits flexibility. Below is the code from above with *static wiring* enabled. The generator knows statically that the `TrackpointStore` interface is only provided by the `InMemoryStore` component. Its `save` operation is called directly:

```
struct void Interpolator_processor_process(
            struct DataStructures_Trackpoint* p,
            void* ___instance) {
   struct compdata_Interpolator* ___castedInstance =
       ((struct Components_compdata_Interpolator*)(___instance));
   InMemoryStore_store_save(p, ___castedInstance->port_store);
   ...
}
```

With regard to performance, we conclude that mbeddr generates reasonably efficient code, both in terms of overhead and performance. It can certainly be used for soft realtime applications on reasonably small processors. We are still a unsure about hard realtime applications. Even though Smartmeter and the Synthesizer are promising, more experience is needed in this area.

In addition, additional abstractions to describe worst-case execution time and to support static scheduling are required. However, these can be added to mbeddr easily, so in the long term, we are convinced that mbeddr is a very capable platform for hard realtime applications.

Summing up, the mbeddr default extensions have proved extremely useful in the development of the various systems. Their tight integration is useful, since it avoids the mismatch between various different abstractions encountered when using different tools for each abstraction. This is confirmed by the developers of the pacemaker, who report that *the fact that the extensions are directly integrated into C, as opposed to the classical approach of using external DSLs or separate modeling tools, reduces the hurdle of using higher-level extensions and removes any potential mismatch between DSL code and C code.*

5.2.2 C Considered Unsafe

The mbeddr C implementation already makes some changes to C that improve safety. For example, the preprocessor is not exposed to the developer; its use cases (constants, macros, `#ifdef`-based variability, `pragmas`) have first-class alternatives in mbeddr that are more robust and type-safe. Size-independent integer types (such as `int` or `short`) can only be used for legacy code integration; regular code has to use the size-specific types (`int8`, `uint16`, etc.). Arithmetic operations on pointers or `enums` are only supported after an explicit cast; and mbeddr C has direct support for `boolean` types instead of treating integers as Booleans.

> **Smartmeter:** Smartmeter is partially based on code received from the hardware vendor. This code has been refactored into mbeddr components; in the process, it has also been thoroughly cleaned up. Several problems with pointer arithmetic and integer overflow have been discovered as a consequence of mbeddr's stricter type system. ◄

More sophisticated checks, such as those necessary for MISRA-compliance, can be integrated as modular language extensions. The necessary building blocks for such an extension are annotations (to mark a module as MISRA-compliant), checking rules (to perform the required checks on modules marked as MISRA-compliant), as well as the existing AST, type information and data-flow graph (to be able to implement these additional checks).

Finally, the existing extensions, plus those potentially created by application developers, support writing code at an appropriate abstraction level. The potentially unsafe lower-level code is generated, reducing the probability of mistakes.

> **Smartmeter:** Smartmeter combines components and state machines, decoupling message assembly and parsing from the application logic in the server component. Parsing messages according to their definition is notoriously finicky and involves a lot of direct memory access and pointer arithmetic. This must be integrated with state-based behavior to keep track of the protocol state. State machines, as well as declarative descrip-

tions of the message structure[15] make this code much more robust and maintainable. ◄

5.2.3 *Program Annotations*

The physical units are an example of program annotations. Program annotations are data that improves the type checking or other constraints in the IDE, but have no effect on the running program.

> **Smartmeter:** Extensive use is made of physical units. According to Table 5.2, there are 102 unit declarations in the Smartmeter project. Smart meters deal with various currents and voltages, and distinguishing and converting between these using physical units has helped uncover several bugs. For example, one code snippet squared a temperature value and assigned it back to the original variable (T = T * T;). After adding the unit K to the temperature variable, the type checks associated with the units extension discovered this bug immediately and it was fixed easily. Units also help a lot with the readability of the code. ◄

As part of mbeddr's tutorials, an example extension has been built that annotates data structures with information about which layer of the system is allowed to write and read these values. By annotating program modules with layer information, the IDE can now check basic architectural constraints, such as whether a data element is allowed to be written from a given program location.

In discussions with a prospective mbeddr user other use cases for annotations were discovered. Instead of physical units, types and literals could be annotated with coordinate systems. The type checker would then make sure that values that are relative to a local coordinate system and values that are relative to a global coordinate systems are not mixed up. In the second use case, program annotations would have been used to represent secure and insecure parts of a crypto system, making sure that no data ever flows from the secure part to the insecure part. Neither customer project materialized, though.

5.2.4 *Static Checks and Verification*

Forcing the user to use size-specific integer types, providing a `boolean` type instead of interpreting integers as Boolean, and prohibiting the preprocessor are all steps that make a program more easily analyzable by the built-in type checker. The physical units serve a similar purpose. In addition, the integrated verification tools provide an additional level of analysis. By integrating these verification tools directly with the language (they rely on domain-specific language extensions) and integrating the tool into the IDE, it is much easier for users to adopt static analyses.

---

[15] This is an extension that is currently being built.

Smartmeter: Decision tables are used to replace nested `if` statements, and the completeness and determinism analyses (Section 4.5) have been used to uncover bugs. The protocol state machines are model-checked. This uncovered bugs introduced when refactoring the protocol implementation from the original C code supplied by the vendor to mbeddr state machines. ◄

Pacemaker: The core behavior of the pacemaker is specified as a state machine. To verify this state machine and to prove correctness of the code, two additional C extensions have been developed. One supports the specification of nondeterministic environments for the state machine (simulating the human heart), the other allows the specification of temporal properties (expressing the correctness conditions for the state machine in the face of its nondeterministic environment). All three – the state machine, the environment and the properties – are transparently translated to C code and verified with CBMC. ◄

Park-o-Matic: It was attempted to use formal analyses for verifying various aspects of the state machine. However this attempt failed, because the analyses were only attempted *after* the state machine was fully developed, at which point it was tightly connected to complex data structures via complex guard conditions. This complexity thwarted the model checker. ◄

The overall experience with the formal analyses is varied. Based on the (negative) experience with Park-o-Matic and the (positive) experience with Smartmeter and Pacemaker, we conclude that a system has to be designed for analyzability to avoid running into scalability issues. In Park-o-Matic, analysis was attempted for an almost finished system, in which the modularizations necessary to keep the complexity at bay were not made.

5.2.5 *Process Support*

mbeddr directly supports requirements and requirements tracing (Section 4.8), product line variability (Section 4.9) and prose documentation that is tightly integrated with code (Section 4.7). This directly addresses the three process-related challenges identified earlier. All of them are directly integrated with the IDE, work with any language extension and are often themselves extensible. For example, new attributes for requirements or new kinds of paragraphs for documents can be defined.

Smartmeter: Smartmeter also make use of requirements traces: during the upcoming certification process, these will be useful for tracking if and how the customer requirements have been implemented. Because of their orthogonal nature, the traces can be attached to the new language concepts specifically developed for Smartmeter. ◄

Pacemaker: Certification of safety-critical software systems requires requirements tracing; mbeddr's ubiquitous support makes it painless to use. Even though this is only an demo system for the Pacemaker Challenge, it is nonetheless an interesting demonstration how domain-specific abstractions, verification, requirements and requirements tracing fit together. ◄

Lego Mindstorms: Lego being what it is, it is easy to develop hardware variants. We have used mbeddr's support for product line variability to reflect the modular hardware in the software: sensor components have been statically exchanged based on feature models. ◄

The requirements language has been proven very useful. In fact, it has been used as a standalone system for collecting requirements (briefly discussed in Section 11.3). Tracing has also proved to be useful, in particular because it works out of the box with any language.

The documentation language has not been used much in the six example systems, since it is relatively new. However, we are currently in the process of porting the complete mbeddr user guide to the documentation language. The tight integration with code will make it very easy to keep the documentation in sync with an evolving mbeddr.

Experience with product line support is more varied. The definition of feature models and configuration works well (which is not surprising, since it is an established approach for modeling variability). Experience with mapping the variability onto programs using presence conditions is mixed. It works well if the presence condition is used to remove parts of programs that are not needed in particular variants. However, once references to variable program parts get involved, the current, simple approach starts to break down:

```
{feature1 || feature2}
int32 speed = 100;

void aFunction(int32 s) {
  speed = s;
}
```

This program is invalid, because the reference to `speed` from within `aFunction` breaks if `feature1` and `feature2` are both not selected. The program could be fixed if the same presence condition (or a more restrictive one) is attached to either the assignment `speed = s` or to the whole function. Checking for such problems is currently not supported, but it could be added in a generic way so that it would still work with any language.

It becomes even more tricky once the type system gets involved. Consider the following example:

```
[float <- int32 if feature1] speed = 100.0;

void aFunction(int32 s) {
  speed = s;
}
```

This expresses that the type of `speed` is `float` by default, and `int32` if `feature1` is selected. In this case, the default value `100.0` would be invalid. Similarly, the type of the argument s would also have to vary consistently. In short, a variability-aware type system would be required. At this point it is not clear whether this is feasible algorithmically and in terms of performance. Also, without enhancement of MPS itself it is probably not possible to build such a variability-aware type system generically, i.e. without explicit awareness of the underlying language. This would be unfortunate, since extensions would have to built in a variability-aware way.

5.3 OTHER CONCERNS

In addition to the explicitly stated challenges from Section 3.2, mbeddr must also fulfill a number of additional properties, discussed in this section. These include scalability (Section 5.3.1), usability (Section 5.3.2), infrastructure integration (Section 5.3.4) and interoperability with textual code (Section 5.3.5).

5.3.1 *Scalability*

In terms of scalability, there are two potential problems: the generation time and the performance of the editor.

Generation Time   The granularity of generation in MPS are models, which are the files that contain program nodes. If a project consists of several models, then only those models that have been changed are regenerated when the developer hits `Make Project`. So, during development, the relevant time with respect to generator performance is the time it takes to generate a single model. We have performed measurements that show that the time for generation scales linearly with the number of program nodes in a model. Table 5.2 shows the data, and Figure 5.1 shows the resulting diagram that reveals the linearity. For an equivalent of 100,000 lines of C code, the total build time (generation plus compile and link) is roughly 20 seconds. Most developers are not willing to wait longer than 5 to 10 seconds when they hit `Make Project`, which means at roughly 50,000 LOC of equivalent C code developers should start modularizing their system into several models.

Once the user starts modularizing their system into several models, the total generation time goes up, of course, but since only one model is typically generated after an incremental change[16] by the developer, one can reasonably assume that dozens of models can be used in a single system. This indicates that mbeddr may be able to handle systems of up to 1 million LOC equivalent in terms of generation performance.

> **Smartmeter:** The Smartmeter system, the largest system built with mbeddr so far, is currently ca. 109,431 nodes. Using the ratios between generated LOC and number of nodes derived from the above data, this corresponds

---

[16] This assumes that no cross-model transformations are applied. This is true for most of mbeddr's extensions. An exception is product-line variability, which is inherently cross-cutting.

Roots	Nodes	generated LOC	$\frac{LOC}{no.\,of\,nodes}$	t_{gen}	t_{make}
20	3,168	8,448	2.6	2.2 s	0.3
32	5,854	16,532	2.8	4.4 s	0.7 s
56	11,226	32,876	2.9	7.1 s	1.2 s
104	16,651	65,564	3.9	14.0 s	2.8 s
149	21,617	96,477	4.4	18.0 s	4.0 s

Table 5.3 This table shows the time it takes to generate C from mbeddr models. The table shows the number of roots, the number of nodes, as well as the LOC of generated C. It then reports the time to generate the C code, as well as the time to compile and link it. It was measured on a Macbook Pro 11', 2.9 GHz Intel Core i7, 8 GB 1600 MHz DDR3 RAM. As the diagram in Figure 5.1 shows, the generation time increases roughly linearly. The table also shows the ratio between number of nodes and generated LOC. The ratio increases with the number of roots. This is because each root is generated into a .c and a .h file, each with its own LOC overhead (double inclusion guards, include statements).

to between 262,000 and 480,000 LOC generated (ratios between 2.6 and 4.4). Running wc on the generated code counts 312,342 LOC. Table 5.2 shows the numbers of instances of important concepts. ◀

The model used for the measurements above is the mbeddr tutorial default-Extensions model. It uses all mbeddr languages, which means that all the generators of these languages are engaged. The generation process comprises

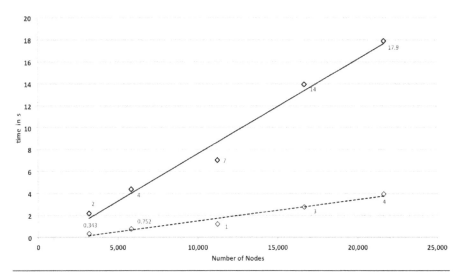

Figure 5.1 This diagram shows the generation time (solid line), as well as the time it takes to compile and link the generated code (dashed line), depending on the number of nodes in the model. The lines in the plot are a linear fit for the data in Table 5.2.

59 mapping configurations ("generation steps") in 10 different phases. The generation times get lower if fewer languages are used. Figure 5.2 shows the effect. The solid line represents the data for the model from the earlier benchmark. The dashed line is a model that uses fewer languages; the generation process comprised 41 mapping configurations in 9 phases. Finally, the dotted line is C only, without only the few built-in extensions; it comprises 4 phases and 27 mapping configurations. There are two conclusions we can draw from this data:

- If only plain C is used, the generation time is of the same order of magnitude as the call to make. In other words, using mbeddr without any extensions leads to duplication in "compile time".

- The difference between plain C vs. few languages is much larger than the difference between few vs. many languages, even though the difference in the number of mapping configurations is relatively similar. However, the number of generation phases is quite different (10 vs. 9 vs. 4). So for the generation time, the deciding factor is the number of phases, not the number of transformations[17].

Editor Performance   Editor performance in MPS is driven by several factors. The first one is the rendering of the cells in the editor. The second factor is the resolutions of scopes and other structural constraints. The third factor are the type system rules. To find out the limits of scalability of the editor, the following experiment was performed. The Components module in the defaultExtensions model in the tutorial was taken as the benchmark. The contents of the module were automatically duplicated. Two time periods were measured: the time it took for the editor to open after a double click on the module, and the time it took for the editor to react when trying to enter a new function. The experiment was performed with realtime type checking enabled, and with realtime type checking disabled. In this case, the type checks can be explicitly requested by pressing F5. The results are shown in Table 5.4.

It is obvious that the type system is what limits editor scalability, which is proportional to the size of single module (root node). Somewhere around 1,000 LOC it becomes prohibitively slow when realtime type checking is enabled. Switching off the realtime type checking, one can probably go up to 10,000 LOC until the editor starts feeling sluggish. The performance of the type system depends on the number and complexity of typing rules used, so switching off realtime type checking for complex languages is an option. In addition, the following steps are currently being investigated to improve type system performance:

---

[17] Phases are automatically computed by the generation scheduler based on the relative priorities between transformations. Since a new phase *always* leads to a complete copy of the models in memory, it is not surprising that this is what costs performance.

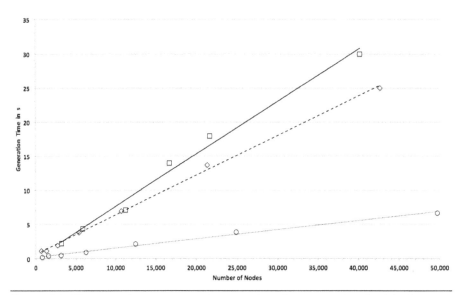

Figure 5.2 The more languages and generation phases are involved in the generation process, the longer the generation time (for similarly sized models). The solid line uses essentially all of mbeddr's extensions, resulting in 10 phases, the dashed line uses only some of the extensions (9 phases), and the dotted line is plain C (4 phases). The fact that the effect is not obvious for small models and short generation times is probably due to the interference of multitasking and/or garbage collection on the benchmark computer.

- Several of mbeddr's typing rules use the `when concrete` keyword, which forces the type system engine into serial operation. Together with the JetBrains team we are investigating whether some of these typing rules can be formulated in a way that does not require serialization.

- Many of the slow typing rules relate to the physical units. Performing the symbolic unit simplifications as part of the realtime type checking may be overloading the declarative type checker. Extracting the unit checking into a separate checking phase may be necessary.

- More generally, MPS evaluates all typing rules in realtime, or not at all (by switching off realtime type checking). A more granular approach, similar to what Xtext provides, may be useful. In Xtext, constraints can be marked as FAST, NORMAL and SLOW. Fast rules are executed essentially on every keypress, normal rules are executed on save, and slow rules are executed only on demand. We are discussing with JetBrains whether such a facility makes sense for MPS as well.

Summing up, developers have to make sure that single roots do not contain more than 1,000 to 2,000 LOC, depending on the complexity of the language. If, for some reason, bigger roots are required, switching off the realtime type checking makes roots with up to 10,000 lines feasible.

	Add Function		Open Editor	
LOC	Without TS	With TS	Without TS	With TS
280	0 s	0 s	0 s	0 s
510	0 s	0.1 s	0 s	0.5 s
970	0 s	0.5 s	0.8 s	4 s
1,883	0.1 s	1.0 s	1.2 s	6 s
3,718	0.2 s	3.0 s	2.1 s	10 s
7,393	0.4 s	-	4.5 s	- s
14,740	1.0 s	-	8.2 s	- s

Table 5.4 Editor scalability as measured by the time it takes for the editor to react to an attempt to enter a new function and by the time it takes to open the editor, depending on the size of the module shown in the editor. Lines of code (LOC) refers to the "lines as projected" in the MPS editor, not to the generated LOC.

5.3.2 Usability

Projectional editing has advantages: it contributes to enabling the modularization, extension and composition of languages, it supports mixing textual and non-textual notations (for example, in decision tables), allows annotations of programs (as in product line and traceability support) and it supports partial projection of programs (as in product line support).

However, projectional editing also has drawbacks. First, while MPS' user experience comes very close to real text editing (see Section 6.2.1), there are some idiosyncrasies users have to get used to, such as selecting parts of programs along the tree as opposed to selecting along the linear text. Experience shows that after a few days the editor is no longer perceived as a disadvantage; some people actually prefer it to normal text editors. However, users have to get through the first few days of adapting to the editor.

> **Park-o-Matic:** One of the Park-o-Matic developers was extremely skeptical about the projectional editor at the start of the project. After a few weeks, she reported that she is actually quite comfortable with the editor, and misses some of its editing gestures when using Eclipse. ◄

In an ongoing study[18] on the usability of MPS, where ca. twenty MPS users were asked to fill in a questionnaire, the first results are positive.

A few things are impossible with projectional editors. One of them is putting comments around *certain* code segments. Commenting is easily supported for entire subtrees. However, cross-tree comments, as in `boolean b = true /*|| false*/;` are not possible, since the `true` node is a child of the `OrExpression`. It remains to be seen whether this is a significant issue in practice. So far, users did not complain about this specific issue.

---

[18] This study was not specific to mbeddr; users of other MPS-based languages were interviewed as well. The study was performed with Janet Siegmund and Thorsten Berger. The results have not been analyzed or published; this thesis only a few preliminary results.

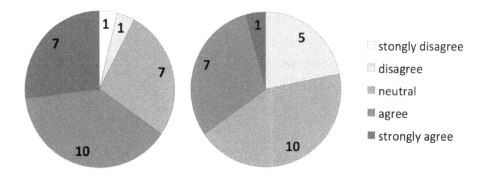

Figure 5.3 **Left:** This diagram shows the level of agreement with the statement *"I can work productively with MPS"*. The majority agrees or agrees strongly. **Right:** The second diagram shows agreement and disagreement for *"It was easy to get used to programming in MPS"*. The results for this question is overall agreement. This is in line with our experience that, once users have gotten used to MPS (and its editor) they can work productively with it.

5.3.3 *Learnability*

mbeddr is a comprehensive system that addresses a variety of aspects in embedded software engineering. The reason for this variety is that mbeddr first and foremost serves as an example for the *Generic Tools, Specific Languages* approach; for this to be convincing, it is important that mbeddr be comprehensive and address many different kinds of languages. However, this has the potential to overwhelm (new) users and hamper learnability.

In our experience, this is not a significant problem in mbeddr for the following three reasons. First, the extensions provide linguistic abstractions for concepts that are usually well-known to the users: state-based behavior, interfaces and components or test cases. They only have to learn the language, not the underlying concepts.

> **Smartmeter:** One of the Smartmeter developers (not the mbeddr team member) has a background in component-oriented software development in C. He was very happy to be able to mix C with a real component language in mbeddr. He said that, for this reason alone, he does not want to go back to plain C. ◄

Second, the additional language features are easily discoverable because of the IDE support. Third, and most important, these extensions are modularized, and any particular application developer will only use those extensions that are relevant to whatever their current program addresses. This avoids overwhelming the user with too much "stuff" at a time.

> **Pacemaker:** The pacemaker team reports that the learning curve for C programmers who want to use mbeddr takes ca. 2 days, to become accustomed to projectional editors and to the default extensions. ◄

The assumption underlying the first point (that new users already understand the concepts underlying the mbeddr languages) has been true for all the mbeddr users involved in all the systems built so far. Hence they did not report any particular challenges in learning mbeddr. If this assumption does not hold, learnability may be a bigger problem.

5.3.4 *Infrastructure Integration*

Since models are not stored as readable text, but rather as an XML document, infrastructure integration can be challenging. MPS integrates with mainstream version control systems including CVS, Subversion and git, and also supports diff/merge based on the projected syntax. We have a lot of experience with using MPS in a team of eight people in the research project during language development. Except for a few bugs in MPS (fixed in the meantime), teamwork has always worked well. Since application developers use the same approach, we assume that this will also be the case for application developers.

Smartmeter: The Smartmeter team currently has three developers and uses git as the version control system. So far it has worked well. ◄

Park-o-Matic: Park-o-Matic uses subversion. The team has not reported any issues. ◄

However, the projected diff/merge is only supported *inside* MPS, so a diff shown on the command line or the browser (for example as part of the gerrit[19] code review tool) will show the XML and is hence not useful. None of the systems built with mbeddr so far uses gerrit, so this has not been a problem so far.

Another important aspect of infrastructure integration is building the software and running the tests on a continuous integration server. Since MPS supports a command-line build via `ant`, this integration works in principle. The documentation for this aspect of MPS is limited, so setting up the respective MPS classpath can be challenging. Since mbeddr provides a wizard for creating the `ant` file with all necessary settings for mbeddr application projects, this problem is not relevant to end users.

Smartmeter: The Smartmeter project, for example, is built completely on a Teamcity integration server. Unit tests are executed automatically. ◄

A problem with build server integration is that the command line build via ant is slow. Remember from Table 5.2 that the pure generation time for the tutorial `defaultExtensions` model is 2.2 seconds. When running that same build on the command line, it takes ca. 30 seconds. The difference, ca. 27 seconds, is the time it takes to start up MPS for the generation job. This unacceptably long and needs to be shortened significantly. Unfortunately, MPS' architecture does not support starting only the generator component,

---

[19] https://code.google.com/p/gerrit/

which would presumably be faster. The good news is that as the project becomes bigger, these 27 seconds do not get longer; only the actual generation time increases according to Table 5.2.

5.3.5 *Interoperability with Textual Code*

Additional effort is required to integrate with legacy code. As a consequence of the projectional editor, textual sources cannot simply be used in mbeddr. The remainder of this section addresses handling header files and implementation files separately (cf. Section 4.10).

mbeddr provides an importer for header files as a means of connecting to existing libraries. However, this importer currently cannot handle #ifdef-based product line variability. Users have to specify a specific configuration to be imported. Also, header files often contain platform-specific keywords or macros. Since they are not supported by mbeddr C, these have to be removed before they can be imported. The header importer provides a regex-based facility to remove these platform specifics before the import.

> **Smartmeter:** As its processor, Smartmeter uses a member of Texas Instrument's MSP 430 series[20]. Smartmeter extensively calls into processor-specific header files supplied by Texas Instruments. Since there are many variants of the MSP 430, the header files are full of mutual includes and #ifdefs. Only a very small subset of the overall set of header files is actually used by Smartmeter, since it is known exactly which processor variant is used. To simplify the import in terms of variability and sheer size, the team has identified the variant-specific header file that is necessary for Smartmeter and has imported just this file. The import of this file worked reasonably well, with only few manual fixes after the automated import. ◄

> **Lego Mindstorms:** When the Lego Mindstorms system was built, no header file importer was available for mbeddr. However, the system used only about 30 relatively simple NXT OSEK API functions. The corresponding external module has been manually created. For projects that use small and well-defined APIs, this approach is perfectly feasible. ◄

The Smartmeter project, which is heavily based on an existing code base, also drives the need for a complete source code importer (including .c files, not just header files), which is currently being developed.

The parser behind this importer will also be integrated into MPS' paste handler, so textual C source can be pasted into the projectional editor. Copy and pasting from MPS to text works by default as long as the syntax of the code is textual. The reverse is not true, however – it has to be built specifically.

> **Smartmeter:** In Smartmeter, the complete code for a smartmeter application had been made available to the development team by the processor vendor. It was decided to reimplement it completely in mbeddr. No

---

[20] http://msp430.com

importer for C files was available at the time, so the required code was retyped into mbeddr. In the process, the code was structured into components with well-defined interfaces, thereby increasing quality, testability and modularity in the way discussed in Section 4. ◄

The integration of legacy code described in this section is clearly a disadvantage of projectional editing, and a robust importer for header files is definitely required. However, we feel that for dealing sensibly with legacy code in the context of mbeddr, the code should be partitioned into components and other higher-level abstractions. It is not yet clear how important a source code importer is in this context.

5.4 RELATIONSHIP TO KUHN'S SURVEY

[Kuhn et al., 2012] present an empirical study of the problems that currently plague model-driven development in the industry. They performed in-depth interviews with 12 engineers from General Motors who use mainstream model-driven development tools (mostly Matlab/Simulink, IBM Rhapsody and MS Word) for embedded software development. Since the study fits well with the mbeddr story it is interesting to discuss. The next paragraphs analyze how and why mbeddr improves on the problems identified in the study.

Diffing   Diffing between various versions of the same model is insufficiently supported. Because of the fear of missing a change, developers have resorted to manually written comments that describe each change. Sometimes they even use a textual diff tool on the generated source. In some cases they create screenshots of a new version of a model, mark the changes with a red pen, and send the picture back to the owner of the model to incorporate the changes. When stating their requirements towards model diffing, they suggested that a facility like the diff support for code would be just what they needed.

mbeddr improves on this situation, since any model or program can be diffed (and merged) with the diff and merge tooling provided by MPS. This works for any language, regardless of abstraction level and notation, as long as MPS is used for diffing and merging (as discussed in the previous subsection).

Point-to-Point Tracing   Traceability between implementation artifacts (code, model) and requirements is very important to all engineers interviewed in the study. The current tool-chain only provides document-to-document traceability, which is not granular enough. Traceability is required on the level of model or program elements, for any level of abstraction. Currently, the engineers rely on naming conventions and ticket IDs (as defined by their issue tracker) as a workaround. Since only very limited tool support is provided, this approach is tedious and error-prone.

mbeddr solves this problem completely by providing element-level traceability from arbitrary program elements to requirements or other high-level specifications. The traces are actual references and not just based on name equality. Tracing works for program elements expressed in any language, representing any abstraction level. Since all languages live inside the same language workbench, consistent tracing is much simpler than across a set of non-integrated (and often non-extensible) tools.

Problem-Specific Expressibility   The engineers interviewed in the study complained about the need for problem-specific expressibility, i.e. the ability to define their own "little languages" for particular abstractions relevant in the domain. The study cites two particular examples. One refers to the ability for domain experts to use concise visual notations when they describe requirements, and then generate code from the resulting diagrams. The other example identifies support for physical units as a major problem in the (Matlab-based) implementation models. They reverted to Hungarian notation[21] to encode unit information into signal and variable names ("The printed list of all prefixes used in the system fills four pages").

mbeddr improves on this situation generally and specifically. The ability to extend existing languages with domain-specific concepts allows application developers to plug in their own "little languages" and generate abstractions available in the base language. Admittedly, mbeddr does not yet support graphical languages, as requested by the engineers in the study. However, it is safe to assume that the same kind of problems will arise with predefined textual languages. mbeddr also helps specifically with the two problems discussed in the study. mbeddr's requirements language can be extended with arbitrary domain-specific languages, and the models that become part of the requirements in this way can be used directly in the implementation of the final system. Also, mbeddr ships with a language extension for physical units that can be used with C or any of its other extensions.

Long Build Times   The engineers in the study report build times of the model-driven tool-chain in the range of several hours – in contrast to ca. 30 minutes in the old, C-based tool-chain. These long build times prevent exploratory development of control algorithms, especially while in the car on the test track: whenever a change had to be made, the test drive had to be rescheduled for another day. Ideally, developers should be able to apply (certain kinds of) changes at runtime and continue the test drive immediately.

mbeddr does not provide an out-of-the-box solution for this problem, but it can help. To be able to change parts of a system on the fly, two approaches can be used (both suggested in the study). The first one relies on interpretation or data-driven development, where the behavior of a part of a system can be changed at runtime, for example, by changing the values of configuration parameters. To enable this approach, these configuration parameters have to be integrated with the hard-coded algorithm, and the constraints on the values of the parameters have to be described in a rigid way to prevent misconfiguration. Specific extensions of C (or other languages) can be developed with mbeddr, where the parameters and their constraints can be described suc-

---

[21] http://en.wikipedia.org/wiki/Hungarian_notation

cinctly, integrated with the hard-coded algorithm. Static consistency checking and IDE support is provided as well, which potentially makes this approach more robust than the ad-hoc XML-file based descriptions of configurability often used today.

The second approach for improving turn-around times mentioned in the study is hot-swapping of code in the field. To make this possible, the underlying system must be partitioned well, and the interfaces between different program parts must be clearly defined and enforced. mbeddr's interfaces and components, plus a suitable DSL for defining the partitioning of the target binary, can help to solve this problem. Note that better modularity and clearer interfaces reduce build times in general, since there is no need to regenerate the whole system when a part changes. Together with mbeddr's support for testing and mocking, this can improve testability. Taken together, these two approaches can reduce turn-around times during the development phase.

Graphical Notations   The paper does not identify the graphical notations provided by the mainstream tools used by the engineers as a point of friction. However, the paper does point out a set of problems with graphical notations[22] and the limited set of abstractions provided by the modeling tools (such as scopes or subroutines). Another problem is reported to be the fact that diagrams have no obvious reading direction, which is compensated by modeling guidelines. Developers report struggling with reading visual models to make sure they do not miss important parts. The paper states that:

> [..] when offered an alternative to visual programming, engineers seem to prefer non-visual representations.

In the available tools these were forms and tree views. It is reasonable to assume that, if textual notations had been available, these would have been preferred over trees and forms, since the developers said that they miss "programming" in other parts of the paper. The discussion of the visual notations provided by the tools used in the study also points out the following:

> While this language is visual, it does not seem to be an actual abstraction from source code. Even worse, as we learned through our interviews, the level of abstraction seems to be lower than high-level source code. For example, engineers reported that they struggled to introduce abstraction such as nested scopes of variable visibility, enumerators, or refactoring duplicated code into a new method.

mbeddr takes a fundamentally different approach. First, it generally relies on textual, symbolic and tabular notations. Second, since it starts out from C, existing C abstraction mechanisms such as the nested scopes of variable visibility or enumerators are supported. The IDE supports various refactorings.

---

[22] The paper points out that these problems apply to the notations and tools used in the study, but may not be generalizable to graphical notations in general.

Third, additional domain-specific abstractions can be added at any time, in a modular way.

Summing up, the paper draws a rather bleak picture of today's mainstream use of model-driven development in embedded software (and our experience is certainly in line with this picture). mbeddr improves on several of the problems discussed in the study.

Summary — *This chapter discusses the experience from several projects conducted with mbeddr, which seem to confirm that mbeddr is a productive environment for embedded software development. The various example systems also show that domain-specific extension is useful for the end user and feasible in terms of efforts and extensibility of the mbeddr core system. To validate the overall* **Generic Tools, Specific Languages** *approach, however, the validation also has to include the construction of mbeddr itself. Chapter 10 provides this validation. To provide context, Part III of the thesis introduces language workbenches, language modularity and JetBrains MPS. It also discusses how many of mbeddr's languages have been implemented.*

Part III

Implementing mbeddr with Language Engineering

Language Workbenches and MPS

Abstract — *Language workbenches are tools for efficiently developing and using general-purpose and domain-specific languages. JetBrains MPS is an example of such a language workbench that emphasizes the integration and composition of sets of languages. It supports the implementation of a wide range of language aspects including structure, editor, type system, refactoring, transformations and debugging. MPS' most distinguishing feature is its projectional editor, which, in addition to helping with language composition, also supports a wide range of notations, including textual, tabular and symbolic. This chapter illustrates the basics of building languages with MPS and introduces a simple language that acts as the basis for the discussion on language modularization and composition in the next chapter.*

6.1 OVERVIEW

The Meta Programming System[1] is a projectional language workbench available as open source software under the Apache 2.0 license. It was initiated by JetBrains founder and president Sergey Dmitriev, and has been developed continuously over the last ten years[2]. The term *language workbench* was coined by Fowler [2005]. He defines a language workbench as a tool with the following characteristics, all exhibited by MPS:

1. users can define languages which are fully integrated with each other.

2. the primary source of information is a persistent abstract representation.

3. a DSL is defined in three parts: schema, editor(s), and generator(s).

4. language users manipulate a DSL through a projectional editor.

5. a language workbench can persist incomplete/contradictory data.

For the *Generic Tools, Specific Languages* approach, the most important statement in this definition is *languages which are fully integrated with each other*. It is not enough for a language workbench to address the definition of a single language: it must be possible to define sets of languages, and, while each of them should be a well-defined module, it is also essential to be able to define how these languages integrate. MPS is particularly good at this.

---

[1] http://jetbrains.com/mps

[2] MPS has not been developed as part of this thesis. However, a lot of feedback has been provided to JetBrains based on the experience gained during the development of mbeddr, which is likely MPS' most advanced and demanding use case.

This chapter introduces MPS as a language workbench. It starts out by discussing MPS' most distinguishing feature, the projectional editor, in Section 6.2. It then looks at MPS' support for modular, multi-stage transformations in Section 6.3. Section 6.4 discusses the various aspects of language definition supported by MPS. To further illustrate how MPS works, Section 6.5 discusses the development of a simple language. The next chapter then discusses several ways of composing languages, both conceptually and in terms of the implementation with MPS. A comparison of MPS with other language workbenches and language implementation techniques can be found at the end of the next chapter (Section 7.5), because modularization and composition is an important aspect of this comparison.

6.2 PROJECTIONAL EDITING

For textual languages, text editors are traditionally used to enter character sequences that represent programs. Based on a grammar, a parser then checks the text for syntactic correctness and constructs an abstract syntax tree (AST) from the character sequence. The AST contains all the data expressed by the text, but ignores notational details. It is the basis for all downstream analysis and processing.

Projectional editing does not rely on parsers. As a user edits a program, the AST is modified *directly*. A projection engine then creates some representation of the AST with which the user interacts, and which reflects the resulting changes (Figure 6.1). This approach is well-known from graphical editors: when editing a UML diagram, users do not draw pixels onto a canvas and a "pixel parser" then creates the AST. Rather, the editor creates an instance of uml.Class as a user drags a class from the palette onto the canvas. A projection engine renders the diagram by drawing a rectangle for the class. Programs are stored using a generic tree persistence format (such as XML). This approach can be generalized to work with any notation, including textual.

In projectional editors, every program element is stored as a node with a unique ID (UID). References between program elements are represented as

Figure 6.1 **Left:** In parser-based systems a user sees and manipulates the concrete textual syntax of a program. A parser then (re-)constructs the AST from the text (going from the AST to the concrete syntax requires extra care to retain formatting, and is not supported out of the box by most parsers – hence the dotted line). **Right:** In projectional editing, while the user still *sees* a concrete syntax, an editing gesture *directly* changes the AST. No parser is involved, and the AST must never be reconstructed from a flat text structure. Instead, the concrete syntax is projected from the AST. Storage is based on the abstract syntax.

references to the UID, so the AST is actually a graph. These references are established during program editing by directly selecting reference targets from the code completion menu. This is in contrast to parser-based environments in which a reference is expressed as a string in the source text and a separate name resolution phase resolves the target AST element.

What makes projectional editing interesting for language workbenches in general, and for mbeddr in particular, are the following two characteristics. First, the approach can deal with arbitrary syntactic forms including textual, symbolic/mathematical, tabular and graphical[3]. This means that much richer notations can be used *in an integrated fashion*, improving the programming experience for the application developer. An example from mbeddr is the decision table shown in Figure 3.1. Traditionally the tools for building textual and tabular/symbolic/graphical editors were very different in terms of their architecture and user experience, and integrating them seamlessly was a lot of work, and sometimes impossible. Projectional editing solves this problem. Second, if independently developed languages are composed, the resulting composite program will *never* be syntactically ambiguous. This is in contrast to mainstream parser-based systems that rely on a limited grammar class such as LR or LL(k), where such compositions are often ambiguous and require invasive change to the composite grammar to resolve the ambiguities.

Traditionally, projectional editing has also had a number of problems. The most important of them are discussed in the following subsections: editor usability (Section 6.2.1), language evolution (Section 6.2.2), infrastructure integration (Section 6.2.3) and tool lock-in (Section 6.2.4). These sections also look at the extent and the way in which MPS solves these issues.

6.2.1 *Editor Usability*

In principle, projectional editing is simpler than parsing, since there is no need to "extract" the syntactic structure from a linear textual source. The challenge for projectional editors lies in making them convenient to use for end users. Traditionally, projectional editors have had a bad reputation, because users had to construct the syntax tree more or less manually, instead of "just typing". MPS has solved this problem to a large extent; the editing experience is comparable to traditional text editors (cf. Section 5.3.2). Here are some of the approaches MPS uses to achieve this.

Code Completion and Aliases   Every language concept that is legal at a given program location is available in the code completion menu. In naive implementations, users have to select the language concept based on its name and instantiate it. This is inconvenient. In MPS, language concepts define an alias, allowing users to "just type" the alias to immediately instantiate the

---

[3] MPS does not yet support graphical syntax, but will in 2014. Other projectional editors, such as Intentional Software's Domain Workbench [Simonyi et al., 2006] support graphical notations already.

concept. By making the alias the same as the leading keyword (for example, `if` for an `IfStatement`), users can "just type" the code.

Side Transforms   Side transforms make sure that expressions can be entered conveniently. Consider a local variable declaration `int a = 2;`. If this should be changed to `int a = 2 + 3;` the `2` in the init expression needs to be replaced by an instance of the binary `+` operator, with the `2` in the left slot and the `3` in the right. Instead of removing the `2` and manually inserting a `+`, users can simply type `+` on the right side of the `2`. The system performs the tree restructuring that moves the `+` to the root of the subtree, puts the `2` in the left slot, and then puts the cursor into the right slot, so the user can enter the second argument. This means that expressions (or anything else) can be entered linearly, as expected. For this to work, operator precedence has to be specified, and the tree has to be constructed taking these precedences into account. In MPS, precedence is specified by a number associated with each operator, and whenever a side transformation is used to build an expression, the tree is automatically reshuffled to make sure that those operators with a higher precedence number are further down in the tree.

Delete Actions   Delete actions are used to similar effect when elements are deleted. Deleting the `3` in `2 + 3` first keeps the plus, with an empty right slot. Deleting the `+` then removes the `+` and puts the `2` at the root of the subtree.

Wrappers   Wrappers support instantiation of concepts that are actually children of the concepts allowed at a given location. Consider again a local variable declaration `int a;`. The respective concept could be `LocalVariableDeclaration`, a subconcept of `Statement`, to make it legal in method bodies (for example). However, users simply want to start typing `int`, i.e. entering the content of the `type` field of the `LocalVariableDeclaration`. A wrapper can be used to support entering `Type`s where `LocalVariableDeclaration`s are expected. Once a `Type` is selected, the wrapper implementation creates a `LocalVariableDeclaration`, puts the `Type` into its `type` field, and moves the cursor into the `name` slot. Summing up, this means that a local variable declaration `int a;` can be entered by starting to type the `int` type, as expected.

Smart References   Smart references achieve a similar effect for references (as opposed to children). Consider pressing `Ctrl-Space` after the `+` in `2 + 3`. Assume further, that a couple of local variables are in scope and that these can be used instead of the `3`. The local variables should be available in the code completion menu. However, technically, a `VariableReference` has to be instantiated first, whose `variable` slot is then made to point to any of the variables in scope. This is tedious. Smart references trigger special editor behavior: if in a given context a `VariableReference` is allowed, the editor *first* evaluates its scope to find the possible targets, then puts those targets into the code completion menu. If a user selects one, *then* the `VariableReference` is created, and the selected element is put into its `variable` slot. This makes the reference object effectively invisible in terms of the editing experience.

Smart Delimiters Smart delimiters are used to simplify inputting list-like data, in which elements are separated with a specific separator symbol. An example is argument lists in functions: once a parameter is entered, users can press comma, i.e. the list delimiter, to instantiate the next element.

6.2.2 *Language Evolution*

If the language changes, existing instance models temporarily become out-dated, in the sense that they were developed for the old version of the language. If the new language is not backward compatible, these existing models have to be migrated to conform to the updated language.

Since projectional editors store the models as structured data in which each program node points to the language concept it is an instance of, the tools have to take special care that such "incompatible" models can still be opened and then migrated, manually or by a script, to the new version of the language. MPS supports this feature, and it is also possible to distribute migration scripts with (updated) languages to run the migration automatically. It is also possible to define quick fixes that run *automatically*; so whenever a concept is marked as `deprecated`, this quick fix can trigger an automatic migration to a new concept[4].

6.2.3 *Infrastructure Integration*

Today's software development infrastructure is typically text-oriented. Many tools used for diff and merge, or tools like `grep` and regular expressions, are geared towards textual storage. Programs written with parser-based textual DSLs and stored as plain text integrate automatically and seamlessly with these tools.

In projectional IDEs, special support must be provided for infrastructure integration. Since the concrete syntax is not pure text, a generic persistence format is used, typically based on XML. While XML is technically text as well, it is not practical to perform diff, merge and the like on the level of the XML-based storage format. Therefore, special tools need to be provided for diff and merge. MPS provides integration with the usual version control systems and handles diff and merge in the IDE, using the concrete, projected syntax[5]. Figure 4.20 shows an example of an MPS diff. However, it clearly is a drawback of projectional editing and the associated abstract syntax-based storage that many well-known text utilities do not work. For example, web-based diffs in github or gerrit are not very helpful when working with MPS.

---

[4] The key to making this possible is that MPS stores programs on the meta-meta level. This allows XML files that represent programs that no longer conform to the language structure to still be opened. By using MPS' reflection, the raw data stored in these files can be accessed. This way a migration script can "recover" the stored data that corresponds to the old language structure and transform it to the new (current) one.

[5] Note that since every program element has a unique ID, *move* can potentially be distinguished from *delete/create*, providing richer semantics for diff and merge.

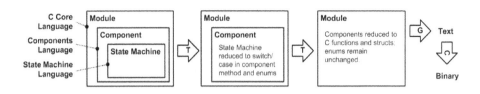

Figure 6.2 Higher-level abstractions such as state machines or components are transformed (T) to their lower-level equivalent. C text is generated from the C program, (G), that is subsequently compiled (C).

Also, copy and paste with textual environments may be a challenge. MPS, for example, supports pasting a projected program that has a textual-looking syntax into a text editor. These is no automatic support for the way back from a textual environment to the projectional editor. However, special support for specific languages can be provided via *paste handlers*. Such a paste handler is available for Java, for example: when a user pastes Java text into a Java program in MPS, a parser is executed that builds the respective MPS tree. While this already works reasonably well for Java, it has to be developed specifically for each language used in MPS. If a grammar for the respective language is available for a Java-based parser generator, it is relatively simple to provide such an integration.

6.2.4 *Tool Lock-In*

In the worst case, textual programs can be edited with any text editor. Unless one is prepared to edit XML, programs expressed with a projectional editor *always* require that editor to edit programs. This leads to tool lock-in. However, as soon as one takes IDE support into account, both the textual and the projectional approaches lock users into a particular tool. Also, there is essentially no standard for exchanging language definitions between the various language workbenches[6]. So the effort of implementing a language is always lost if the tool must be changed.

6.3 MULTI-STAGE TRANSFORMATION

A transformation maps one program tree or graph to another one. In the context of processing programs expressed with DSLs, the languages used to express these two graphs will usually be different: a more high-level and domain-specific language is mapped to a more general one (Figure 6.2).

However, for modular language extension and composition, transformations have to be composable as well. In particular, it must be possible to chain

---

[6] There is *some* support for exchanging the abstract syntax based on formalisms such as MOF or Ecore, but most of the effort for implementing a language is in areas other than the abstract syntax.

144

transformations, where the result of one transformation acts as the input to another. To avoid unnecessary overhead in this case, intermediate transformations should be AST-to-AST mappings. Only if a subsequent tool requires textual input (for example, an analysis tool or a compiler) should textual output be generated. To make a set of transformations extensible, the following features, both supported by MPS, are required.

First, several transformations for the same model have to be supported, executable either in parallel, creating several products from a single input, for example, configuration files and visualizations, or alternatively, creating different, alternative products from a given input, for example, for realizing different non-functional characteristics of an extension; the static component connections discussed in Section 4.4 are an example.

Second, dependencies between transformations must be specified in a relative way, and the transformation engine must compute a global transformation sequence based on the transformations configured for a particular program. This supports plugging in additional transformations into the chain without invasive modification of other transformations (see, for example, the transformation of mocks in Section 8.5). In MPS, a transformation specifies a relative priority (`before`, `together with`, or `after`) relative to the transformations it depends on.

Many transformation engines do not support the second item. While they provide languages to express transformation, they often do not address the extensible composition of transformations. Eclipse Xtend[7] is an example that does not explicitly address composition. In contrast, Stratego [Bravenboer et al., 2008] provides higher-order functions to orchestrate transformations.

6.4   MPS LANGUAGE ASPECTS

In MPS, the ingredients of languages are called *concepts*. A concept has several aspects, including structure, editor, or type systems. Like other language workbenches, MPS comes with a set of DSLs for language definition, a separate DSL for each language aspect. MPS is bootstrapped, so these DSLs are built (and can be extended) with MPS itself. Figure 6.3 provides an overview of the most important aspects of MPS language definition. The following paragraphs briefly introduce every language aspect supported by MPS.

Structure   The structure, or abstract syntax or metamodel, has been discussed earlier. In terms of structure, a language concept consists of a name, child concepts, references to other concepts and primitive properties (`integer`, `boolean`, `string` or an enumeration). A concept may also extend *one* other concept and implement any number of concept interfaces. In addition, a concept can also have *static* properties, children and references; MPS refers to those as *concept* properties/children/references. The definition of a new concept always starts with the structure.

---

[7] http://eclipse.org/xtext

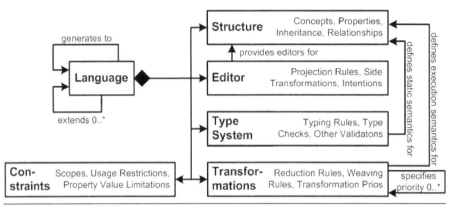

Figure 6.3 In MPS, a language consists of several aspects. The figure shows the most important ones (*language structure* is MPS' term for abstract syntax). In addition, languages can specify refactorings, find-usages strategies, migration scripts and debuggers. Languages can make use of other languages in their definition and generate down to other languages. Transformations specify priorities relative to other transformations; MPS calculates a global transformation schedule based on these priorities.

Editor   The editor aspect defines the concrete syntax, or the projection rules. Each concept has exactly one editor unless a concept inherits the editor from its super-concept[8]. Interface concepts do not have editors, but they may define editor *components* that can be embedded into other editors. Editors consist of cells, where each cell may contain a constant (i.e. a keyword or a symbol), a property value (such as the name), a child cell, a reference cell or a collection of other cells. In fact, the editor for a concept is defined in two parts: the editor for the concept in the primary editor, as well as the concept's representation in the inspector (essentially a properties view). The editor aspect also defines (some) *actions* and keymaps. These determine the reaction of MPS if a specific key is pressed in given cell or when a node is deleted.

Actions   The actions aspect contains mostly wrappers and side transformations (as discussed in Section 6.2.1).

Behavior   The behavior aspect essentially contains methods defined on concepts. Such methods can implement arbitrary behavior and can be called on each instance of the concept. Note that concept interfaces can not only declare methods (as in Java), but can also provide an implementation. In that sense, interfaces are more like Scala traits.

Constraints   The constraints aspects comprises scopes for references (i.e., the set of valid target nodes beyond their type), constraints for properties

---

[8] Future versions of MPS will support the definition of several independent editors for a single concept, leading to the ability to change the representation of a program at any time.

(value ranges, regular expressions), as well as context dependencies for concepts. The latter allows restrictions on where a concept can be used; for example, an `assert` statement may be restricted to anywhere *under* a test case.

Type System   The type system is used to specify typing rules for concepts. These include inference rules (the type of a variable reference is the type of the variable referenced by it), subtyping rules (`int` is a subtype of `float`) and checking rules. The latter are essentially Boolean expressions that evaluate any part of the model[9]. For example, they can be used to check for name uniqueness or naming conventions. The type system aspect may also contain quick fixes that can be used to resolve errors reported by type system rules.

Intentions   Intentions are similar to quick fixes in that they can be activated via `Alt-Enter` and selected from the menu that pops up. They are different in that an intention is not associated with an error, but just generally with a concept. For example, an intention could allow a user to mark a type as `const` by selecting `Make Const` from the intentions menu of a `Type`.

Refactorings   Refactorings are similar to intentions in that they change the structure of a program. They are also typically associated with a specific concept. There are several differences though: a refactoring shows up in the `Refactorings` menu, it can have a keyboard shortcut associated with it, it can be written to be able to handle several nodes at a time, and it can query the user for input before it is executed.

Generator   The generator aspect is used to define mappings of subtrees to other subtrees. MPS relies on multi-stage transformations, where only the last one creates text and all others are tree-to-tree mappings. The generator aspects contains the tree-to-tree mappings, and the textgen aspect (discussed below) handles the final to-text transformation. A generator consist of mapping configurations that contain transformation rules. There are different kinds of rules that transform nodes in different ways. For example, a reduction rule replaces any instance of a concept with the tree fragment created by the template associated with the reduction rule. Note that IDE support is available for the target language in the transformation template. A generator may also contain procedural mapping scripts.

Textgen   The textgen aspect for a language concept defines the mapping of the concept to a text buffer. This should only be used for the concept of a base language such as Java, C or XML. Any higher-level concepts that create programs expressed in a base language should use generators (discussed in the previous paragraph).

Find Usages   The Find Usages aspect supports custom finders: when the `Find Usages` item is selected from the context menu of a node, the custom finders show up there. Instead of finding *all* usages of a node, these custom

---

[9] These are usually known as constraints in other language workbenches or modeling tools.

finders can filter based on the usage context. For example, for a local variable a finder may only show usages where the variable is used on the left side of an assignment statement (i.e., is assigned).

Dataflow The dataflow aspect constructs a dataflow graph for a program. For each language concept, a dataflow builder can be defined whose task is to construct the dataflow graph fragment for the respective concept. Based on this program-specific dataflow graph, a set of generic dataflow analyses can be performed.

Scripts The scripts aspect contains migration or enhancement scripts for language concepts. They are useful in handling language migration problems.

6.5 IMPLEMENTING A DSL WITH MPS

This section illustrates language definition with MPS with a simple `entities` language. This language will also be used in the next chapter as the basis for demonstrating language modularization and composition. Some example code is shown below.

```
module company                          // continued...
  entity Employee {                       entity Department {
    id: int                                 id: int
    name: string                            description: string
    role: string                          }
    worksAt: Department                 }
    freelancer: boolean
  }
```

Structure and Syntax Figure 6.4 shows a UML diagram of the concepts involved in the `entities` language. Language definition in MPS always starts with the structure. The following code shows the definition of the `Entity` concept. `Entity` extends `BaseConcept`, the top-level concept similar to `java.lang.Object` in Java. It implements the `INamedConcept` interface to inherit a `name` property. It declares a list of children of type `Attribute` in the `attributes` role.

```
concept Entity extends BaseConcept implements INamedConcept
  is root: true
  children:
    Attribute attributes 0..n
```

Editors in MPS are based on cells. Cells are the smallest unit relevant for projection. Consequently, defining an editor consists of arranging cells and defining their content. Different cell types are available. Figure 6.5 explains the editor for `Entity`. The editors for the other concepts are defined similarly.

Type System Language developers specify typing rules for language concepts. To calculate and check types for a program, MPS "instantiates" these rules for each instance of the concept, resulting in a set of type equations for a program. These equations contain type values (such as `int`) as well as type variables, which stand in for the type of program elements whose type has not yet been calculated. MPS then solves the set of type equations, trying to assign type values to the type variables in such a way that all the equations for a program are free from contradictions. If a contradiction arises, this is flagged as a typing error. For the `entities` language, only two simple typing rules are needed. The first one specifies the type for the `Type` nodes themselves (for example, the `int` node in attributes such as `int age;`):

```
rule typeof_Type for Type as t {
    typeof(t) :==: t.copy;
}
```

This rule has the (semantically irrelevant) name `typeof_Type`, and applies to the language concept `Type` (`int` or `string` are subconcepts of the abstract `Type` concept). The `typeof(...)` operator creates a type variable associated with a program element – in this case, with an instance `t` of `Type`. The type is calculated by cloning `t` itself. In other words, if the type system engine needs to find the type of an `int` program element, that type is `int` as well. This may be a bit confusing, because instances of `Type` (and its subconcepts) play two roles. First, they are part of the program itself if they are explicitly specified in attributes (`int age;`). Second, they are also the objects with which the type system engine works. Cloning the program element expresses that types represent themselves in the type system engine[10]. Another typing rule

---

[10] A clone is needed because if the node itself were used, it would be "ripped out" of the AST by the type system engine. A node can be owned either by the AST or by the type system engine.

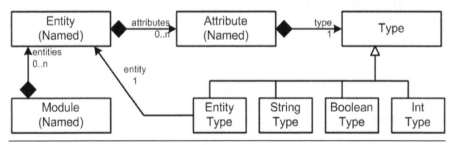

Figure 6.4 The abstract syntax of the entities language. An `Entity` has `Attributes` which have a `Type` and a name. `EntityType` extends `Type` and references `Entity`. This adapts entities to types (cf. the Adapter pattern [Gamma et al., 1995]). Concepts like `EntityType` which have exactly one reference are called *smart references* and are treated specially by MPS: instead of proposing to explicitly instantiate the reference concept and then selecting the target, the code completion menu shows *the possible targets* of the reference directly. The reference concept is implicitly instantiated once a target is selected.

```
editor for concept Entity
    node cell layout:
        [/
            [> entity { name } { <]
            [>        (> % attributes %              <) <]
                        /empty cell: <default>
            }
        /]
```

Figure 6.5 The editor for `Entity`. The outermost cell is a vertical list `[/ .. /]`. The first line contains a horizontal list `[> .. <]` that contains the keyword `entity`, the `name` property and an opening curly brace. The second line uses indentation `-->` and a vertical arrangement of the contents of the `attributes` collection `(> .. <)`. Finally, the third line contains the closing curly brace.

defines the type of the `Attribute` as a whole to be the type of the attribute's `type` property:

```
rule typeof_Attribute for Attribute as a {
    typeof(a) :==: typeof(a.type);
}
```

This rule answers the question of what the type system engine's type should be for instances of `Attribute`. Note how this equation has two type variables and no type values. It simply propagates the type of the attribute's specified type (the `int` in `int age;`) to be the type of the overall attribute. Note how the two typing rules discussed in this section work together to calculate the type of the `Attribute` from the type specified by the user: the type of the specified type is calculated by cloning, and then this type is propagated to the type of the whole attribute.

One more rule has to be defined that is not strictly part of the type calculation. It is a constraint that checks the uniqueness of attribute names for any given `Entity`:

```
checking rule check_Entity for Entity as e {
    set<string> names = new hashset<string>;
    foreach a in e.attributes {
        if (names.contains(a.name)) {
            error "duplicate attribute name" -> a;
        }
        names.add(a.name);
    } }
```

This rule does *not* establish typing equations, it just checks a property of the program (note the *checking* in the rule header). It checks attribute name uniqueness based on a set of the names, and reports an error if it finds a duplicate. It annotates the error with the attribute `a`, so the editor can highlight the respective program element.

Generator From `entities` models, Java Beans are generated. Since Java is available in MPS (called the BaseLanguage), the generation is actually a model-to-model transformation: from the `entities` model, a Java model is generated. MPS supports several kinds of transformations. The default case is the template-based transformation which maps ASTs onto other ASTs. Alternatively, one can use an API to manually construct the target tree.

MPS templates look like text generation templates known from tools such as Xpand[11], Jet[12] or StringTemplate[13], since they use the concrete syntax of the target language in the template. However, this concrete syntax is projected like any other program, and the IDE can provide support for the target language *in the template* (details of the support for the target language in templates is discussed in Related Work, Section 7.5). This also means that the *template code itself* must be valid in terms of the target language.

Template-based generators consist of mapping configurations and templates. Mapping configurations define which elements are processed by which templates. For the `entities` language, a root mapping rule and reduction rules are needed. *Root mapping rules* create new root nodes from existing root nodes. In this case, a Java class is generated from an `Entity`. *Reduction rules* are in-place transformations. Whenever the engine encounters an instance of the specified source concept somewhere in a model, it replaces the element with the result of the associated template. In this case, the various types (`int`, `string`, etc.) are reduced to their Java counterparts. Figure 6.6 shows a part of the `entities` mapping configuration.

Figure 6.7 shows the `map_Entity` template. It generates a complete Java class from an input `Entity`. To understand how templates work in MPS, the generation of Java fields for each `Entity Attribute` is discussed next:

- In MPS, a template developer first writes structurally correct example code in the target language. To generate a field into a class for each `Attribute` of an `Entity`, one would first add a field to a class (see `aField` in Figure 6.7).

- Then macros are attached to those program elements in the example code that have to be replaced with elements from the input model during the transformation. In the `Attribute` example in Figure 6.7, the first step is to attach a `LOOP` macro to the whole field. It contains an expression `node.attributes;` where `node` refers to the input `Entity` (this code is entered in the Inspector window and is not shown in the screenshot). This expression returns the set of `Attributes` from the current `Entity`, making the `LOOP` iterate over all attributes of the entity and create a field for each of them.

- At this point, each created field would be *identical* to the example code to which the `LOOP` macro was attached (`private int aField;`). To make

---

[11] http://www.eclipse.org/modeling/m2t/?project=xpand

[12] http://www.eclipse.org/modeling/m2t/?project=jet

[13] http://www.stringtemplate.org/

```
┌                               ┐
│ concept           Entity      │ --> map_Entity
│ inheritors        false       │
│ condition         <always>    │
│ keep input root   true        │
└                               ┘
```

reduction rules:

```
┌                        ┐
│ concept      IntType   │ --> <T  int  T>
│ inheritors   false     │
│ condition    <always>  │
└                        ┘
```

```
┌                          ┐
│ concept      EntityType  │ --> <T  ->$ Double  T>
│ inheritors   false       │
│ condition    <always>    │
└                          ┘
```

Figure 6.6 The mapping configuration for the `entities` language. The root mapping rule for `Entity` specifies that instances of `Entity` should be transformed with the `map_Entity` template, which produces a Java class and is shown in Figure 6.7. The reduction rules use inline templates, i.e. the template is embedded in the mapping configuration. For example, the `IntType` is replaced with the Java `int` and the `EntityRefType` is reduced to a reference to the class generated from the target entity. The `->$` is a reference macro. It contains code (not shown) that "rewires" the reference (that points to the `Double` class *in the template code*) to a reference to the class generated from the target entity.

the generated field specific to the particular `Attribute` currently iterated over, more macros are used. A `COPY_SRC` macro is used to transform the `type`. `COPY_SRC` copies the input node (the Inspector specifies the current attribute's `type` as the input here) and applies reduction rules (those defined in Figure 6.6) to map types from the `entities` language to Java types. Finally, a property macro (the `$` sign around `aField`) is used to change the `name` property of the currently generated field to the name of the current source `Attribute`.

Most regular template engines mix template code and target language code, separating them with some kind of escape character. In MPS, instead regular, valid target language code is annotated with macros. Macros can be attached to arbitrary program elements. In this way the target language code in templates *is always structurally correct*, but it can still be annotated to control the transformation. Annotations are a generic MPS mechanism not specific to transformation macros, and are discussed in Section 7.4.5.

Summary — *Based on the foundation laid in this chapter, more advanced aspects of MPS and mbeddr can be tackled. In particular, the next chapter systematically*

```
┌root template┐
│input Entity │
└             ┘
public class $⎡map_Entity⎤ extends <none> implements <none>

  $LOOP$⎡private $COPY_SRC$⎣int⎦ $⎣aField⎦; ⎤

  public map_Entity( ) {
  }

  $LOOP$⎡public void $⎣setter⎦($COPY_SRC$⎣int⎦ newValue) {⎤
        │ <<placeholder>> pre-set : $⎣attr⎦              │
        │ this.aField = newValue;                        │
        └}                                               ┘

  $LOOP$⎡public $COPY_SRC$⎣int⎦ $⎣getter⎦() {⎤
        │ return aField;                     │
        └}                                   ┘
```

Figure 6.7 The template for creating a Java class from an Entity. The generated class contains a field, a getter and a setter for each of the Attributes of the Entity. The running text explains the details.

discusses language modularization and composition, which serves as an enabler for mbeddr. Chapters 8 and 9 then discuss the implementation of mbeddr itself, illustrating the power of MPS to realize Generic Tools, Specific Languages.

Language Composition and MPS

Abstract — *Language modularization and composition is the backbone of* Generic Tools, Specific Languages. *Based on the two dimensions of syntactic mixing and dependencies, this chapter identifies four major composition techniques: referencing, reuse, extension and embedding. In addition, restriction, annotations and extension composition are special cases of the four major techniques. All of these techniques are supported by MPS, and this chapter provides simple examples that act as the basis for the discussion of the implementation of mbeddr languages discussed in Chapters 8 and 9. The chapter concludes by comparing and contrasting MPS' approach with other approaches to language composition.*

7.1   INTRODUCTION

As mentioned in the introduction to Chapter 6, language composition is an important capability provided by language workbenches. This is for several reasons. One reason is the rising level of complexity of target platforms. For example, web applications consist of business logic on the server, a database backend, business logic on the client as well as presentation code on the client. Most of these are implemented with their own set of languages, and these have to be integrated in some way when applications are developed for this platform. A particular language stack could use Java, SQL, JavaScript and HTML.

The second reason driving multi-language programming is the increasing popularity of DSLs. Since these are specialized and often small languages that are optimized for expressing programs in a particular domain, several such languages will have to be composed to implement a complete system. DSLs may be used to describe technical domains (for example, database querying, user interface specification or scheduling) or business domains (such as insurance contracts, refrigerator cooling algorithms or state-based programs in embedded systems). mbeddr's extensions to C can be seen as a set of DSLs for embedded software development – these all have to be integrated in some way.

The combined use of multiple languages in a single system raises the question of how the syntax, semantics, and the development environments (IDEs) of the various languages can be integrated. In particular, syntactic composition has traditionally been hard [Kats et al., 2010]. Adding a requirement for decent IDE support, such as code completion, syntax coloring, static error checking, refactoring or debugging for the syntactically composed languages makes the challenge even harder. In some rare cases, syntactic integration between *specific* pairs of languages has been built, for example, embedded SQL in Java [Bravenboer et al., 2010]. A more systematic approach for language and IDE modularization and composition is required to provide IDE support for *arbitrary* combinations of languages.

Language and IDE modularization and composition addresses the following concerns. First, the concrete and the abstract syntax of the two languages have to be composed. This may require the embedding of one syntax into another. This, in turn, requires modular syntax definitions. Second, the static semantics (constraints and type system) have to be integrated. For example, existing operators have to be overridden for new types. Third, the execution semantics have to be combined as well. In practice, this may mean mixing the code generated from the composed languages, or composing the generators or interpreters. Finally, the IDE services have to be composed as well.

This chapter discusses the challenge of language and IDE modularization and composition; it proceeds as follows: Section 7.2 defines terms and concepts used throughout the chapter. Section 7.3 introduces four composition approaches and provides a rationale for why these four approaches are discussed, and not others: referencing, reuse, extension and embedding. The main section of the chapter is Section 7.4 which shows the implementation of the four composition approaches in MPS.

The discussion in Section 7.4 is based on a set of languages that compose in various ways with the entities language developed in Section 6.5: the uispec language illustrates referencing with entities. relmapping is an example of reuse with separated generated code. rbac illustrates reuse with intermixed generated code. uispec_validation demonstrates extension (of the uispec language) and embedding with regards to the expressions language. Extension is also illustrated by extending MPS' built in BaseLanguage, a variant of Java.

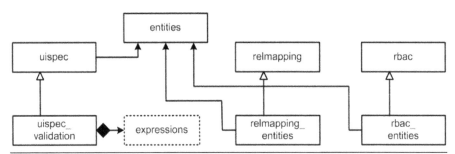

Figure 7.1 entities is the central language. uispec defines UI forms for the entities. uispec_validation adds validation rules, and embeds a reusable expressions language. relmapping provides a reusable database mapping language, relmapping_entities adapts it to the entities language. rbac is a reusable language for specifying access control permissions; rbac_entities adapts this language to the entities language.

Programs are represented in two ways: concrete syntax and abstract syntax. A language definition comprises both concrete syntax and abstract syntax, as well as rules for mapping one to the other. *Parser-based* systems map the concrete syntax to the abstract syntax. Users interact with a stream of characters, and a parser derives the abstract syntax tree (AST) by using a grammar. *Projectional* editors go the other way round: user editing gestures directly change the AST, the concrete syntax being a mere projection that looks (and mostly feels) like text. MPS is a projectional editor.

The abstract syntax of programs is primarily a tree of program *elements*. Every element (except the root) is contained by exactly one parent element. Syntactic nesting of the concrete syntax corresponds to a parent-child relationship in the abstract syntax. There may also be any number of non-containment cross-references between elements, established either directly during editing (in projectional systems) or by a linking phase that follows parsing.

A program may be composed from several program *fragments* that may reference each other. Each fragment f is a standalone AST. In file-based tools, a fragment corresponds to a file. E_f is the set of program elements in a fragment.

A language l defines a set of language *concepts* C_l and their relationships. The term *concept* is used to refer to concrete syntax, abstract syntax plus the associated type system rules and constraints, as well as a definition of its semantics. In a fragment, each program element e is an instance of a concept c defined in a language l. The *concept-of* function co is defined to return the concept of which a program element is an instance: $co(element) \Rightarrow concept$. Similarly, the *language-of* function lo returns the language in which a given concept is defined: $lo(concept) \Rightarrow language$. Finally, the *fragment-of* function fo returns the fragment that contains a given program element: $fo(element) \Rightarrow fragment$.

The following sets of relations between program elements are defined. Cdn_f (short for *children*) is the set of parent-child relationships in a fragment f. Each $c \in Cdn$ has the properties *parent* and *child*. Since fragments are primarily trees and Cdn_f essentially represents this tree structure, both *parent* and *child* reside in the same fragment, so $child \in E_f$ and $parent \in E_f$. $Refs_f$ (short for *references*) is the set of non-containment cross-references between program elements in a fragment f. Each reference $r \in Refs_f$ has the properties *from* and *to*, which refer to the two ends of the reference relationship. Finally, an inheritance relationship applies the Liskov Substitution Principle [Liskov & Wing, 1994] to language concepts: a concept *sub* that extends another concept *super* can be used in places where an instance of *super* is expected. Inh_f (short for *inheritances*) is the set of inheritance relationships for a fragment f. Inh_f is a unidirectional relationship from the perspective of *sub* pointing to *super*.

Note that *Refs* and *Inh* can be used for languages as well (as $Refs_l$ and Inh_l). On fragment level, these relations look at particular program nodes. At language level they refer to the definitions of the nodes, i.e., language concepts. Since Inh_l is seen from the perspective of sub, the referenced $super$ may reside in another language.

An important concern in language and IDE modularization and composition is the notion of independence. An *independent language* does not depend on other languages. It can be defined as follows:

$$\forall r \in Refs_l \mid lo(r.to) = lo(r.from) = l \tag{7.1}$$
$$\forall s \in Inh_l \mid lo(s.super) = lo(s.sub) = l \tag{7.2}$$
$$\forall c \in Cdn_l \mid lo(c.parent) = lo(c.child) = l \tag{7.3}$$

An *independent fragment* is one where all references stay within the fragment:

$$\forall r \in Refs_f \mid fo(r.to) = fo(r.from) = f \tag{7.4}$$

Homogeneous fragments are distinct from *heterogeneous* fragments. A homogeneous fragment is one in which all elements are expressed with the same language:

$$\forall e \in E_f \mid lo(e) = l \tag{7.5}$$

As elaborated by Harel & Rumpe [2004] the execution semantics of a language l is defined by mapping the syntactic constructs of l to concepts from the semantic domain S of the language. Different representations of S and the mapping $l \rightarrow S$ exist. Harel and Rumpe prefer to use mathematical formalisms as S because their semantics are well known, but acknowledge that other formalisms are useful as well. In this thesis the semantics of a language l is considered to be defined via a *transformation* that maps a program expressed in l to a program in another language l_2 that has the same *observable behavior*. The observable behavior can be determined in various ways, for example using a sufficiently large set of test cases. A discussion of alternative ways to define language semantics is beyond the scope of this thesis, and, in particular, interpretation is not discussed as an alternative to transformations in this chapter. This decision is driven partly by the fact that, in my experience, transformations are the most widely used approach for defining execution semantics in real-world language workbenches.

The chapter emphasizes *IDE* modularization and composition in addition to *language* modularization and composition. IDE services refers to syntax highlighting, code completion and static error checking, refactoring, quick fixes, support for testing, debugging and version control integration. When composing languages in MPS, these services are (mostly) automatically composed as well. As a consequence, this chapter does not discuss IDE services explicitly.

7.3   CLASSIFICATION OF COMPOSITION APPROACHES

This chapter defines and discusses the following four modularization and composition approaches: referencing, extension, reuse and embedding. Below

	homogeneous	heterogeneous
independent language dependencies	Reuse	Embedding
dependent	Referencing	Extension

homogeneous   heterogeneous
fragment structure

Figure 7.2 The four modularization and composition approaches are distinguished regarding their fragment structure and language dependencies. The dependencies dimension captures whether or not the languages have to be designed specifically for a specific composition partner. The fragment structure dimension captures whether or not the composition approach supports mixing of the concrete syntax of the composed languages.

is an intuitive description of each approach; stricter definitions follow in the remainder of the chapter.

Referencing   Referencing refers to the case in which a program is expressed in two languages A and B, but the parts expressed in A and B are kept in separate homogeneous fragments (files), and only name-based references connect the fragments. The referencing language has a direct dependency on the referenced language. An example for this case is a language that defines user interface (UI) forms for data structures defined by another language. The UI language references the data structures defined in a separate program.

Extension   Extension also allows a dependency of the extending language to the extended language (also called base language). However, in this case the code written in the two languages resides in a single, *heterogeneous* fragment, i.e. syntactic composition is required. An example is mbeddr's extension of C with new types, operators or literals.

Reuse   Reuse is similar to referencing in that the respective programs reside in separate fragments, connected only by references. However, in contrast to referencing, no direct dependencies between the languages are allowed. An example would be a persistence mapping language that can be used together with *different* data structure definition languages. To make this possible, the persistence mapping language cannot depend on any particular data definition language.

Embedding   Embedding combines the syntactic integration introduced by extension with not having dependencies introduced by reuse: *independent* languages can be used in the same *heterogeneous* fragment. An example is embedding a reusable expression language into another DSL. Since neither of the two composed languages can have direct dependencies, the same expression language can be embedded into *different* DSLs, and a specific DSL could integrate *different* expression languages.

As can be seen from the above descriptions, the four approaches are distinguished regarding fragment structure and language dependencies, as illustrated in Figure 7.2 (other classifications have been proposed; these are discussed in Section 7.5). Figure 7.3 shows the relationships between fragments and languages in these cases. These two criteria are essential for the following reasons. *Language dependencies* capture whether a language has to be designed with knowledge about a particular composition partner in order to be composable with that partner. It is desirable in many scenarios that languages be composable *without* previous knowledge about possible composition partners. *Fragment structure* captures whether the composed languages can be syntactically mixed. Since modular concrete syntax can be a challenge, this is not always easily possible, though often desirable.

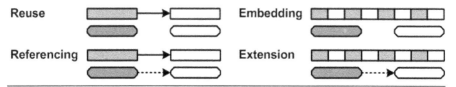

Figure 7.3 The relationships between fragments and languages in the four composition approaches. Boxes represent fragments, rounded boxes are languages. Dotted lines are dependencies, solid lines references/associations. The shading of the boxes represent the two different languages.

7.4 LANGUAGE COMPOSITION WITH MPS

This section discusses the four language and IDE modularization and composition techniques introduced in Section 7.3, plus an additional one that works only with a projectional editor such as MPS. The four major techniques are defined with a concise prose definition plus a set of formulas. Each technique is then illustrated with a detailed example based on the `entities` language introduced in the previous chapter[1].

7.4.1 *Language Referencing*

Language referencing enables *homogeneous* fragments with cross-references among them, using *dependent* languages (Figure 7.4).

A fragment f_2 depends on f_1. f_2 and f_1 are expressed with languages l_2 and l_1, respectively. l_2 is called the *referencing* language, and l_1 the *referenced* language. The referencing language l_2 depends on the referenced language l_1 because at least one concept in the l_2 references a concept from l_1. While equations (7.2) and (7.3) (from Section 7.2) continue to hold, (7.1) does not.

---

[1] I have decided against using mbeddr examples in this systematic and introductory chapter to keep the overall complexity lower. The next chapter shows how mbeddr's C extensions have been built.

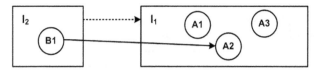

Figure 7.4 Referencing: language l_2 depends on l_1, because concepts in l_2 reference concepts in l_1. (Rectangles represent languages, circles represent language concepts, and UML syntax is used for the lines: dotted = dependency, arrows = associations, hollow-triangle-arrow for inheritance.)

Instead

$$\forall r \in \textit{Refs}_{l_2} \mid lo(r.from) = l_2 \wedge (lo(r.to) = l_1 \vee lo(r.to) = l_2) \qquad (7.6)$$

From a concrete syntax perspective, such a reference is a simple identifier, (possibly with dots). This terminal can easily be redefined in the referencing language and does not require reusing and embedding non-terminals from the referenced language. Hence no syntactic composition is required in this case.

The `uispec` language serves as an example for referencing; it defines UI forms for `entities`. Below is an example. This is a *homogeneous* fragment, expressed only in the `uispec` language. Only the identifiers of the referenced elements (such as `Employee.name`) have been added to the referencing language, as discussed in the previous paragraph. However, the fragment is *dependent*, since it references elements from another fragment (expressed in the `entities` language).

```
form CompanyStructure
  uses Department
  uses Employee
  field Name: textfield(30) -> Employee.name
  field Role: combobox(Boss, TeamMember) -> Employee.role
  field Freelancer: checkbox -> Employee.freelancer
  field Office: textfield(20) -> Department.description
```

Structure and Syntax   The abstract syntax for the `uispec` language is shown in Figure 7.5. The `uispec` language extends[2] the `entities` language, which means that concepts from the `entities` language can be used in the definition of the `uispec` language. A `Form` owns a number of `EntityReferences`, which in turn reference an `Entity`. Below is the definition of the `Field` concept. It has a `label` property, owns exactly one `Widget` (hence the cardinality of 1) and refers to the `Attribute` it edits.

---

[2] MPS uses the term *extension* whenever the definition of one language uses or refers to concepts defined in another language. This is not necessarily an example of language extension as defined in this thesis.

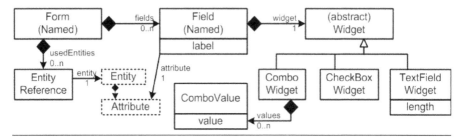

Figure 7.5 The abstract syntax of the `uispec` language. Dotted boxes represent classes from another language (here: the `entities` language). A `Form` contains `EntityReference`s that connect to an `entities` model. A `Form` also contains `Field`s, each referencing an `Attribute` from an `Entity` and containing a `Widget`.

```
concept Field extends BaseConcept
  properties:
    label: string
  children:
    Widget      widget    1
  references:
    Attribute  attribute  1
```

Note that there is no composition of concrete syntax, since the programs written in the two composed languages remain separated into their own fragments. No grammar ambiguities or clashes between names of concepts may occur in this case.

Type System   There are limitations regarding which widget can be used with which attribute type. For example, a checkbox widget can only be used with Boolean attributes. The typing rule below implements these checks and is defined in the `uispec` language. It references types from the `entities` language. A `checking rule` is used to illustrate how constraints can be written that do not use the inference engine introduced earlier.

```
checking rule checkTypes for Field as f {
  node<Widget> w = f.widget;
  node<Type> t = f.attribute.type;
  if (w.isInstanceOf(CheckBoxWidget) &&
      !(t.isInstanceOf(BooleanType))) {
    error "checkbox can only be used with booleans" -> w;
  }
  if (w.isInstanceOf(ComboWidget) &&
      !(t.isInstanceOf(StringType))) {
    error "combobox can only be used with strings" -> w;
  }
}
```

Generator   The defining characteristic of referencing is that the two languages only *reference* each other, and the instance fragments are dependent, but homogeneous. No syntactic integration is necessary. In this example, the generated code exhibits the same separation. From a `Form`, a Java class is generated that uses Java Swing to render the UI. It uses the Beans generated from the `entities`: they are instantiated, and the setters are called. The generators are separate but they are *dependent*, since the `uispec` generator knows about the names of the generated Java Beans, as well as the names of the setters and getters. This dependency is realized by defining a set of behavior methods on the `Attribute` concept that are called from both generators. The code below shows these methods. Note that the colon in the code represents the node cast operator and binds tightly; the code casts the `Attribute`'s parent to `Entity` and then accesses the `name` property.

```
concept behavior Attribute {
  public string qname()
          { this.parent:Entity.name + "." + this.name;}
  public string setterName() { "set" + this.name.toFirstUpper(); }
  public string getterName() { "get" + this.name.toFirstUpper(); }
}
```

7.4.2 Language Extension

Language extension enables *heterogeneous* fragments with *dependent* languages (Figure 7.6). A language l_2 extending l_1 adds additional language concepts to those of l_1. l_2 is called the *extending* language, and l_1 the *base* language. To allow the new concepts to be used in the context of l_1, some of them typically extend concepts in l_1. While l_1 remains independent, l_2 is dependent on l_1:

$$\exists i \in \mathit{Inh}(l_2) \mid i.sub = l_2 \wedge (i.super = l_2 \vee i.super = l_1) \qquad (7.7)$$

A fragment f contains language concepts from both l_1 and l_2:

$$\forall e \in E_f \mid lo(e) = l_1 \vee lo(e) = l_2 \qquad (7.8)$$

In other words f is *heterogeneous*. For heterogeneous fragments (1.3) no longer holds, since:

$$\forall c \in \mathit{Cdn}_f \mid (lo(co(c.parent)) = l_1 \vee lo(co(c.parent)) = l_2) \wedge$$
$$(lo(co(c.child)) = l_1 \vee lo(co(c.child)) = l_2) \qquad (7.9)$$

Note that copying a language definition and changing it does not constitute a case of extension, because the approach is not modular – it is invasive. Also, native interfaces that supports calling one language from another (such as calling C from Perl or Java) is not extension; rather it is a form of language referencing. The fragments remain homogeneous.

As an example, the MPS BaseLanguage is extended with block expressions and placeholders. These concepts make writing generators *that generate Base-Language code* much simpler. Figure 7.7 shows an example.

A block expression is a block that can be used where an `Expression` is expected [Bravenboer et al., 2005]. It can contain any number of statements; `yield` can be used to "return values" from the block. A block expression can be seen as an "inlined method" or a closure that is defined and called directly. The generator of the block expression from Figure 7.7 transforms it into a method and calls the generated method from the location where the block expression is used:

```
aEmployee.setName( retrieve_name(aEmployee, widget0) );
...

public String retrieve_name(Employee aEmployee, JComponent w) {
  String newValue = ((JTextField) w).getText();
  return newValue;
}
```

Structure and Syntax The `exprblocks` language extends MPS' BaseLanguage. The block expression is used in places where the base language expects an `Expression`, so a `BlockExpression` must extend `Expression`. Consequently, fragments that use the `exprblocks` language can now use `BlockExpressions` in addition to the concepts provided by BaseLanguage. The fragments become *heterogeneous*.

```
concept BlockExpression extends Expression implements INamedConcept
  children:
    StatementList   body   1
```

Type System The type of the `yield` statement is the type of the expression that is `yield`ed, specified by `typeof(aYield) :==: typeof(aYield.result)` (the type of `yield 1;` is `int`, because the type of `1` is `int`). Since the `BlockExpression` is used as an expression, it has to have a type as well: the type of the `BlockExpression` is the common supertype of the types of all `yields` used in the block expression:

```
var resultType;
for (node<BlockExpressionYield> y:
```

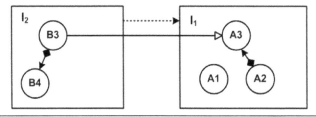

Figure 7.6 Extension: l_2 extends l_1. It provides additional concepts B3 and B4. B3 extends $A3$, so it can be used as a child of $A2$, plugging l_2 into the context provided by l_1. Consequently, l_2 depends on l_2.

```
$LOOP$[->$[o].->$[split]({$COPY_SRC$[String]n = $SWITCH$[null]; name: $[aName]);
                        yield n;
```

Figure 7.7 Block expressions (rendered with a shaded background) are basically anonymous inline methods. Upon transformation, an actual method is generated that contains the block content, and the block expression is replaced with a call to this generated method. Block expressions are used mostly when implementing generators; this screenshot shows a generator that uses a block expression.

```
        blockExpr.descendants<BlockExpressionYield>) {
    resultType :>=: typeof(y.result);
  }
  typeof(blockExpr) :==: resultType;
```

This equation iterates over all `yield` statements in a block expression and establishes an equation between the current `yield`'s type and a type variable `resultType`. It uses the `:>=:` operator to express the fact that the `resultType` must be the same or a supertype of the type of each `yield`. The only way to make *all* these equations true (which is what the type system solver attempts to do) is to assign the common supertype of all `yield` types to `resultType`. This `resultType` is then associated with the type of the overall block expression.

Generator   The generator reduces `BlockExpressions` to BaseLanguage. It transforms a heterogeneous fragment (BaseLanguage plus `exprblocks`) to a homogeneous fragment (BaseLanguage only). The first step is the creation of the additional method for the block expression, as shown in Figures 7.8 and 7.9.

```
concept     BlockExpression
inheritors false
condition   <always>
-->
  weave_BlockExpression
  context : (node, genContext, operationContext)->node< > {
            node<ClassConcept> cls = node.ancestor<ClassConcept, +>;
            genContext.get copied output for (cls);
        }
```

Figure 7.8 A weaving rule is used to create an additional method for a block expression. A weaving rule processes an input element (a `BlockExpression`) by creating another element *in a different location*. The `context` function defines the target location. In this example, it simply gets the class in which the particular block expression is defined, so the additional method is generated into that same class. The called template `weaveBlockExpression` is shown in Figure 7.9.

The template shown in Figure 7.9 shows the creation of the method. The mapping label (`b2M`) creates a mapping between the `BlockExpression` and the created method. This label is used to refer to this generated method when generating the method call that replaces the `BlockExpression` (Figure 7.10).

```
<TF b2M   public $COPY_SRC$[string] $[amethod]($LOOP$v2P[ $COPY_SRC$[int] $[a]]) {   TF>
              $COPY_SRCL$[return "hallo"; ]
          }
```

Figure 7.9 This generator template creates a method from the block expression. It uses COPY_SRC macros to replace the `string` type in the template with the computed return type of the block expression, inserts a computed name using a property macro (`$[]`), adds a parameter for each referenced variable outside the block (with the help of a LOOP macro), and inserts all the statements from the block expression into the body of the method (using a COPY_SRCL macro attached to the return statement). The b2M (block-to-method) mapping label is used later when generating the call to this generated method (shown in Figure 7.10 directly below). The macros contain expression that return the to-be-created property values or the nodes that must be inserted.

Another concept introduced by the `exprblocks` language is the `PlaceholderStatement`. This extends `Statement` so that it can be used in function bodies. It is used to mark locations at which subsequent generators can add additional code. These subsequent generators will use a reduction rule to replace the placeholder with whatever they want to put at this location. It is a means to build extensible generators, as shown below.

```
public void caller() {
    int j = 0;
    <TF [ ->$[callee]($LOOP$[$COPY_SRC$[j]]) ] TF>;
}
```

Figure 7.10 This generates the call to the method generated in Figure 7.9. The reference macro ->$[] around the `callee` dummy method is used to "reroute" the invocation to generated method. The expression behind the the reference macro (not shown) uses the b2M mapping label to retrieve the correct method; that label had been attached by the generator that created the method in Figure 7.9. The variables from the call's environment are passed in as actual arguments using the LOOP and COPY_SRC macros.

Extension comes in two flavors. One feels like actual extension, the other more like embedding. This section has described the extension flavor: provide (a little, local) additional syntax (block expressions and placeholders) to an otherwise unchanged language (BaseLanguage). The programs still essentially look like BaseLanguage programs, but in a few particular places, something is different. Extension with embedding flavor is when a completely new language is created that uses some of the syntax provided by a base language. An example could be a state machine language that reuses Java's expressions in guard conditions. This use case *feels* like embedding, since syntax from

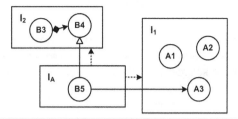

Figure 7.11 Reuse: l_1 and l_2 are independent languages. Within an l_2 fragment, nodes in a fragment expressed with l_1 should still be referenceable. To do this, an adapter language l_A is added that uses extension and referencing to adapt l_1 to l_2.

the base language is embedded in the new language, but in terms of the classification (Section 7.3) it is still extension. True embedding would prevent a dependency between the state machine language and Java. Embedding is discussed in Section 7.4.4.

7.4.3 *Language Reuse*

Language reuse enables *homogenous* fragments with *independent* languages. Consider two independent languages l_2 and l_1 and two fragment f_2 and f_1. f_2 depends on f_1, so that:

$$\exists r \in Refs_{f_2} \mid fo(r.from) = f_2 \land fo(r.to) = f_1$$

Since l_2 is independent, its concepts cannot directly reference concepts in l_1. This makes l_2 reusable with different languages, in contrast to language referencing, where concepts in l_2 reference concepts in l_1. l_2 is called the *context* language and l_1 the *reused* language.

A way of realizing dependent fragments with independent languages is by using an adapter language l_A (cf. [Gamma et al., 1995]) that contains concepts that *extend* concepts in l_2 and *reference* concepts in l_1 (Figure 7.11). One could argue that in this case reuse is just a combination of referencing and extension. This is true from an implementation perspective, but it is worth describing as a separate approach, because it enables the combination of two *independent languages* with an adapter *after the fact*, so no pre-planning during the design of l_1 and l_2 is necessary.

Reuse covers the case in which a language has been developed independently of its reuse context. The respective fragments remain homogeneous. Two alternative cases are covered in the remainder of this section. In the first one (a persistence mapping language) the generated code is separate from the code generated from the `entities` language. The second one, a language for role-based access control, describes the case in which the generated code has to be "woven into" the `entities` code.

`relmapping` is a reusable language for mapping arbitrary data to relational tables. It supports the definition of relational table structures, but leaves the actual mapping of the source data to these tables unspecified. When the language is adapted to a specific context, this mapping has to be provided. The left side of the code below shows the reusable part. A database is defined that contains tables with columns. Columns have (database-specific) data types. The right side shows the database definition code when it is reused with the `entities` language; each column is mapped to an entity attribute.

```
database CompanyDB              database CompanyDB
  table Departments               table Departments
    number id                       number id <- Department.id
    char descr                      char descr <-Department.description
  table People                    table People
    number id                       number id <- Employee.id
    char name                       char name <- Employee.name
    char role                       char role <- Employee.role
    char isFreelancer               char isFreelancer <-
                                                 Employee.freelancer
```

Structure and Syntax   Figure 7.12 shows the structure of the `relmapping` language. The abstract concept `ColumnMapper` serves as a hook: if this language is reused in a different context, this hook is extended in a context-specific way.

The `relmapping_entities` language extends `relmapping` and adapts it for reuse with the `entities` language. To this end, it provides a subconcept of `ColumnMapper`, the `AttributeColMapper`, which references an `Attribute` from the `entities` language as a means of expressing the mapping from the attribute to the column. The `relmapping` language projects the column mapper – and its context-specific subconcepts – on the right of the field definition, resulting in heterogeneous fragments.

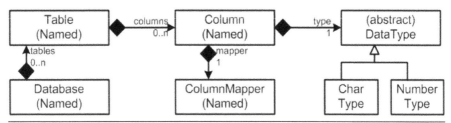

Figure 7.12 A `Database` contains `Tables` which contain `Columns`. A column has a name and a type. A column also has a `ColumnMapper`. This is an abstract concept that determines where the column gets its data from. It is a hook intended to be specialized in sublanguages, specific to the particular reuse context.

Type System The type of a column is the type of its `type` property. In addition, the type of the column must also conform to the type of the column mapper, so the concrete subtype must provide a type mapping as well. This "typing hook" is implemented as an abstract behavior method `typeMappedToDB` on the `ColumnMapper`. The typing rules then look as follows:

```
typeof(column)        :==: typeof(column.type);
typeof(column.type)   :==: typeof(column.mapper);
typeof(columnMapper)  :==: columnMapper.typeMappedToDB();
```

The `AttributeColMapping` concept implements this method by mapping `Int-Type` to `NumberType`, and everything else to `CharType`:

```
public node<> typeMappedToDB()
                overrides ColumnMapper.typeMappedToDB {
  node<> attrType = this.attribute.type.type;
  if (attrType.isInstanceOf(IntType)) {
    return new node<NumberType>();
  }
  return new node<CharType>();
}
```

Generator The generated code is separated into a reusable base class generated by the generator of the `relmapping` language and a context-specific subclass, generated by `relmapping_entities`. The generic base class contains code for creating the tables and for storing data in those tables. It contains abstract methods for accessing the data to be stored in the columns. The dependency structure of the generated fragments, as well as the dependencies of the respective generators, resembles the dependency structure of the languages: the generated fragments are dependent, and the generators are dependent as well: they share the name and implicitly the knowledge about the structure of the class generated by the reusable `relmapping` generator.

```
public abstract class CompanyDBBaseAdapter {

  private void createTableDepartments() {
    // SQL to create the Departments table }
  private void createTablePeople() {
    // SQL to create the People table }

  public void storeDepartments(Object applicationData) {
    Insert i = new Insert("Departments");
    i.add( "id", getValueForDepartments_id(applicationData));
    i.add( "descr", getValueForDepartments_descr(applicationData));
    i.execute();
  }

  public void storePeople(Object applicationData) { // like above }
  public abstract String valueForDepartments_id(Object appData);
```

```
public abstract String valueForDepartments_descr(Object appData);
    // abstract methods for obtaining the data to be stored in the
    // respective table columns - to be implemented by subclass.
}
```

The subclass generated by the generator (shown below) in the `relmapping_-entities` language implements the abstract methods defined by the generic superclass. The interface, represented by the `appData` object, has to be generic, so that any kind of user data can be passed in. Note how this class references the Beans generated from the `entities`.

```
public class CompanyDBAdapter extends CompanyDBBaseAdapter {

    public String valueForDepartments_id(Object appData) {
        Object[] arr = (Object[]) appData;
        Department o = (Department) arr[0];
        return o.getId();
    }
    public String valueForDepartments_descr(Object appData) {
        Object[] arr = (Object[]) appData;
        Department o = (Department) arr[0];
        return o.getDescription();
    }
}
```

Interwoven generated code

`rbac` is a language for specifying role-based access control. The code below shows an example fragment when used together with `entities`: it references entities (`Department`) and attributes (`Employee.name`) defined in some `entities` fragment.

```
users: user mv: Markus Voelter
       user ag: Andreas Graf
       user ke: Kurt Ebert

roles: role admin: ke
       role consulting: ag, mv

permissions: admin, W: Department
             consulting, R: Employee.name
```

Structure and Syntax   The structure is shown in Figure 7.13. Like `relmapping`, `rbac` provides a hook `Resource` to adapt it to context languages. The sublanguage `rbac_entities` provides two subconcepts of `Resource`, namely `AttributeResource` to reference to an `Attribute`, and `EntityResource` to refer to an `Entity`, to define permissions for entities and their attributes.

Type System   No type system rules apply here, because none of the concepts added by the `rbac` language are typed or require constraints regarding the types in the `entities` language.

170

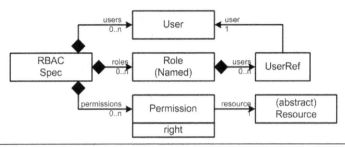

Figure 7.13 The language structure of the `rbac` language. An `RBACSpec` contains `Users`, `Roles` and `Permissions`. Users can be members in several roles. A permission assigns a role and right (read, write) to a `Resource` (such as an `Entity` or an `Attribute`).

Generator   What distinguishes this case from the `relmapping` case is that the code generated from the `rbac_entities` language is *not* separated from the code generated from the `entities`; the convenient base class/subclass approach cannot be used. Instead, a permission check is required *inside* the setters of the Java Beans. Here is some example code:

```
public void setName(String newValue) {
  // check permission (from rbac_entities language)
  if (!new RbacSpecEntities().hasWritePermission("Employee.name")) {
    throw new RuntimeException("no permission");
  }
  this.name = newValue;
}
```

The generated fragment is homogeneous (it is all Java code), but it is *multi-sourced*, since several generators contribute to the same fragment. To implement this, several approaches are possible:

- AspectJ[3] could be used. This would allow separate Java artifacts (all single-sourced) to be generated, "mixed" together by the aspect weaver. While this would be a simple approach in terms of MPS (because only singled-sourced artifacts need to be generated), it fails to illustrate advanced MPS generator concepts (the point of this subsection), which is why the approach is not used here.

- An interceptor framework (see the Interceptor pattern by Buschmann et al. [1996b]) could be added to the generated Java Beans, with the generated code contributing specific interceptors. This would effectively mean building a custom aspect-oriented programming (AOP) solution. This approach is not used either, for the same reason that AspectJ is not used.

---

[3] http://www.eclipse.org/aspectj/

- Additional code could be "injected" into the generation templates of the existing `entities` generator from the `rbac_entities` generator. This would make the generators *woven*, as opposed to just dependent. However, weaving generators in MPS is not supported.

- A hook in the generated Java beans code could be defined, with the `rbac_entities` generator contributing code to this hook. The generators remain dependent because they share knowledge about the way the hook works. This is the approach used in the remainder of this section.

Notice that only the AspectJ solution would work *without any pre-planning* from the perspective of the `entities` language, because it avoids mixing the generated code artifacts (mixing is handled by AspectJ). All other solutions require the original `entities` generator to "expect" extensions. In this case, the `entities` generator was modified to generate a `PlaceholderStatement` (Figure 7.14) into the setters. The placeholder acts as a hook at which subsequent generators can add statements.

The `rbac_entities` generator contains a reduction rule for `Placeholder-Statements`. If the generator encounters a placeholder (that has been put there by the `entities` generator), it replaces it with code that checks for the permission (Figure 7.15). To make this work, the generator priorities have to specify that this generator runs *strictly after* the `entities` generator (since the `entities` generator has to create the placeholder before it can be replaced) and *strictly before* the BaseLanguage generator (which transforms BaseLanguage code into Java text for compilation). Priorities specify a partial ordering (cf. the `strictly before` and `strictly after`) on generators and can be set in a generator properties dialog. Note that specifying the priorities does not introduce additional language dependencies; modularity is retained.

7.4.4 *Language Embedding*

Embedding enables *heterogeneous* fragments with *independent* languages. Similar to reuse, there are two independent languages l_1 and l_2, but instead of just having references between two homogeneous fragments, instances of concepts from l_2 are now *embedded* in a fragment f expressed with l_1:

```
$LOOP$ public void $ setter ($COPY_SRC$ int  newValue) {
         <<placeholder>> pre-set : $ attr
         this.aField = newValue;
       }
```

Figure 7.14 This generator fragment creates a setter method for each attribute of an `Entity`. The `LOOP` iterates over all attributes. The `$` macro computes the name of the method, and the `COPY_SRC` macro on the argument type computes the type. The placeholder is used later to insert the permission check.

```
┌                                                                          ┐
│ concept     PlaceholderStatement                                         │
│ inheritors false                                                         │
│ condition   (node, genContext, operationContext)->boolean {              │
│                  node.name.equals("pre-set");                            │
│                }                                                         │
└                                                                          ┘
    -->
content node:
public void dummy() {
  ┌                                                                      ┐
  <TF │ {{ // transparent block                                   TF> │
      │ // check permissions (from rbac_entities)                         │
      │ if (!new ->$⌈RbacSpecEntities⌉().currentUserHasWritePermission("$⌈res⌉ │
      │      ")) { throw new RuntimeException("no permission"); }          │
      │ }}                                                                 │
  └                                                                      ┘
}
```

Figure 7.15 This reduction rule replaces `PlaceholderStatement`s with a permission check. Using the condition, only those placeholders whose identifier is `pre-set` are matched. This identifier has been defined in the template in Figure 7.14. The inserted code queries another generated class that contains the actual permission check. A runtime exception is thrown if the check fails.

$$\forall c \in Cdn_f \mid lo(co(c.parent)) = l_1 \land$$
$$(lo(co(c.child)) = l_1 \lor lo(co(c.child)) = l_2)) \qquad (7.10)$$

Unlike language extension, where l_2 depends on l_1 because concepts in l_2 extend concepts in l_1, there is no such dependency in this case. Both languages are independent. l_2 is called the *embedded* language and l_1 the *host* language. Again, an adapter language can be used to achieve this (embedding *without* adapters in described Section 7.4.5). However, in this case concepts in l_A do not just reference concepts from l_1. Instead, they contain them. The diagram is similar to Figure 7.11, but with a containment link between B5 and A3.

As an example, an existing `expressions` language is embedded into the `uispec` language without modifying either the `uispec` language or the expression language, since, in the case of embedding, none of them may have a dependency on the other. Below is an example program using the resulting language that uses expressions after the `validate` keyword:

```
form CompanyStructure
  uses Department
  uses Employee
  field Name: textfield(MAX_NAME_LEN) -> Employee.name
                  validate lengthOf(Employee.name) < MAX_NAME_LEN
  field Role: combobox(Boss, TeamMember) -> Employee.role
  field Freelancer: checkbox -> Employee.freelancer
        validate if (isSet(Employee.worksAt))
                    Employee.freelancer == true
                else
                    Employee.freelancer == false
  field Office: textfield(20) -> Department.description
```

Structure and Syntax A new language `uispec_validation` is created that extends `uispec` and also extends `expressions`. Figure 7.16 shows the structure. To be able to use the validation expressions, the user has to use instances of `ValidatedField` instead of plain `Field`s. `ValidatedField` is also defined in `uispec_validation` and is a subconcept of `Field`.

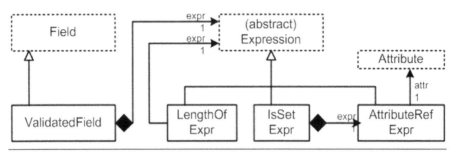

Figure 7.16 The `uispec_validation` language defines a subtype of `uispec.Field` that contains an `Expression` from a reusable `expressions` language. The language also defines a couple of additional expressions, including the `AttributeRefExpr`, which can be used to refer to attributes of entities.

To support the migration of existing models that already contain `Field` instances, an intention is created. An intention is an in-place model transformation that can be triggered by the user by selecting it from the intentions menu accessible via `Alt-Enter`. This particular intention is defined for a `Field`, so the user can press `Alt-Enter` on a `Field` and select `Add Validation`[4]. This transforms an existing `Field` into a `ValidatedField`, so that a validation expression can be entered. The core of the intention is the following script, which performs the actual transformation:

```
execute(editorContext, node)->void {
  node<ValidatedField> vf = node.replace with new(ValidatedField);
  vf.widget = node.widget;
  vf.attribute = node.attribute;
  vf.label = node.label;
}
```

As mentioned, the `uispec_validation` language extends the `uispec` and `expressions` languages. `ValidatedField` has a property `expr` that contains the actual `Expression`. As a consequence of polymorphism, any existing subconcept of `Expression` defined in the `expressions` language can be used here. So without doing anything else, one could write 20 + 40 > 10, since integer literals and the + and > operators are defined as part of the embedded `expressions` language. However, to express useful field validations, entity attributes must be referenceable from within validation expressions. The `AttributeRefExpr` (as shown in Figure 7.16) is created to achieve this. Also,

---

[4] Alternatively, a way for people to just type `validate` on the right side of a field could be implemented to trigger this transformation.

174

the `LengthOfExpr` and `IsSetExpression` are created as further examples of how to adapt an embedded language to its new context (the `uispec` and `entities` languages in the example). As an example, the following is the structure definition of the `LengthOfExpr`:

```
concept LengthOfExpr extends Expression
  children: Expression expr 1
```

The `AttributeRefExpr` references entity attributes. However, it may only reference attributes of entities that are used in the `Form` within which the validation expression resides. The code below defines the necessary scoping rule:

```
(model, scope, referenceNode, enclosingNode) -> sequence<node< >> {
  nlist<Attribute> res = new nlist<Attribute>;
  node<Form> form = enclosingNode.ancestor<Form>;
  for (node<EntityReference> er: form.usedEntities)
    res.addAll(er.entity.attributes);
  return res;
}
```

Notice that, in terms of the concrete syntax, the actual embedding of the expressions into the `uispec_validation` language is not a problem because of how projectional editors work. No ambiguities can arise.

Type System   Primitive types such as `int` and `string` are defined in the `entities` language *and* in the reusable expression language. Although they have the same names, they are not the same concepts, so the two sets of types must be mapped. For example, the type of the `IsSetExpression` is `expressions.BooleanType` so it fits in with the `expressions` language. The type of the `LengthOfExpr`, which takes an `AttributeRefExpression` as its argument, is `expressions.IntType`. The type of an attribute reference is the type of the attribute's `type` property, as in `typeof(attrRef) :==: typeof(attrRef.attr.type)`. However, consider the following code:

```
field Freelancer: checkbox -> Employee.freelancer
    validate if (isSet(Employee.worksAt))
                then Employee.freelancer == false
                else Employee.freelancer == true
```

This code states that if the `worksAt` attribute of an employee is set, then its `freelancer` attribute must be `false`, else it must be `true`. It uses the `==` operator from the `expressions` language. However, that operator expects two `expressions.BooleanType` arguments, but the type of the `Employee.freelancer` is `entities.BooleanType`. In effect, the typing rules for the `==` operator in the `expressions` language have to be overridden. The expressions language contains overloaded operation rules which specify the resulting type for an `EqualsExpression` depending on its argument types. Below is the code in the `expressions` language that defines the resulting type to be `boolean` if the two arguments are `expressions.BooleanType`. The keywords `left`/`right` `operand type` and the `operation type` function signature are predefined; only the (`new node<...>`) expressions must be manually written:

```
[concept      MultiExpression]  --> <T  $COPY_SRC$[1] * $COPY_SRC$[2]  T>
[inheritors false            ]
[condition   <always>        ]


[concept      FalseLiteral]  --> <T  false  T>
[inheritors false         ]
[condition   <always>     ]


[concept      BooleanType]  --> <T  boolean  T>
[inheritors false        ]
[condition   <always>    ]


[concept      IfExpression]  --> <T  $COPY_SRC$[true] ?
[inheritors false         ]           $COPY_SRC$[true] : $COPY_SRC$[true]  T>
[condition   <always>     ]
```

Figure 7.17 A number of reduction rules that map the reusable `expressions` language to BaseLanguage (Java). Since the languages are very similar, the mapping is trivial. For example, a `MultiExpression` is mapped to a ∗ in Java; the left and right arguments are reduced recursively through the `COPY_SRC` macro.

```
operation concepts: EqualsExpression
  left operand type: new node<BooleanType>
  right operand type: new node<BooleanType>
  operation type: (op, leftOperandType, rightOperandType)->node< > {
    new node<BooleanType>;
  }
```

To override these typing rules for `BooleanType` from the `entities` language, the `uispec_validation` provides another overloaded operation specification:

```
operation concepts: EqualsExpression
  one operand type: new node<BooleanType> // entities.BooleanType!
  operation type: (op, leftOperandType, rightOperandType)->node< > {
    node<BooleanType>;  // expressions.BooleanType
  }
```

Generator   For the generator, the following two alternative approaches can be used. The first alternative uses the `expressions` language's existing to-text generator and wraps the expressions in some kind of `TextWrapperStatement`. A wrapper is necessary because text cannot simply be embedded in BaseLanguage – this would not work structurally. The alternative is to write a (reusable) transformation from `expressions` to BaseLanguage; these rules would be used as part of the transformation of `uispec_validation` code to BaseLanguage. Since many DSLs will map code to BaseLangauge, it is worth the effort to write a reusable generator from `expressions` to BaseLanguage expressions. The second alternative is chosen here.

The actual expressions defined in the `expressions` language and those of BaseLanguage are almost identical, so this generator is trivial. A new lan-

```
┌                           ┐
│ concept    AttributeRefExpr │  --> content node:
│ inheritors false            │      public void dummy() {
│ condition  <always>         │          Object anObj = null;
└                           ┘          <TF [ ->$[anObj].->$[toString]() ] TF>;
                                   }
```

Figure 7.18 References to entity attributes are mapped to a call to their getter method. The template fragment (inside the `<TF .. TF>`) uses reference macros (`->$`) to "rewire" the reference to the Java Bean instance, and the `toString` method call to a call to the getter.

guage project `expressions.blgen` is created, and reduction rules are added. Figure 7.17 shows some of these reduction rules.

Reduction rules for the new expressions added in the `uispec_validation` language (`AttributeRefExpression`, `isSetExpression`, `LengthOfExpr`) are necessary as well. Those rules are defined in `uispec_validation`. As an example, Figure 7.18 shows the rule for handling the `AttributeRefExpression`. The validation code itself is "injected" into the UI form via the same placeholder reduction, as in the case of the `rbac_entities` language.

7.4.5 *Language Annotations*

In a projectional editor, the concrete syntax of a program is projected from the AST. A projectional system always goes from abstract syntax to concrete syntax, never from concrete syntax to abstract syntax (as parsers do). This has the important consequence that the concrete syntax does not have to contain all the data necessary to build the AST, which, in the case of parsers, is necessary. This has two consequences:

- A projection may be *partial*. The abstract syntax may contain data that is not shown in the concrete syntax. The information may, for example, only be changeable via intentions (see Section 7.4.4), or the projection rule may project some parts of the program only in some cases, controlled by some kind of configuration.

- It is also possible to project *additional* concrete syntax that is not part of the concrete syntax definition of the original language. Since the concrete syntax is never used as the information source, such additional syntax does not confuse the tool (in a parser-based tool the grammar would have to be changed to take into account this additional syntax in order not to derail the parser).

This section discusses the second alternative. It represents a variant of embedding (no dependencies, but syntactic composition). The mechanism MPS uses for this is called *annotations*; their use has already been illustrated in the context of generator templates (Section 6.5): an annotation can be attached to arbitrary program elements and can be shown together with the concrete syntax of the annotated element. This section uses this approach to implement an alternative approach for the entity-to-database mapping. Using this approach, the mapping from entity attributes to database columns can be stored directly in the `Entity`, resulting in the following code:

```
module company
  entity Employee {
    id: int -> People.id
    name: string -> People.name
    role: string -> People.role
    worksAt: Department -> People.departmentID
    freelancer: boolean -> People.isFreelancer
  }

  entity Department {
    id: int -> Departments.id
    description: string -> Departments.descr
  }
```

This is a heterogeneous fragment, consisting of code from `entities`, as well as the annotations (for example, `-> People.id`). From a concrete syntax perspective, the column mapping is embedded in the `Entity`. In the AST the mapping information is also actually stored in the `entities` model. However, the definition of the `entities` language does not know that this additional information is stored and projected "inside" entities. The `entities` language is not modified.

Structure and Syntax   An additional language `relmapping_annotations` is defined which extends the `entities` language as well as the `relmapping` language. This language contains the following concept:

```
concept AttrToColMapping extends NodeAnnotation
  references:
    Column column 1
  properties:
    role = colMapping
  concept links:
    annotated = Attribute
```

`AttrToColMapping` concept extends `NodeAnnotation`, a concept predefined by MPS. Concepts that extend `NodeAnnotation` have to provide a `role` property and an `annotated` concept link. Structurally, an annotation is a child of the node it annotates. So the `Attribute` has a new child of type `AttrToColMapping`, and the reference that contains the child is called `@colMapping` – the value of the `role` property prepended with `@`. The `annotated` concept link points to the concept *to which this annotation can be added*. `AttrToColMapping`s can be annotated to instances of `Attribute`.

While structurally the annotation is a child of the annotated node, the relationship is reversed in the concrete syntax: The editor for `AttrToColMapping`

```
editor for concept AttrToColMapping
  node cell layout:
    [- [> attributed node <] -> ( % column % -> * R/O model access * ) -]
```

Figure 7.19 The editor for the `AttrToColMapping` embeds the editor of the concept
it is annotated to (using the `attributed node` cell). It then projects the reference
to the referenced column. This gives the editor of the annotation control of whether
and how the editor of the annotated element is projected.

wraps the editor for `Attribute`, as Figure 7.19 shows. A slight drawback of
this approach is that, since the annotation is not part of the original language,
it cannot just be "typed in": it must be attached to nodes via an intention.

It is possible to define the annotation target to be `BaseConcept`, which
means the annotation can be attached to *any* program element. This is useful
for generic metadata such as documentation, requirements traces or presence
conditions in product line engineering (discussed in Sections 4.8 and 4.9).
MPS' template language uses this approach as well. Note that this is a way
to support embedding generically, *without* the use of an adapter language.
The reason why this generic approach is useful mostly for metadata is related
to semantics: since the annotations can be composed *with any other language*
without an adapter, the semantics must be generic as well, i.e. not related
to any particular target language. This is true for the generic metadata mentioned above.

Type System   The same typing rules are necessary as in `relmapping_enti-`
`ties` described previously. They reside in `relmapping_annotations`.

Generator   The generator is also similar to the one for `relmapping_entities`.
It takes the `entities` model as the input, and then uses the column mappings
in the annotations to create the entity-to-database mapping code.

7.4.6 *Language Restriction*

Mernik et al. [2005] suggest restriction as another means of language modularization and composition. In the context of this thesis, however, restriction
is considered a special case of extension: a restriction is implemented as a set
of additional constraints on an existing language. The restrictions live in a
separate language that extends the restricted language. As usual in the case
of extension, the language that defines these restrictions has a dependency on
the restricted language.

Restrictions are often used together with extension or embedding. For
example, in the example in Section 7.4.4, the validation expressions may be
restricted to only use arithmetic expressions, comparison expressions and the
special expressions built for the purpose (`AttributeRefExpr` or `LengthOfExpr`),
and not all the other expressions potentially available in a reusable expression
language.

Another example is the restriction on use of `return` statements in the block expressions introduced in Section 7.4.2. As a consequence of how block expressions are generated to Java, `return` statements cannot be used inside a block expression. To express such a restriction, a `can be ancestor` constraint is defined for the `BlockExpression` in the `blockexpr` language:

```
concept constraints for BlockExpression {
  can be ancestor:
    (operationContext, scope, node, childConcept, link)->boolean {
      childConcept != concept/ReturnStatement/;
    }
}
```

The `childConcept` variable represents the concept of which an instance is about to be added under a `BlockExpression`. The constraint expression has to return `true` if the respective `childConcept` is valid in this location. True is returned if the `childConcept` is not a `ReturnStatement`. Note how this constraint is written *from the perspective of the ancestor* (the `BlockExpression`). MPS also supports writing constraints from the perspective of the child. This is important to keep dependencies pointing in the right direction.

7.4.7 Extension Composition

Erdweg et al. [2012] suggest another composition mechanism called *extension composition*. This refers to the ability of using several independently developed extensions of a base language together in the same program. This feature is extremely important to exploit the benefits of extension.

The reason why it is worth mentioning explicitly is this. As discussed in this chapter, extension implies that when defining the extension language, the base language is known, so the extension language can be defined in a way that is compatible with the base language. In particular, syntactic ambiguities can be avoided. However, in extension composition, several independently developed extensions to the same base language are combined in a single program. While each of the extensions can be designed to be compatible with the common base language, they cannot be designed to be compatible with *each other*, since, at the time of developing either of the two, it is not known that they will be used together in the future. The same issue arises if several languages are embedded into a common host language.

MPS supports extension composition, and mbeddr uses it extensively: all C extensions discussed in this thesis can be used together in a single program. As a consequence of MPS' projectional editor, no ambiguities may arise. The following illustrates how MPS handles potential ambiguities:

Same Concept Name: Two languages (independent extensions or embeddings) may define concepts with the same name as the host language. This will not lead to ambiguity because concepts have a unique ID as well. A program element will use this ID to refer to the concept whose instance it represents.

Same Concrete Syntax: The projected representation of a concept is not relevant to the functioning of the editor. The program would still be unambiguous to MPS even if *all elements had the same notation*. Of course it would be confusing to the users. However, users can always see the qualified name of the instantiated concept in the inspector as a means of disambiguation.

Same Alias: If two concepts that are valid at the same location use the same alias, then, as the user types the alias, it is not clear which of the two concepts should be instantiated. This problem is solved by MPS opening the code completion window and requiring the user to select which alternative to choose explicitly. Once the user has made the decision, the unique ID is used to create an unambiguous program tree.

7.5 RELATED WORK

This section discusses related work regarding the core contribution of this thesis: language engineering, language workbenches and extensible IDEs.

Parsers and Grammars MPS is a projectional editor, and does *not* use grammars and parsers. As this chapter has demonstrated, this enables language and IDE modularization and composition. This section discusses the fundamental limitations and recent advances of parser-based tools in this respect.

Kats et al. [2010] describe the trade-offs with non-declarative grammars. Grammar formalisms that cover only subsets of context-free grammars are not closed under composition and composed grammars are likely to be outside of the respective grammar class. Composition (without invasive change) is prohibited. Formalisms that implement full context-free grammars avoid this problem and compose much better.

Most mainstream parser generators (such as ANTLR [Parr & Quong, 1995]) do not support the full set of context-free grammars and hence face problems with composition. In contrast, version 2 of the Syntax Definition Formalism (SDF2, [Visser, 1997]) does support full context-free grammars. Based on a scannerless GLR parser, it parses tokens and characters in a context-aware fashion. There will be no ambiguities if grammars are composed that both define the same token or production *in different contexts*. This allows, for example, embedding of SQL into Java (as Bravenboer et al. discuss by Bravenboer et al. [2010]). However, if the same syntactic form is used by the composed grammars *in the same location*, manual disambiguation becomes necessary. In SDF2, disambiguation is implemented via quotations and antiquotations ("escape characters"), which are defined in a third grammar that defines the composition of two other independent grammars [Bravenboer & Visser, 2004]. The SILVER/COPPER system described by Wyk et al. [2008] instead uses disambiguation functions written specifically for each combination of ambiguously composed grammars. In MPS disambiguation is never necessary – in the worst case, the user makes the disambiguating decision by picking the correct concept from the code completion menu. Given a set of extensions for a language, SILVER/COPPER allows users to include a subset of these extensions into a program as needed (demonstrated for Java in AbleJ [Wyk et al., 2007] and for SPIN/Promela in AbleP [Mali & Wyk, 2011]). A similar approach is discussed for an SDF2-based system by Bravenboer & Visser [2007]. However, ad-hoc inclusion only works as long as the set of included extensions (presumably developed independently of each other) *are not ambiguous* with regards to each other. Otherwise disambiguation has to be used. Again, MPS does not have this limitation.

Polyglot, an extensible compiler framework for Java [Nystrom et al., 2003] also uses an extensible grammar formalism and parser to supports adding, modifying or removing productions and symbols defined in a base grammar. However, since Polyglot uses the LALR grammar class, users must make sure *manually* that the base language and the extension remains LALR.

Monticore is another parser-based tool that generates parsers, metamodels and editors based on extended grammar. Languages can extend each other and can be embedded within each other [Krahn et al., 2010]. An important idea is the ability to not regenerate the parsers or any of the related tools for a composed language. However, ambiguities have to be avoided manually.

Macro systems support the definition of additional syntax for existing languages (i.e. they can be seen as some form of language extension). The new syntax is reduced in place to valid base language code. The definition of the syntax and the transformation is expressed with special host language constructs, not with a separate meta language. Macro systems differ with regard to the degree of freedom they provide for the extension syntax, and whether they support extensions of type systems and IDEs. The most primitive macro system is the C preprocessor, which performs pure text replacement during macro expansion. The Lisp macro system is more powerful because it is aware of the syntactic structure of Lisp (see Guy Steele's *Growing a Language* keynote [Jr., 1999]). An example of a macro system with limited syntactic freedom is the Java Syntactic Extender [Bachrach & Playford, 2001], in which each macro has to begin with a unique keyword, and only a limited set of syntactic forms is supported. In OpenJava [Tatsubori et al., 1999], the locations where macros can be added is limited. More fine-grained extensions, such as new operators, are not possible. Some of the C extensions developed in mbeddr are macro-style (they are reduced in place to the corresponding C code). However, MPS enforces no limitations on the granularity, syntax or location of such extensions, and supports extending the type system and the IDE.

MPS' template language provides IDE support for the target language *in the template*. In traditional text-generation template languages this is not possible, because it requires support for language composition: the target language must be embedded in the template language. However, there are examples of template languages that support this, built on top of modular grammar formalisms. An example is the Repleo template language [Arnoldus et al., 2007], which is built on SDF2. However, as explained in the discussion on

SDF above, SDF requires the definition of an additional grammar that defines how the host grammar (template language in this case) and the embedded grammar (target language) fit together (quotations). In MPS, any target language can be marked up with template annotations. No separate language has to be defined for the combination of template and target language.

Projectional Editing   This section discusses other tools, that, like MPS, are based on a projectional editor. The section focuses on flexibility and in particular on usability, since MPS is groundbreaking in this space.

An early example of a projectional editor is the Incremental Programming Environment (IPE, [Medina-Mora & Feiler, 1981]). It provides a projectional editor and an integrated incremental compiler. It supports the definition of several notations for the same program (supported by MPS from late 2013) as well as partial projections. However, the projectional editor forces users to build the program tree top-down. For example, to enter 2+3, users first have to enter the + and then fill in the two arguments. This is tedious and forces users to be aware of the language structure at all times. In contrast, as illustrated in Section 6.2.1, MPS supports editing that resembles linear text editing, particularly for expressions. IPE also does not address language modularity. In fact it comes with a fixed, C-like language, and does not have a built-in facility for defining new languages. Another projectional system is GANDALF [Notkin, 1985]. Its ALOEGEN component generates projectional editors from a language specification. It has the same usability problems as IPE. This is nicely expressed by Porter [1988]: *Program editing will be considerably slower than normal keyboard entry although actual time spent programming non-trivial programs should be reduced due to reduced error rates.*

The Synthesizer Generator [Reps & Teitelbaum, 1984] also supports projectional editing. However, at the fine-grained expression level, textual input and parsing is used. This destroys many of the advantages of projectional editing in the first place, because simple language composition *at the expression level* is prohibited. This thesis shows that extensions of expressions are particularly important to tightly integrate an embedded language with its host language. MPS does not use this parsing "trick", and instead supports projectional editing also on the expression level, with convenient editing gestures.

The Intentional Domain Workbench [Simonyi et al., 2006] is a contemporary projectional editor that has been used in real projects. While not too much has been published about it, it is well-known that it supports mixing graphical, tabular and textual notations.

Modular Compilers   Language extension does not just include modular concrete syntax. It also requires the extension or composition of static semantics and transformations.

Many systems (including SILVER [Wyk et al., 2008] mentioned above, JastAdd [Hedin & Magnusson, 2003] and LISA [Mernik et al., 2002]) describe static semantics using attribute grammars. These associate attributes with AST elements. An attribute can hold arbitrary data about the element (such as its type). Forwarding [Wyk et al., 2002] is a mechanism that improves the modularity of attribute grammars by delegating the look-up of an attribute value to another element. While MPS' type system can be seen as associating a type attribute with AST elements using the `typeof` function, it is different from attribute grammars. Attribute values are calculated by *explicitly* referring to the values of other attributes, often recursively. MPS' type system rules are declarative. Developers specify typing rules for language concepts and MPS "instantiates" each rule for each AST element. A solver then solves all type equations in that AST. In this way the typing rules of elements contributed by language extensions can *implicitly* affect the overall typing of the program.

For language extension the execution semantics is usually defined by a transformation to the base language. van Wyk shows that this is valid only if the changes to the AST are local, avoiding unintended interactions between independently developed extensions used in the same program [Wyk et al., 2008]. In MPS such local changes are performed with reduction rules. Based on the experience with mbeddr, it is also feasible to add additional elements to the AST *in selected places*. In MPS, this is achieved using weaving rules. However, in both local reduction and selective adding, there is no way to detect in advance whether using two extensions in the same program will conflict semantically or not.

As mentioned before, the Stratego [Bravenboer et al., 2008] term rewriting-based transformation engine separates the transformations themselves from the orchestration of sets of transformations. The latter is achieved with several predefined strategies that can be parameterized with the actual transformations. This way, the same transformations can be reused in different contexts. The facility can also be used to define the global order of independently developed transformations.

Extensible Tools and Language Workbenches   While projectional tools always requires an IDE for editing programs, textual languages can be used with any text editor. Modular languages have already been discussed above; modular IDEs and full-blown language workbenches are discussed here.

Early examples include the Synthesizer Generator [Reps & Teitelbaum, 1984] (mentioned above) and the Meta Environment [Klint, 1993], which provides an editor for languages defined via ASF+SDF. Rascal [Klint et al., 2009] and Spoofax [Kats & Visser, 2010] provide Eclipse-based IDE support for SDF-based languages. In both cases the IDE support for composed languages is still limited (for example, at the time of this writing, Spoofax only provides syntax highlighting for an embedded language, but no code completion), but improving rapidly. To implement semantics, Rascal uses a Java-like language that has been extended with features for program construction, transformation and analysis. Spoofax uses term rewriting based on Stratego [Bravenboer et al., 2008], which supports transformation composition based on higher-order strategies. An interesting tool is SugarJ [Erdweg et al., 2011] also based on SDF2, which supports library based language extension, which can be seen as a sophisticated macro system. Spoofax-based IDE support is available as well [Erdweg et al., 2011].

LISA [Mernik et al., 2002] (mentioned earlier) supports the definition of language syntax and semantics (via attribute grammars) in one integrated specification language. It then derives, among other things, a syntax-aware text editor for the language, as well as various graphical and structural viewing and editing facilities. Users can use inheritance and aspect-orientation to define extended languages. The use of this approach for incremental language development is detailed by Mernik & Zumer [2005]. However, users have to make sure manually that sub-grammars remain unambiguous with respect to the base grammar. The same is true for the combination of independently developed grammars.

Eclipse Xtext[5] generates sophisticated text editors from an EBNF-like language specification. Syntactic composition is limited, since Xtext is based on ANTLR [Parr & Quong, 1995], which is a two phase LL(k) parser. It is possible for a language to extend *one* other language. Concepts from the base language can be used in the sub-language. and it is possible to redefine grammar rules defined in the base language. Combination of independently defined extensions or embedding is not supported. Xtext's abstract syntax is based on EMF Ecore[6], so it can be used together with any EMF-based model transformation and code generation tool (such as Xtend, Xpand, ATL, and Acceleo, all part of Eclipse Modeling[7]). Static semantics is based on constraints written in Java or on third-party frameworks that support declarative description of type systems, such as XTS[8] or XSemantics[9]. Xtext comes with Xbase, an expression language that can be used as the basis for custom DSL [Efftinge et al., 2012]. Xbase also comes with a framework that simplifies the creation of interpreters and compilers for Xbase-based DSLs.

An interesting comparison can be made with the Renggli et al's Helvetia [Renggli et al., 2010]. This supports language embedding and extension of Smalltalk using *homogeneous* extension, which means that the host language (Smalltalk) is also used for *defining* the extensions. In contrast to macro systems, it can embed languages with full-blown grammars. The authors argue that the approach is independent of the host language and could be used with other host languages as well. While this is true in principle, the implementation strategy relies heavily on the unique aspects of the Smalltalk system, which are not available for other languages, and in particular, not for C. Also, since extensions are defined in the host language, the complete implementation would have to be redone if the approach were used with another language. This is particularly true for IDE support, where the Smalltalk IDE is extended using this IDE's APIs. mbeddr uses a *heterogeneous* approach which does not have these limitations: MPS provides a language-agnostic framework for language and IDE extension that can be used with any language, once the language is implemented in MPS.

---

[5] http://eclipse.org/Xtext

[6] http://eclipse.org/emf

[7] http://eclipse.org/modeling

[8] http://code.google.com/a/eclipselabs.org/p/xtext-typesystem

[9] http://xsemantics.sourceforge.net

Cedalion [David H. Lorenz, Boaz Rosenan, 2011] is a host language for defining internal DSLs, based on a projectional editor and logic programming semantics. Both Cedalion and language workbenches such as MPS aim to combine the best of both worlds from internal DSLs (combination and extension of languages, integration with a host language) and external DSLs (static validation, IDE support, flexible syntax). Cedalion starts out from internal DSLs and adds static validation and projectional editing, the latter avoiding ambiguities resulting from combined syntaxes. Language workbenches start from external DSLs and add modularization, and, as a consequence of implementing GPLs with the same tool, optional tight integration with GPL host languages. Cedalion could not be used for mbeddr though, since mbeddr requires its own base language (C), and the logic-based semantics would not have been a good fit.

An older line of work is focused on meta-CASE tools that aim at rapid development of CASE tools in order to support customized development methodologies [Ferguson et al., 2000]. They support specifying a metamodel and a typically *visual* notation; editors are then synthesized. Tools that implement this approach range from academic tools such as Pounamu [Grundy & Hosking, 2007] to industry quality tools based on Eclipse [Grünbacher et al., 2009]. MetaEdit+ [Tolvanen & Kelly, 2009] is one of the most well-known tools used in this space. It was and is used in several industry projects. The focus of mbeddr is different: it focuses on mixed-notation languages and on the incremental extension of languages, general-purpose and domain-specific. This goes far beyond the creation of (often relatively high-level) graphical modeling languages.

Domain-Specific Tools based on Language Workbenches   mbeddr is an example of instantiating a language workbench to build a domain-specific tool. While we believe that mbeddr is one of the largest and most sophisticated examples of this class of tools, it is not the only one. For example, WebDSL [Visser, 2007] is a set of DSLs for building (form-based) web applications based on Spoofax. mobl [Hemel & Visser, 2011] is a similar approach for mobile web applications. WebDSL in particular has proven to be useful for realistically sized applications, as exemplified by the `researchr.org` website. In contrast to mbeddr, both WebDSL and Spoofax are not incremental extensions of a general-purpose language, and are based on a parser-based language workbench. The only other example that uses a projectional workbench is Intentional's Pension Workbench, discussed in a presentation on InfoQ titled *Domain Expert DSLs*[10].

Summary — *This chapter demonstrated a number of techniques for language modularization and composition. As the discussion of related work shows, MPS has a number of advantages compared to existing tools. These have been exploited in the implementation of mbeddr, as Chapters 8 and 9 illustrate.*

---

[10] http://www.infoq.com/presentations/DSL-Magnus-Christerson-Henk-Kolk

186

Implementing mbeddr Languages

Abstract — *mbeddr's features, as demonstrated in Chapter 4, require many different kinds of extensions to C, fully exploiting MPS' capabilities for language modularization and composition. This chapter illustrates how some interesting aspects of the mbeddr languages are implemented, including extensions of top level constructs, statements, expressions as well as types and literals. The chapter also discusses how to plug in alternative transformations, annotate programs with meta data and restrict the language. Integration of new languages, new prose words and new requirements details is also discussed. The example extensions are selected to illustrate the various aspects of language definition supported by MPS, including structure, editor, type system and transformations.*

8.1 INTRODUCTION

C can be partitioned into expressions, statements, functions, etc. These are factored into separate language modules to make each of them reusable without pulling in all of C. The `expressions` language is the most fundamental language. It depends on no other language and defines the primitive types, the corresponding literals and the basic operators. Support for pointers and user-defined data types (`enum`, `struct`, `union`) is factored into the `pointers` and `udt` languages respectively. `statements` contains the procedural part of C, and the `modules` language covers modularization. Figure 8.1 shows an overview of some of the languages and constructs. This implementation of C must be extensible in the following ways to ensure that meaningful systems can be built (see also table Table 8.1):

Top Level Constructs   Top level constructs (on the level of functions or `struct` declarations) are necessary. This enables the integration of test cases or new programming paradigms relevant in particular domains such as state machines, or interfaces and components.

Statements   New statements, such as `assert` or `fail` statements in test cases, must be supported. If statements introduce new blocks, then variable visibility and shadowing must be handled correctly, just as in regular C. Statements may have to be restricted to a specific context; for example the `assert` or `fail` statements must *only* be used in test cases and not in any other statement list.

Expressions   New kinds of expressions must be supported. An example is the decision table expression that represents a two-level decision tree as a

187

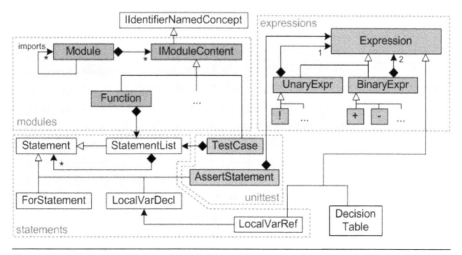

Figure 8.1 Anatomy of the mbeddr language stack: the diagram shows some of the language concepts, their relationships and the languages that contain them.

two dimensional table (Figure 4.4). Another example is references to event arguments in state machines.

Types and Literals   New types, for example, for matrices, complex numbers or quantities with physical units, must be supported. This also requires defining new operators and overriding the typing rules for existing ones. New literals may also be required: for example, physical units could be attached to number literals (as in `10kg`), or vectors may use the familiar vertical arrangement of their elements.

Transformation   Alternative transformations for existing language concepts must be possible. For example, in a module marked as `safe`, the expression `x + y` may be translated to `addWithBoundsCheck(x, y)`, a call to an `inline` function that performs bounds-checking in addition to adding `x` and `y`.

Metadata Decoration   It should be possible to add metadata such as trace links to requirements or product line variability constraints to arbitrary program nodes, without changing the concept of the node.

Restriction   It should be possible to define contexts that restrict the use of certain language concepts. Like any other extension, such contexts must be definable *after* the original language has been implemented, without invasive change. For example, the use of pointer arithmetic should be prohibited in modules marked as `safe`, or the use of real numbers should be prohibited in state machines that are intended to be model checked (model checkers do not support real numbers).

New Languages   It must be possible to add new languages. These may be completely independent of C or reuse some parts of C (for example, expres-

	Structure	Editor	Behavior	Scoping	Type System	Constraints	Transform
Top level Contents	Tests Mocks					Tests	Tests
Statements	Safeheap		Safeheap	Safeheap	Safeheap		SM Triggers
Expressions	Dec. Tables Postconds.	Dec. Tables			Dec. tables Postconds.		
Types and Literals		Matrices		Units	Units Matrices		
Alternative transform							Ranges
Metadata	Traces	Traces			Arch. constr.		Variants
Restriction						Tests Arch. constr.	
Separate language	OS Config	OS Config		OS Config	OS Config	OS Config	OS Config
Extending requirements	Req. Data		Req. Data	Req. Data			
New words in prose	Words			Words		Words	Words

Table 8.1 This table provides an overview of the remainder of this chapter. It relates the means of extension (row headers), the discussed language aspect (column headers) and the examples (content cells). The examples are covered in the following sections: Test cases and assert statements 8.2, State machine triggers 8.4, transformation of mock components 8.5, `safeheap` statement 8.6, decision tables 8.7, post-conditions 8.8, physical units 8.9, vectors and matrices 8.10, range checking 8.11, requirements traces 8.12, product line variability 8.13, architecture constraints 8.14, OS configuration 8.15, additional requirements data 8.16, and new words in prose blocks 8.17.

sions). They may also define new entities that can be referenced from C. An example would be a configuration for an operating system that declares tasks, memory regions or interrupts.

New Requirements Details mbeddr supports languages that are not directly related to C, such as the requirements language. Such languages may also have to be extended, for example, with ways to add business rules directly to requirements.

Documentation Words Finally, mbeddr makes use of blocks of prose text in various contexts, such as comments, requirements descriptions or documents. It must be possible to add new kinds of words (i.e., nodes rendered in prose blocks). An example would be words that reference function arguments that can be used in function documentation comments.

This section illustrates the implementation of test cases. Test cases were introduced in Section 4.2. The test cases themselves are a top-level construct, and the `assert` and `fail` statements available inside test cases are statement-level extensions.

Structure `Module`s own a collection of `IModuleContent`s, an interface that acts as the supertype of everything that can reside directly in a module. All top-level constructs, such as C's `Function`s, `struct`s or `typedef`s, implement `IModuleContent`. `IModuleContent` extends MPS' `IIdentifierNamedConcept` interface, which provides a `name` property. `IModuleContent` also defines a Boolean property `exported` that determines whether the respective module content is visible to modules which import this module. This property is queried by the scoping rules that determine which elements can be referenced from within any given module. Since the `IModuleContent` interface can also be implemented by concepts in other languages, new top-level constructs such as the `TestCase` in the `unittest` language can implement this interface, as long as the respective language has a dependency on the `modules` language, which defines `IModuleContent`. Figure 8.1 shows some of the relevant concepts and languages.

Constraints A test case contains a `StatementList`, so any C statement can be used in a test case. `StatementList` becomes available to the `unittest` language through its dependency on the `statements` language. `unittest` also defines additional statements: `assert` and `fail`. They extend the abstract `Statement` concept defined in the `statements` language. This makes them valid in *any* statement list, for example in a function body. This is undesirable, since the transformation of `assert`s into C depends on them being used in a `TestCase`. To enforce this, a `can be child` constraint is defined (see below). This constraint restricts an `AssertStatement` to be used only inside a `TestCase` by checking that at least one of its ancestors is a `TestCase`.

```
concept constraints AssertStatement {
  can be child
    (context, scope, parentNode, link, childConcept)->boolean {
      parentNode.ancestor<TestCase>.isNotNull;
    }
}
```

Transformation The new language concepts in `unittest` are reduced to C concepts: the `TestCase` is transformed to a `void` function without arguments and the `assert` statement is transformed into a `report` statement defined in the logging language. The `report` statement, in turn, is transformed into a platform-specific way of reporting an error (console, serial line or error memory). Figure 8.2 shows an example of this two-step process.

8.3 EMBEDDING STATE MACHINES IN COMPONENTS

Ideally, independently developed extensions should be usable together in the same program *without* explicitly designing them for any particular combination (this is extension composition as explained in Section 7.4.7). For example, any concept that implements the `IModuleContent` interface can be used alongside any other `IModuleContent` in a single program as long as their transformations do not interfere with each other.

However, sometimes it is not so simple. For example, while state machines have been designed to be used as top-level concepts in modules (they implement `IModuleContent`), they should also be usable in components. Those, however, expect their contents to implement `IComponentContent`. The mismatch can be resolved by using the Adapter pattern [Gamma et al., 1995]: a new concept `SmCompAdapter` is defined which implements `IComponentContent` and contains a `State Machine`. The editors can be built in a way that users do not notice this adapter element when entering or reading the code. The adapter concept lives in a separate language, so neither the `components` nor the `statemachines` languages have a dependency on each other.

8.4 TRANSFORMING STATE MACHINE TRIGGERS

State machines are top-level extensions (for an example, see Section 4.6) and have to be transformed into an `enum` for the states, an `enum` for the events, a `struct` that holds the state machine's data (variables, current state), and a function that implements the behavior. The function takes two arguments: a `struct` that represents a state machine instance as well as the event the instance is supposed to consume[1].

The `trigger` statement is a statement-level extension which fires an event into a state machine instance (for example, `trigger(aStatemachineInstance,`

---

[1] The actual implementation is a little more complicated, since events can also have arguments. This is ignored here for reasons of brevity.

```
test case exTest {        void test_exTest {        void test_exTest {
  int x = add(2, 2);        int x = add(2, 2);         int x = add(2, 2);
  assert(0) x == 4;         report                     if (!(x == 4)) {
}                             test.FAIL(0)                 printf("fail:0");
                              on !(x == 4);            }
                          }                          }
```

Figure 8.2 Two-stage transformation of `TestCase`s. The `TestCase` is transformed into a C function using the logging framework to output error messages. The `report` statement is in turn transformed into a `printf` statement if code is generated for the Windows/Mac environment. It would be transformed into something else if code were generated for the actual target device, a choice configured by the user in the build configuration.

anEvent)). It must be transformed to a call to the function that implements the state machine behavior, supplying the `struct` instance that corresponds to the instance of the triggered state machine, plus the `enum` literal that represents the event. Figure 8.3 shows the respective transformation rule. It has three parts: the part above the `->` specifies that the transformation rule applies to instances of `TriggerSMStatement`. The part enclosed in `<TF ..   TF>` is called the *template fragment*. Its content replaces the `TriggerSMStatement` during execution of the transformation. The rest of the code is used for scaffolding. Scaffolding is necessary for the following reason: as mentioned earlier, the code inside the template must be valid C code, *even in the template* (this is why MPS can provide IDE support for the code in the template). So to be able to generate a reference, the template must contain a node that can be referenced by the reference, even if it is not intended to generate the referenced node, because it already exists in the output AST. So, for example, to be able to write a function call in the template, there first has to be a function (`smExecuteFunction`), to be able to reference an `enum` literal, there has to be an `enum`, and so on. During the execution of the transformation, references are "rewired" using the `->$` macro. Its embedded expression returns the target for the reference, typically an element that already exists (or has been created by the transformation) in the output AST.

In the case discussed here, a call to a function with two arguments must be generated, so the scaffolding has to contain a function with two arguments as well – and they must have the correct type, to avoid getting type errors *in the template*. Please see the caption of Figure 8.3 for further details.

The transformation rule above is an example of a *reduction* rule. Reduction rules *replace* the input node with the code generated by the template associ-

```
concept     TriggerSMStatement
inheritors false
condition   <always>
--> module dummy {
        enum eventEnum { e1; e2; }
        struct instanceData { };
        var instanceData theStatemachine;
        void smExecFunc(instanceData* instance, eventEnum event){ }
        void someMethod() {
            <TF  { ->$ smExecFunc (&$COPY_SRC$ theStatemachine , ->$ e1 );} TF>
        } }
```

Figure 8.3 Transformation macros are used to replace dummy nodes (such as the reference e1) with the code created by the transformation based on the input node. Reference macros (`->$`) are used to wire up references, and `$COPY_SRC$` macros are used to replace entire nodes. Behind each macro is an expression that computes the node that should be used to replace the dummy node. For example, behind the `$COPY_SRC$[theStatemachine]` is an expression that returns the variable that holds the instance data for the current state machine instance. More details about transformations are discussed in the running text.

ated with the rule. MPS also supports various other kinds of rules, including conditional root rules, which create a new node without a specific input element, and weaving rules, which create a new node at a specified location different from the input node's location in the output tree.

8.5 TRANSFORMING A MOCK COMPONENT

Mock components (discussed in Section 4.4) are a special kind of component that declaratively express the behavior they expect to see on their provided ports in the context of a test case. They are a top-level extension, but they are transformed to regular components, *not* to plain C. Here is an example:

```
mock component PasswordMock {
  total number of calls is 3
  sequence {
    step 0: energyDataAccess.hasMeterStatus return false;
      assert 0: parameter expectedStatus:
                  expectedStatus == PASSWORD_OK
    step 1: energyDataAccess.hasMeterStatus return false;
    step 2: setPasswordHandler.processCommand return true;
```

These expectations are transformed into implementations of the component operations that track invocations and check whether the expectations are met. For this to work, the mock-to-component transformation has to run *before* the component-to-C transformation. To achieve this, the mock-to-components generator specifies a `strictly before` constraint relative to the components-to-C generator. Based on the specified relative priorities, MPS computes an overall order comprising four separate phases. The following code shows the overall mapping configuration for a program that uses mocks, components, unit tests, and, of course, C:

```
[1]  core.removeCommentedCode
[2]  ext.components.mock
[3]  ext.components.main, core.unittest
[4]  core.ctext
```

Phase 1 removes commented code, since it should not end up in the resulting C text file. Phase 2 runs the mock component transformation. As expected, it runs *before* the components-to-C transformation, which runs in phase 3, together with the unit-test-to-C transformation. Phase 4 finally generates the resulting C text.

8.6 SAFEHEAP STATEMENT

The basics of integrating new statements have been discussed in the previous sections, for example, when `assert` and `fail` extended the `Statement` concept inherited from the C core languages. This section focuses on statements that require handling local variable scopes and visibilities. To do so, the implementation of the `safeheap` statement is illustrated, which automatically frees dynamically allocated memory (an example is shown in Figure 8.4). The variables introduced by the `safeheap` statement must only be visible inside its body, and they must shadow variables of the same name declared in outer scopes (such as the `a` declared in the second line of the `measure` function in Figure 8.4).

```
int8_t measure() {
  int8_t result = 0;
  int8_t* a = malloc(sizeof int8_t);
  safeheap(int8_t* a = malloc(10 * sizeof int8_t)) {
    for (int8_t i = 0; i < 10; i++) { (a[i]) = readSensor(); }
    // th Error: cannot pass a safe heap var to a function ss a heap var to function
    result = calcAverage(a);
  }
  // accessing a here would the one declare outside the safeheap
  return result;
}
```

Figure 8.4 A `safeheap` statement declares heap variables which can only be used inside its body. When control flow leaves the body, the memory is automatically freed. Notice also how an error is reported if the variable tries to escape.

Structure   Like any statement in C, the `safeheap` statement extends the abstract concept `Statement`. It contains a `StatementList` as its `body`, as well as a list of `SafeHeapVars`. These extend `LocalVarDecl`, a pre-condition for integrating with the existing mechanism for handling local variable shadowing (explained below).

Behavior   `LocalVarRefs` are expressions that reference a `LocalVarDecl`. A scope constraint determines the set of visible variables for a given `LocalVarRef`. This constraint is implemented by plugging into mbeddr's generic local variable scoping mechanism using the following approach. The constraint ascends the containment tree until it finds a node which implements the concept interface `ILocalVarScopeProvider` and calls its `getLocalVarScope` method. A `LocalVarScope` has a reference to an outer scope, which is set by finding *its* `ILocalVarScopeProvider` ancestor, effectively building a hierarchy of `LocalVarScopes`. To get at the list of the visible variables, the `LocalVarRef` scope constraint calls the `getVisibleLocalVars` method on the innermost `LocalVarScope` object. This method returns a flat list of `LocalVarDecls`, taking into account that variables owned by a `LocalVarScope` that is *lower* in the hierarchy shadow variables of the same name from a *higher* level in the hierarchy. So, to plug the `SafeHeapStatement` into this mechanism, it has to implement `ILocalVarScopeProvider` and implement the following two methods:

```
public LocalVarScope getLocalVarScope(node<> ctx, int stmtIdx) {
  LocalVarScope scope = new LocalVarScope(
      getContainedLocalVars());
  node<ILocalVarScopeProvider> outerScopeProvider =
```

```
        this.ancestor<ILocalVarScopeProvider>;
    if (outerScopeProvider != null)
      scope.setOuterScope(outerScopeProvider.
                          getLocalVarScope(this, this.index));
    return scope;
  }

  public sequence<node<LocalVariableDecl>> getContainedLocalVars() {
    this.vars; // the list of SafeHeapVars
  }
```

getContainedLocalVars returns the LocalVarDecls that are declared between
the parentheses of a safeheap statement (see the example in Figure 8.4).
getLocalVarScope constructs a scope that contains these variables and then
builds the hierarchy of outer scopes by relying on its ancestors that also implement ILocalVarScopeProvider. The index of the statement that contains
the reference is passed in to make sure that only variables declared *before* the
reference site are visible.

Type System   To make the safeheap statement work correctly, the variables declared and allocated in the safeheap statement must not escape from
the safeheap's body. To prevent this, an error is reported if a reference to
a safeheap variable is passed to a function (see the code below). This type
system rule reports an error if a reference to a local variable declared and
allocated by the safeheap statement is used in a function call.

```
checking rule check_safeVarRef for LocalVarRef as lvr {
    boolean isInSafeHeap =
      lvr.ancestor<SafeHeapStatement>.isNotNull;
    boolean isInFunctionCall =
      lvr.ancestor<FunctionCall>.isNotNull;
    boolean referencesSafeHeapVar =
      lvr.var.parent.isInstanceOf(SafeHeapStatement);
    if (isInSafeHeap && isInFunctionCall && referencesSafeHeapVar)
        error "cannot pass a safe heap var to a function" -> lvr;
}
```

8.7   DECISION TABLE EXPRESSIONS

Expressions are different from statements in that they evaluate to a value as
the program executes. During editing and compilation, the *type* of an expression is relevant for the static correctness of the program. So extending a
language in terms of expressions requires extending the type system as well.

Figure 4.4 shows an example decision table expression. It is evaluated to
the expression in a cell c if the column header of c and the row header of c
are true. If none of the condition pairs is true, then the default value, FAIL in
the example, is used as the resulting value. The type of the overall decision
table is the least common supertype of all value expressions. The type of the
header cells has to be Boolean.

Structure   The decision table extends the `Expression` concept defined in the `expressions` language. Decision tables contain a list of expressions for the column headers, one for the row headers and another for the result values. It also contains a child of type `Expression` to hold the default value. The concept defines an alias `dectab` to allow users to instantiate a decision table in the editor. Obviously, for non-textual notations such as the table, the alias will be different than the concrete syntax (in textual notations, the alias is typically made to be the same as the "leading keyword", for example, `assert`).

Editor   Defining a tabular editor is straightforward: the editor definition contains a `table` cell, which delegates to a Java class that implements `ITable-Model`. This is similar to Java Swing. It provides methods such as `getValueAt` `(int row, int col)` or `deleteRow(int row)`, which have to be implemented for any specific table-based editor. To embed another node in a table cell, such as the expression in the decision table, the implementation of `getValueAt` simply returns this node, which supplies its own editor.

Type System   As mentioned above, MPS uses unification in the type system. Language concepts specify type equations that contain type literals (such as `boolean`) as well as type variables (such as `typeof(dectab)`). The unification engine then tries to assign values to the type variables so that all applicable type equations become `true`. New language concepts contribute additional type equations. The code below shows those for decision tables; `dectab` represents a decision table.

```
// calculate the common supertype of all element
// types, reports an error if there is none
var commonElementType;
foreach e in dectab.resultValues {
   infer typeof(e) :<=: commonElementType;
}

// commonElementType must also be
// a supertype of the default value
infer typeof(dectab.defaultValue) :<=: commonElementType;

// the type of the whole decision table expression
// is the common supertype calculated above
typeof(dectab) :==: commonElementType;

// for each of the expressions inside
// the column headers, the type must be Boolean
foreach expr in dectab.colHeaders {
  typeof(expr) :==: <boolean>;
}

// ... same for the row headers
foreach expr in dectab.rowHeaders {
  typeof(expr) :==: <boolean>;
}
```

The interesting part is the first part, where the `commonElementType` is computed. First, a new, unbound type system variable is declared using the `var` keyword. The code then iterates over all elements in the `resultValues` and defines the following equation for each of them:

```
infer typeof(e) :<=: commonElementType;
```

This expresses the fact that the type of the element `e` must be the same as or a subtype of (`:<=:`) the `commonElementType` variable. Note how, through the iteration, *one such equation for each element* is created. The only way in which the type system engine can make *all* of these equations true is to make `commonElementType` represent the common supertype of all of the element types.

New equations are solved along with those for existing concepts. For example, the typing rules for a `ReturnStatement` ensure that the type of the returned expression is the same as or a subtype of the type of the surrounding function. If a `ReturnStatement` uses a decision table as the returned expression, the type calculated for the decision (`typeof(dectab) :==: commonElementType;`) table must be compatible with the return type of the surrounding function.

8.8 POST-CONDITIONS FOR INTERFACE OPERATIONS

Section 4.4 has shown how interface operations can declare pre- and post-conditions. These are Boolean expressions that specify parts of the semantics of the operation: pre-conditions have to be true before the operation is invoked, and if they are true, the post-conditions are guaranteed to be true after the execution of the operation finishes. This section explains how to add an expression that acts as a placeholder for the result value in an operation's post-condition.

Structure   An `Operation` has a list of `PrePostConditions`, an abstract concept that acts as the supertype of `Precondition` and `Postcondition`. It contains a child called `expr` of type `Expression`. In post-conditions, the user must have access to the result of the context operation to express things like *the result value is greater than zero*. To make this possible, a new subconcept of `Expression` is created, the `ResultExpression`:

```
concept ResultExpression extends Expression
```

By making `ResultExpression` a subtype of `Expression`, it can be used anywhere an `Expression` is expected. However, this is *not* what is required in this case; the `ResultExpression` has to be restricted to inside of `PostConditions`. And it should only be allowed if the return type of the owning `Operation` is not `void`, since there is no meaningful result for `void` operations. Both restrictions are implemented by a `can be child` constraint:

```
can be child constraint for ResultExpression {
  (operationContext, scope, parent, link, childConcept)->boolean {
    boolean isUnderPost = parent.ancestor<PostCondition>.isNotNull;
```

```
    boolean isVoid = parent.ancestor<Operation>.returnType.
                    isInstanceOf(VoidType));
    return isUnderPost && !isVoid;
  }
}
```

Type System   The type of the `ResultExpression` must be the return type of
the ancestor `Operation`:

```
rule typeof_ResultExpression for ResultExpression as resultExpr {
    node<Operation> op = resultExpr.ancestor<concept = Operation>;
    typeof(resultExpr) :==: typeof(op.returnType);
}
```

8.9   PHYSICAL UNITS

Physical units are used to illustrate the extension of C with new types and
literals. An example was shown in Figure 4.1.

Structure   Derived and convertible `UnitDeclaration`s are `IModuleContents`.
Derived unit declarations specify a name (`mps` or `kmh`) and the corresponding
SI base units (`m`, `s`) plus an exponent; a convertible unit declaration specifies a name and a conversion formula. The backbone of the extension is the
`UnitType`, which is a composite type that has another type (`int`, `float`) in
its `valueType` slot, plus a unit. The unit is either an SI base unit or a reference to a `UnitDeclaration`. It is represented in programs as `baseType/unit/`.
mbeddr also provides `LiteralWithUnits`, which are expressions that contain
a `valueLiteral` and, like the `UnitType`, a unit (so one can write `100 kmh`).

Scoping   `LiteralWithUnit`s and `UnitType`s reference a `UnitDeclaration`,
which are `IModuleContents`. According to the visibility rules, valid targets for
the reference are the `UnitDeclaration`s in the same module, and the *exported*
ones in all imported modules. This rule applies to *any* reference to *any* module
contents, and is implemented generically in mbeddr. Here is the code for the
scope of the reference to the `UnitDeclaration`:

```
link {unit}
  search scope:
    (model, refNode, enclosingNode, operationContext)
                        ->sequence<node<UnitDeclaration>> {
      enclosingNode.ancestor<IVisibleNodeProvider>.
              visibleContentsOfType(concept/UnitDeclaration/);
    }
```

An interface `IVisibleNodeProvider` (implemented by `Module`s) is used to find
all instances of a given type. The implementation of `visibleContentsOfType`
simply searches through the contents of the current and imported modules
and collects instances of the specified concept. The result is used as the scope
for the reference.

Type System   The use of equations and unification in type system rules has been illustrated earlier. However, there is special support for binary operators that makes overloading for new types easy: overloaded operations containers essentially specify 3-tuples of *(leftArgType, rightArgType, resultType)*, plus applicability conditions to match type patterns and decide on the resulting type. Typing rules for new (combinations of) types can be added by specifying additional 3-tuples. The following piece of code shows the overloaded rules for C's `MultiExpression` when applied to two `UnitType`s:

```
operation concepts: MultiExpression
  left operand type: new node<UnitType>()
  right operand type: new node<UnitType>()
is applicable:
  (op, leftOpType, rightOpType)->boolean {
    node<> resultingValueType = operation type(op,
                leftOpType.valueType , rightOpType.valueType );
    resultingValueType != null;
  }
operation type:
  (op, leftOpType, rightOpType)->node<> {
    node<> resultingValueType = operation type(op,
            leftOpType.valueType, rightOpType.valueType );
    UnitType.create(resultingValueType,
                    leftOpType.unit.toSIBase().add(
                        rightOpType.unit.toSIBase(),
                        1
                    )
                );
  }
```

This code overloads the `MultiExpression` for the case in which both the left and right argument are `UnitType`s. The `is applicable` section checks whether there is a typing rule for the two value types (for example, `int * float`) by trying to compute the resulting value type. If none is found, the types cannot be multiplied. In the computation of the `operation type` a new `UnitType` is created that uses the `resultingValueType` as the value type, then computes the resulting unit by adding up the exponents of component SI units of the two operand types.

While any two units can legally be used with * and / (as long as the resulting unit exponents are computed correctly), this is not true for + and -. There, the two operand types must be the same in terms of their representation in SI base units. This is expressed by using the following expression in the `is applicable` section:

```
leftOpType.unit.isSameAs(rightOpType.unit)};
```

The typing rule for the `LocalVariableDeclaration` requires that the type of the `init` expression must be the same or a subtype of the `type` of the variable. To make this work correctly with units, a type hierarchy for `UnitType`s is required. This is done by defining the supertypes for each `UnitType`. These

```
void vectorDemo() {

    vector<int16, 3> aVector = [1]
                               [2] * 512;
                               [3]

    vector<int16, 3> resultOfCrossProduct = aVector x aVector;

    matrix<int16, 2x3> aMatrix = [1 + 2    2 * 7    42];
                                 [  3        51      24]

                                                       T
    matrix<int16, 3x2> transposedMatrix = aMatrix ;
}
```

Figure 8.5 This function shows the use of vectors and matrices. The extension supports new types (`vector<..>` and `matrix<..>`) and literals. The literals exploit the projectional editor by using the familiar two-dimensional notation. Existing operators are overloaded (e.g., for scalar multiplication ∗) and new operators are defined (e.g., cross product x and transposition T).

supertypes are those `UnitType`s whose unit is the same, and whose `valueType` is a supertype of the current `UnitType`'s value type:

```
subtyping rule supertypeOf_UnitType for UnitType as ut {
  nlist<> res = new nlist<>;
  foreach st in immediateSupertypes(ut.valueType) {
    res.add(UnitType.create(st, ut.unit.copy));
  }
  return res;
}
```

This typing rule computes the direct supertypes of a `UnitType`. It iterates over all immediate supertypes of the current `UnitType`'s value type, wrapped into a `UnitType` with the same unit as the type whose supertypes are calculated.

8.10 VECTORS AND MATRICES

Vectors and matrices are quite useful in many embedded or technical applications. As a consequence of their unique syntax, the projectional nature of the MPS editor is a nice fit. This section looks at the interesting aspects of supporting vectors and matrices, including the editor. Vectors and matrices are an example of a Types and Literals extension. Figure 8.5 shows some example code.

Structure   Vectors are structurally just matrices with one column. Consequently there is a `MatrixLiteral` but no vector literal: a `MatrixLiteral` owns a collection of `MatrixLiteralCol` concepts, which in turn contain `Expressions`.

In terms of types and their operators, matrices and vectors must be treated differently. The two are represented as `MatrixType` and `VectorType` which both implement the `IMatrixType` interface:

```
interface concept IMatrixType
  properties:
    dimensionsRows: integer
  children:
    IType baseType 1
```

This interface specifies the number rows as well as the base type. These are important because the number of rows as well as the base type are relevant for typing: a `vector<int8,3>` is not compatible with a `vector<int16,2>`. The `vector<..>` and `matrix<..>` types are defined as follows:

```
concept VectorType extends Type implements IMatrixType
  concept properties:
    alias = vector

concept MatrixType extends Type implements IMatrixType
  properties:
    dimensionsCols: integer
  concept properties:
    alias = matrix
```

Type System   If `MatrixType` and `VectorType` are used in programs, their type (in terms of the type system engine) is a clone of themselves; this is achieved by the default typing rule for all concepts that inherit from `Type`:

```
rule typeof_Type for Type as t {
    typeof(t) :==: t.copy;
}
```

Vectors are *covariant* regarding their base type: `vector<T,i>` is a subtype of `vector<Q,i>` if T is a subtype of Q. To make this work, a subtyping rule for `VectorType` is needed. Subtyping rules return the collection of super-types for any particular type. The following code implements covariance (`immediateSupertypes` is a built-in type system operator):

```
subtyping rule supertypesOfVectorType for VectorType as vt {
    nlist<IMatrixType> vectorSuperTypes = new nlist<IMatrixType>;
    foreach superType in immediateSupertypes(vt.baseType) {
        node<VectorType> st = new node<VectorType>();
        st.baseType = superType:Type;
        st.dimensionsRows = vt.dimensionsRows; // same num of rows!
        vectorSuperTypes.add(st);
    }
    return vectorSuperTypes;
}
```

A similar subtyping rule has to be defined for `MatrixTypes`. However, if the matrix type has only one column, a corresponding `VectorType` must be among the supertypes.

```
editor for concept MatrixLiteral
  node cell layout:
    [> $ custom cell $ ^(> % cols % /empty cell: <default> <) $ custom cell $ <]
```

Figure 8.6 The definition of the editor for the `MatrixLiteral`. Note how the `custom cells` are used to render the two brackets. Custom cells can draw arbitrary graphics onto the editor's canvas.

Next up is the typing of literals. Consider a matrix that uses values of type `uint8`, `int16` and `double`. The type of this matrix is a `MatrixType` where the base type must be the least common supertype of the element types (in this case a `double`). The following code computes the type for matrix literals:

```
rule typeof_MatrixLiteral for MatrixLiteral as ml {
    var commonElementType;
    foreach e in ml.cols.elements {
      infer typeof(e) :<=: commonElementType;
    }

    node<MatrixType> mt = new node<MatrixType>();
    mt.baseType = commonElementType;
    mt.dimensionsCols = ml.cols.size;
    mt.dimensionsRows = ml.cols.first.elements.size;
    typeof(ml) :==: mt;
}
```

The first part computes the least common supertype of all the element types of the vector; it uses the same approach as the decision table (Section 8.7). The second part then constructs the corresponding `MatrixType` and assigns it to the literal.

Editor   The editor definition for the `MatrixLiteral` is shown in Figure 8.6. It consists of two custom cells that draw the brackets (see below) and a horizontal collection ([> ..   <]) of the columns. A column has its own editor, also discussed below. To make sure the columns have some space between them, a trick is used: a white, vertical bar is used as the separator for the list of columns:

```
list element:
  separator                |
  separator constraint     noflow
  separator style          <no parentClass> {
                             text-foreground-color: white
                             padding-left: 1 spaces
                             padding-right: 1 spaces
                           }
```

The editor for the `MatrixLiteralCol` is simply a vertical list of all the expressions. Two style properties make sure that each expression is horizontally centered, and that the whole vertical list is centered with regard to the line in which the matrix lives:

202

```
horizontal-align: center
default-baseline: collection center
```

Let us now look at the two custom cells which handle the "big brackets" on the left and right side of the matrix. When using the `custom cell` cell type, an object that renders the cell has to be returned. The actual drawing of the cell happens in the `OpeningBracketCell` class. Here is the basic outline of a custom cell implementation:

```
public class OpeningBracketCell extends AbstractCellProvider {

  // constructor, etc.

  public EditorCell createEditorCell(EditorContext context) {
    new EditorCell_Basic(context, this.myNode) {
      public void paintContent(Graphics g, ParentSettings ps) {
        g.setColor(Color.BLACK);
        EditorCell_Collection parent = this.getParent();
        int x = getX();
        int y = parent.getY();
        int height = parent.getHeight();
        g.fillRect(x, y, 2, height);
        g.fillRect(x, y, 4, 2);
        g.fillRect(x, y + height - 2, 4, 2);
      }

      public void relayoutImpl() {
        this.myWidth = 4;
        this.myHeight = 10;
} } };}
```

This class is a subtype of `AbstractCellProvider` and implements the method `createEditorCell` to return a suitable cell. Its `paintContent` is responsible for actually drawing the visual representation.

There are a few things that can be done to improve the editing experience for the user; for example, the following intention lets the user select `Add New Column` from the intentions menu (`Alt-Enter`) to add a new column.

An intention definition consists of three parts. The `description` returns the string that is shown in the intentions popup menu. An optional `isApplicable` section determines under which conditions the intention is available in the menu – this is omitted in the code below, because there is no specific condition. Finally, the `execute` section performs the action associated with the intention:

```
intention addNewMatrixCol for concept MatrixLiteralCol {
  available in child nodes: true

  description(editorContext, node)->string {
    "Add New Column";
  }
```

```
execute(editorContext, node)->void {
    node<MatrixLiteralCol> cc = node.ancestor<MatrixLiteralCol, +>;
    node<MatrixLiteralCol> nc = new node<MatrixLiteralCol>();
    cc.elements.forEach({~it => nc.elements.add new(); });
    cc.add next-sibling(nc);
    editorContext.select(nc.elements.first);
  }
}
```

The intention is available not just on a `MatrixLiteralCol`, but also on all of its children in the tree. This means that when it is invoked, the `node` variable may not actually be a `MatrixLiteralCol`, but one of its child expressions. The first line in the `execute` body compensates for that by retrieving the current ancestor `MatrixLiteralCol`. Next, a new `MatrixLiteralCol` is created, a new (empty) expression is added to it for each expression in the current column, and then the new column `nc` is added as a next sibling to the current one. Finally, the focus is set into the first element of the new column.

Type System   The existing operators must get new type system rules to be able to deal with vectors and matrices. Below is the code that handles the case in which a matrix is multiplied with a scalar value. Similar to the physical units (Section 8.9), an overloaded operations container is used that applies to the case where a `MultiExpression` has a `MatrixType` as the left argument and a numeric type as the right argument. The resulting type is calculated as follows:

```
(op, leftOperandType, rightOperandType)->node<> {
  // determine the least common supertype between the
  // basetype of the  matrix and the primitive on the other
  // side of the binary operator
  set<node<>> nodes = new hashset<node<>>;
  nodes.add(leftOperandType:IMatrixType.baseType);
  nodes.add(rightOperandType);
  set<node<>> leastCommonSupertypes =
      typechecker.getSubtypingManager().
      leastCommonSupertypes(nodes, false);

  // create a matrix type or a vector type
  // depending on what's on the left side
  node<IMatrixType> resultType =
      leftOperandType:IMatrixType.
      cloneForBaseType(leastCommonSupertypes.first:IType);
  return resultType;
}
```

The `typechecker` is used to determine the least common supertype between the base type of the matrix and the primitive on the other side of the binary operator, since this will become the base type of the result type. A `MatrixType` or a `VectorType` is created depending on whether the original non-primitive type was a matrix or a vector; this is handled correctly by the polymorphically

```
editor for concept MatrixTransposeExpr
  node cell layout:
    [> % expression % T <]
```

Figure 8.7 The editor for the `MatrixTransposeExpr` is essentially a horizontal list with the `expression` and the T next to each other. To get the superscript, the `cell layout` property of the collection cell has to be set to `superscript` and the `script-kind:superscript` style property to has to be added to the T.

overloaded `cloneForBaseType` method defined for `IMatrixType`. Similar rules have to be written for the other cases (i.e. matrix/vector and matrix/vector or primitive and matrix/vector). Also, the code has to be generalized for other operators, not just multiplication.

Structure   Additional operators, the cross product x and transposition T, are required as well. The `CrossProductExpression` extends the abstract concept `BinaryArithmeticExpression`, so it directly integrates with the existing facilities regarding editor support and typing. Here is the definition:

```
concept CrossProductExpression extends BinaryArithmeticExpression
  concept properties:
    alias = x
    priolevel = 2000
    shortDescription = cross-product
```

The `prioLevel` determines the operator precedence (the higher the number, the higher the precedence). The value 2000 is the same as the regular multiplication. `shortDescription` is what is shown in the code completion menu behind the actual x symbol. The `MatrixTransposeExpr` is a unary expression; it has an alias of T, a `prioLevel` of 4000 and a `shortDescription` of `transpose`.

Editor   The editor for the cross product is trivial and inherited from the `BinaryArithmeticExpression`: the editor simply projects the two arguments with the alias between them. For the `MatrixTransposeExpr`, the editor is shown in Figure 8.7. To be able to enter the T on the right side of an expression, a right transformation has to be written. Here is the code:

```
right transform actions makeTransposeExpr for Expression
  condition: (operationContext, scope, model, sourceNode)->boolean {
    sourceNode.type.isInstanceOf(MatrixType);
  }
  actions: add custom items (output concept: MatrixTransposeExpr)
    matching text: T
    transform: (operationContext, sourceNode, pattern)->node<> {
      node<MatrixTransposeExpr> n = ew node<MatrixTransposeExpr>();
      sourceNode.replace with(n);
      n.expression = sourceNode;
      PrioUtil.shuffleUnaryExpression(n);
      n;
    }
```

```
┌                                                                          ┐
│ concept    PlusExpression                                                │
│ condition  (node, genContext, operationContext)->boolean {               │
│               node.ancestor< ImplementationModule>.@safeAnnotation != null;│
│            }                                                             │
└                                                                          ┘
  -->
module dummy imports arithmeticOps {
  void dummy() {
     <TF addWithRangeCheck($COPY_SRC$ 1 , $COPY_SRC$ 2 )  TF>;
} }
```

Figure 8.8 This *reduction rule* transforms instances of `PlusExpression` into a call to a library function `addWithRangeChecks`, passing in the left and right argument of the + using the two `COPY_SRC` macros. The `condition` ensures that the transformation is only executed if the containing `Module` has a `safeAnnotation` attached to it. A transformation priority defined in the properties of the transformation makes sure it runs before the C-to-text transformation.

This transformation handles the case in which a `T` is entered on the right side of an `Expression` whose type is `MatrixType`. What is interesting is the call to `PrioUtil.shuffleUnaryExpression(n)`: this reshuffles the tree to take care of precedence as expressed in the `prioLevel` property. It has to be called as part of any left or right transformation that involves expressions.

8.11 RANGE CHECKING

The `safemodules` language defines an annotation to mark modules as `safe` (annotations are discussed in the next subsection). If a module is so annotated, the binary operators such as + or * are replaced with calls to functions that, in addition to performing the addition or multiplication, perform a range check. This is an example of an alternative transformation.

Transformation   The transformation that replaces the binary operators with function calls is triggered by the presence of this annotation on the `Module` which contains the operator. Figure 8.8 shows the code; the `@safeAnnotation != null` checks for the presence of the annotation. As mentioned in Section 8.5, MPS uses priorities to specify relative orderings of transformations. Such a priority is used to express that this transformation runs *before* the final transformation that maps the C tree to C text for compilation (this is done in a property dialog and not shown).

8.12 REQUIREMENTS TRACES

As introduced in Section 7.4.5, annotations are concepts whose instances can be added as children to a node N without this being specified in the definition of N's concept. While structurally the annotations are children of the annotated node, the editor is defined the other way round: the annotation editor

```
editor for concept TraceAnnotation
  node cell layout:
    [> [> attributed node <] ?[> % tracekind % F(> % refs % <) <] <]
```

Figure 8.9 The editor definition for the `ReqTrace` annotation (an example trace annotation is shown in Figure 4.13). It consists of a vertical list `[/ ..  /]` with two lines. The first line contains the reference to the requirement. The second line uses the `attributed node` construct to embed the editor of the program node to which this annotation is attached. So the annotation is always rendered right on top of whatever syntax the original node uses.

delegates to the editor of the annotated element. This allows the annotation editor to add additional syntax *around* the annotated element. Optionally, it is possible to explicitly restrict the concepts to which a particular annotation can be attached. Annotations are used in several places: the `safe` annotation discussed in the previous section, the requirements traces discussed in this section, as well as the product line variability presence conditions discussed in the next section. MPS itself uses annotations as macros in templates.

Structure   The code below shows the structure of the `TraceAnnotation`. Annotations extend the MPS-predefined concept `NodeAnnotation`. They can have an arbitrary child structure (`tracekind, refs`), but they have to specify the `role` (the name of the property that holds the annotated child under its parent) as well as the `annotated` concept (the annotations can only be attached to instances of this concept or subconcepts):

```
concept TraceAnnotation extends NodeAnnotation
  children:
    TraceKind          tracekind   1
    TraceTargetRef     refs        0..n
  concept properties:
    role = trace
  concept links:
    annotated = BaseConcept
```

Editor   As mentioned above, in the editor annotations look as if they *surrounded* their parent node, even though they are in fact children. Figure 8.9 shows the definition of the editor of the requirements trace annotation (and an example is shown in Figure 4.13): it puts the trace on the right side of the annotated node.

Annotations are typically attached to a program node via an intention. As shown in the discussion of vectors and matrices (Section 8.10) intentions are an MPS editor mechanism that lets users select small program transformations from the `Alt-Enter` menu. The one below contributes an entry `Add Trace` to this menu, which attaches a requirements trace to the selected element:

```
intention addTrace for BaseConcept {
  description(node)->string {
    "Add Trace";
  }
  isApplicable(node)->boolean {
    node.ancestor<Module> != null
  }
  execute(editorContext, node)->void {
    node.@trace = new node<TraceAnnotation>();
  }
}
```

The intention is typed to `BaseConcept`, since traces can be attached to arbitrary program elements as long as they are in a module. This is enforced through the applicability condition. The `execute` section puts an instance of `TraceAnnotation` into the `@trace` property of the target node.

8.13 IMPLEMENTING VARIANTS

The transformation implementing product line variability is different from the transformations discussed so far in that it is generic with regard to the transformed languages; presence conditions can be attached to any arbitrary program element. If the presence condition is `false` for the selected configuration during transformation, the respective program element is removed from the program (see the `affectedElement.delete` in the code below). Since this is a generic transformation, it is implemented as a transformation script. In contrast to the template-based approach shown earlier (for example, see Figure 8.3 for state machine triggers and Figure 8.8 for the replacement of + with safer alternatives), a transformation script uses MPS' node API directly to transform the AST.

```
mapping script removePLEStuff
  pre-process input: true
  top-priority group: true
(model, genContext, operationContext)->void {
  node<...> config = // retrieve the configuration that
                     // specifies which variant to generate
  foreach pc in model.nodes<PresenceCondition> {
    if (!(pc.condition.isSelectedInTrafoConfig(config))) {
      node<> affectedElement = pc.parent;
      affectedElement.delete;
} } }
```

The script works as follows. First, it finds the configuration element that specifies which variant should be generated; this is retrieved from the build configuration for the current project. It then finds all `PresenceConditions` in a model and evaluates each of them relative to the selected variant configuration. If a presence condition evaluates to `false`, the script removes the element to which the presence condition is annotated – the parent of the presence condition. Notice how the transformation is put into the `top-priority group`,

```
exported struct EngineStatus {                    [module role: ApplicationLayer]
    int8 speed; ⎡ApplicationLayer: read⎤          module UsingModule imports DataDefinition {
               ⎣DriverLayer: write   ⎦                EngineStatus es;
    int8 rpm; ⎡ApplicationLayer: write⎤               void dummy() {
              ⎣DriverLayer: read    ⎦                    es.rpm = 10;
};                                                       es.speed = 100;
                                                      }
                                                  }
```

Figure 8.10 **Left:** An annotation is used to specify which members of the struct may be read and written by which of the application layer/role. **Right:** If the wrong layer writes to the member, an error is reported. An additional annotation is used to specify the role of an implementation module.

which means it runs in the first phase of the transformation chain *without* explicitly specifying priorities relative to other generators. This is important, because it may not even be known which other transformations are executed for the program, so it is not possible to explicitly declare dependencies relative to them.

8.14 ARCHITECTURE CONSTRAINTS

Imagine enforcing architectural constraints between layers in a system. For example, only modules in the *Driver* layer are allowed to write certain members of a `struct`, and the *Application* layer is allowed to read them. This is an example of a restriction. The first step is the definition of a set of roles (shown below), and then, based on these roles, the permissions for struct members can be specified (see the left part of Figure 8.10). It is also possible to specify which role a module plays; if it assigns to a member for which it has only `read` permissions, an error is reported. The right part of Figure 8.10 shows an example of a permission violation.

```
Access Specification:
    role DriverLayer
    role ApplicationLayer
```

Structure   This extension adds additional metadata to existing language concepts, using annotations to specify the permissions and the module role specification for struct members and modules respectively. These annotations are structurally similar to the requirements traces discussed in Section 8.12.

Editor   The editor for `AccessSpec` annotation embeds the attributed node (i.e. the `Member` it is attached to), and then, on the right side, renders the permissions. An intention is used to be able to attach an `AccessSpec` to a `Member`. The approach for the module role is similar.

Type System   A checking rule for `ImplementationModules` is used to report an error if a module writes to a member for which it does not have the permission. Specifically, it reports an error if a struct member is assigned to which only has a `read` permission for the role declared by the writing module:

```
checking rule check_Access for ImplementationModule as immo {
  if (immo.@moduleRole == null) return;
  node<RoleSpec> moduleRole = immo.@moduleRole.role;
  nlist<AssignmentExpr> aes = immo.descendants<AssignmentExpr>;
  foreach ae in aes {
    if (ae.left.isInstanceOf(AbstractDotExpression)) {
      node<Member> member = ae.left:AbstractDotExpression.
                           member:MemberRef.member;
      if (member.@accessSpec != null) {
        node<Permission> permission =
              member.@accessSpec.permissions.
              findFirst({~it => it.role == moduleRole; });
        if (permission.activity.is(<read>)) {
          error "role " + moduleRole.name +
              " cannot write this member" -> ae.left;
} } } } }
```

Obviously, there should be additional checks. For example, an error must be reported when assigning to a member that has a permission specified from within a module that has *no* role specification: the user has to decide the role of the module, so that the system can verify whether the write access is allowed.

8.15 OS CONFIGURATION

This section discusses the development of new languages that are not directly related to C. An example is operating system configuration, similar to that shown in Figure 10.1 for Lejos/OSEK. This section illustrates a simplified version of such a language. For now, the operating system configuration DSL essentially defines a set of tasks:

```
OS Config:
  task mainTask prio = 1
  task eventHandler prio = 2
  task emergencyHandler prio = 3
```

Structure   A new language `osconfig` is created which contains a new concept, `OSConfig`, which in turn contains operating system configuration items (a collection of `IOSConfigContents`) rendered vertically in the editor. It should be usable as a root node inside models, i.e. it is represented as a separate editor in MPS. This is why its `instance can be root` property is set to `true`:

```
concept OSConfig extends BaseConcept
  instance can be root: true
  children
    IOSConfigContents contents 0..n
```

A concrete concept that represents the task definition can now implement `IOSConfigContents`. It has a `prio` property of type `integer`, and the editor arranges the keyword `task`, its name and the priority in a horizontal collection.

Generator   So far all languages developed in this chapter were extensions of C. Consequently, the generator was a transformation back to C. In the case of the operating system configuration there is no base language – text has to be generated directly. Text generators are different from the generators developed so far; those are actually model-to-model transformations, since they map one MPS tree onto another. Text generators really just write text into a buffer. Assuming the textual representation is similar to the syntax used in MPS, the text generator for `OSConfig` looks as follows:

```
text gen component for concept OSConfig {
  extension: (node)->string {
    "osconfig";
  }
  encoding: utf-8

  (node, context, buffer)->void {
    append {OSConfig} \n ;
    append \n ;
    foreach c in node.contents {
      append ${c} \n ;
    }
  }
}
```

A `text gen` component specifies the encoding and the file extension, as well as the contents of the file. Notice that it does *not* specify the name of the file – this is taken from the `OSConfig` node itself. However, the `OSConfig` does not have a name. This problem can be solved by implementing the `INamedConcept` interface. However, this requires the specification of a name for each `OSConfig`, which does not make sense, since the name of the `OSConfig` should automatically be the name of the model in which it resides. This can be achieved by implementing a getter for the name in the constraints section:

```
concept constraints OSConfig {
  property {name}
    get:(node, scope)->string {
      node.model.name;
    }
    set:<default>
    is valid:<default>
}
```

A text generator for `TaskDef` must also be defined. This is not a root concept, so no name, extension or encoding is specified. The `text gen` component is expected to be called (transitively) from a root concept's `text gen` and only appends to the buffer:

```
text gen component for concept TaskDef {
  (node, context, buffer)->void {
    append {task} ${node.name} { } {(} ${node.prio + ""} {}} ;
  }
}
```

Structure   The language developed so far is completely independent of mbeddr C. However, it should still be possible to refer to concepts defined in that language from C code. In the current example, the C code should contain a task implementation that corresponds to the task definitions in the operating system configuration. In classical C, one would have to define a function that has the same name as the task and use a specific signature; maybe some kind of special modifier is necessary. This is the kind of code that will need to be generated ultimately; however, a better programming experience should be provided to the mbeddr user. The example code below shows the new keyword `task`, which represent a task implementation in a C program. The name behind it (`mainTask`) is a reference to a task definition in an `OSConfig`. Pressing `Ctrl-Space` will code-complete to all available task definitions.

```
module Tasks imports nothing {
  task mainTask {
    // code that implements the task's behavior
  }
}
```

A new language `osconfig.cimpl` acts as the adapter between mbeddr C and the OS configuration (the `osconfig` language should be kept independent of C, and C, of course, must remain independent of `osconfig`). `osconfig.cimpl` extends mbeddr's `modules` and `statements` language, and it also extends the `osconfig` language introduced earlier. The language contains a new concept `TaskImpl` that implements `IModuleContent` so it can be used inside modules. It has a single reference to a `TaskDef` as well as a `StatementList` for the body.

Editor   An alias is specified for the concept even though it is technically a smart reference (it has exactly one reference). However, for the `TaskImpl` the special editor behavior associated with smart references should *not* be triggered. Instead, users should first create a `TaskImpl` node by typing `task` in a module and then select the reference to the `TaskDef`.

Scoping   No explicit scope for the `task` reference has to be defined, since the default behavior that puts all the nodes in the current model into the scope is exactly what is required in this case.

Generator   This example assumes that the compiler for the OS (some kind of fictional OSEK) expects a task implementation function to use a special syntax: the example `mainTask` must be translated as follows:

```
task(mainTask) void Tasks_taskimpl_mainTask(void) {
  // here is some code that implements the task
}
```

```
┌─────────────────────┐
│concept    TaskImpl  │ --> content node:
│inheritors false     │     module dummy imports nothing {
│condition  <always>  │        <TF [$ taskPrefix ] exported void $ taskimpl () {  TF>
└─────────────────────┘            $COPY_SRCL$ int8 x;
                                 } taskimpl (function)
                        }
```

Figure 8.11 This reduction rule replaces a `TaskImpl` with a function that uses a special prefix. As explained before, the `<TF..TF>` template fragment encloses the code that should actually replace the input node; the rest is scaffolding. The `$` macros replace the value of string properties, and the `COPY_SRCL` is used to replace the node it is attached to with a list of nodes from the input model. Both kinds of macros specify, via expressions, (not shown, they are edited in MPS' inspector) the values/nodes that replace the node they are attached to.

A generator with a reduction rule is used to create the function. It is shown in Figure 8.11. The generator uses a property macro to adapt the name, as well as a `COPY_SRCL` macro to copy in all the statements of the body. A special modifier is added to the function via an intention. The `[...]` modifier accepts arbitrary text between the brackets and then just outputs that text during text generation. The `taskPrefix` dummy text is used in the template and then annotated with the following macro expression:

```
"task(" + node.task.name + ")";
```

Structure   Another iteration of this example extends the operating system configuration DSL with a way to define memory layouts. Here is some example code:

```
OS Config:
  // tasks as before
  memory layout {
    region ram: 0..1024
    region eprom: endOf(ram)..2048
    region devices: endOf(eprom)..startOf(devices) + sizeOf(ram) * 2
  }
```

The above code adds additional contents to the `OSConfig` node and also reuses C expressions within the regions, using additional expressions to refer to the start, end and size of other regions. These extensions to the `osconfig` language reside in a new language `osconfig.memory`. This demonstrates how an external DSL can make use of specific concepts from C without modifying the original OS configuration DSL. The new language extends `osconfig` as well as mbeddr's `expressions` language.

The `MemoryLayout` implements `IOSContents` so it can be plugged into the `contents` collection of an `OSConfig`. It also contains a collection of `Regions`. Each `Region` has a name and an `Expression` for the start and the end of the region. Since the language extends the C expression language, `Expression` can be used here:

```
concept Region extends BaseConcept
                implements INamedConcept
  children:
    Expression    startsAt  1
    Expression    endsAt    1
  concept properties:
    alias = region
```

The `startOf(..)`, `endOf(..)` and `sizeOf(..)` expressions are new expressions contributed by this language. All three are essentially similar: they extend `Expression` and have a single reference to a `Region`. They also have an alias to prevent smart-reference editor behavior in the editor:

```
concept EndOfExpr extends Expression
  references:
    Region    region    1
  concept properties:
    alias = endOf
```

Scoping The scope for the `region` reference ascends the tree to the parent `OSConfig` object and the returns all child `Regions`.

Constraints The new expressions (`startOf(..)`, `endOf(..)` and `sizeOf(..)`) may only be used below a `MemoryLayout`. A `can be child` constraint can be used, as demonstrated earlier.

Type System The types of the `startsAt` and `endsAt` properties are defined with the rule below. Both cases express that the type of the respective property must be `uint64` or any of its shorter subtypes.

```
rule typeof_Region for Region as r
    infer typeof(r.startsAt) :<=: new node<UnsignedInt64tType>();
    infer typeof(r.endsAt) :<=: new node<UnsignedInt64tType>();
}
```

The type for the `EndOfExpr` and the `StartOfExpr` is simple as well; it is simply the type of the respective expression of the target region:

```
typeof(endOfExpr) :==: typeof(endOfExpr.region.startsAt);
```

For the `SizeOfExpr` it is a bit more interesting, since the type has to be the common supertype of the start and the end:

```
rule typeof_SizeOfExpr for SizeOfExpr as soe {
    infer typeof(soe) :>=: typeof(soe.region.startsAt);
    infer typeof(soe) :>=: typeof(soe.region.endsAt);
}
```

The code above defines *two* typing equations for the same node (`soe`). Both express a same-or-more-general-type relationship (`:>=:`) relative to the respective property. The only way in which the type system engine can make *both* of these rules true is by assigning the common supertype of the two properties to `typeof(soe)` – which is exactly what is needed.

8.16 ADDITIONAL REQUIREMENTS DATA

Section 4.8 has shown that business rules can be embedded directly into annotations (see Figure 4.16). This section provides an overview of how this is implemented.

Structure Like other mbeddr languages, the requirements languages has been designed to be extensible. In particular, the `additional data` slot contains instances of `IRequirementsData`. By implementing this interface, other concepts can plug into the requirements language. The `RCalculation` concept (the concept of the business rules shown in Figure 4.16) implements this interface. `RCalculation` in turn contains an `Expression` to calculate the value of the calculation, and also contains parameters (`RParam`) and test cases (`RTestCase`).

Scoping To be able to reference the parameters from within the expression, the language also contains an `RParamRef` expression that references an `RParam`. It is scoped to only see the parameters in the current `RCalculation`:

```
link {param}
  scope:
    (model, referenceNode, enclosingNode) -> sequence<node<RParam>>{
      node<RCalculation> c = enclosingNode.ancestor<RCalculation>;
      return c.params;
    }
```

Interpreter The test cases are essentially calls to the calculation rule that supplies values for the parameters, plus an expected result value. An interpreter executes the test cases and checks whether the actual result equals the expected value. The interpreter is hooked in as a checking rule:

```
checking rule check_executeTestCase for RTestCase as tc {
  try {
    TestCaseInterpreter ci = new TestCaseInterpreter(tc);
    int actual = ci.calculate(tc.ancestor<RCalculation>.expr);
    int exp = ci.calculate(tc.expected);
    if (actual != exp) {
      error "expected " + exp + ", but was " + actual -> tc;
    }
  } catch (InterpreterException ex) {
    warning "interpreter error: " + ex.getMessage() -> tc;
  }
}
```

The interpreter itself is a Java class that evaluates program nodes. The only interesting aspect of this interpreter is that it is implemented using a special-purpose language extension to MPS' BaseLanguage[2] that simplifies writing interpreters. Figure 8.12 shows a part of the interpreter that uses this extension.

---

[2] MPS' language definition DSLs are built with MPS and can be extended with MPS' own language definition mechanisms.

```
public int calculate(node<Expression> n) {
  dispatch<int> (n) {
    RConstantRef          ⇒ #(it.constant.value)
    RParamRef             . ⇒ #(attrValues[it.param])
    PlusExpression        ⇒ #(it.left) + #(it.right)
    MinusExpression       ⇒ #(it.left) - #(it.right)
    MultiExpression       ⇒ #(it.left) * #(it.right)
    DivExpression         ⇒ #(it.left) / #(it.right)
    NumberLiteral         ⇒ Integer.parseInt(it.value)
    TernaryExpression     ⇒ evalComparison(it.condition) ? #(it.thenExpr) : #(it.elseExpr)
    ParensExpression      ⇒ #(it.expression)
    GSwitchExpression     ⇒ gswitch(it)
    DecTab                ⇒ dectab(it)
    default -1
  };
}
```

Figure 8.12 The `calculate` method is the core of the expression interpreter. It uses a `dispatch` expression, which is an extension to BaseLanguage specifically developed for building interpreters. It takes a node `n` as an argument and then dispatches over the entries based on the concept of `n`. In each of the cases, the `it` expression refers to `n`, but it is already downcast to the case's declared concept, avoiding repeated explicit downcasting. The `#(..)` shortcut recursively invokes the method in which it is used. Note that both `it` and `#` can only be used under a `dispatch`, so they do not pollute BaseLanguage's namespace.

8.17 NEW WORDS IN PROSE BLOCKS

Section 4.7 described how the generic prose text facility can be extended. For example, in documentation comments for functions, it is possible to reference arguments of that function using the `@arg(..)` notation. This section illustrates how this extension is built.

Structure   The multiline prose editor widget works with instances of `IWord`, and by implementing this interface, new language concepts can be "plugged in" into the multiline editor. The word that references arguments is called `ArgRefWord`:

```
concept ArgRefWord implements IWord
  references:
    Argument    arg    1
  concept properties:
    alias = @arg
```

The concept references one `Argument` and uses the `@arg` alias key: typing `@arg` in a comment, followed by `Ctrl-Space`, instantiates an `ArgRefWord` the respective location in the text. The editor is simply a horizontal list of the `@arg` keyword, a couple of symbols and the name of the referenced argument.

Constraints   The constraint below ensures that an `ArgRefWord` can only be used in a comment that resides directly below a function, i.e., it is a function documentation comment:

```
concepts constraints ArgRefWord {
  can be child of
    (node, parent, operationContext)->boolean {
      node<> comment = parent.ancestor<DocumentationComment>;
      node<> owner = comment.parent;
      owner.isInstanceOf(Function)
    }
```

Scoping   A scope for the `arg` reference must be defined, since not all
`Arguments` (anywhere in the model) are allowed; only those owned by the
function to which the documentation comment is attached are valid targets
for the reference:

```
link {arg}
  scope:
    (refNode, enclosingNode)->sequence<node<Argument>>) {
      enclosingNode.ancestor<Function>.arguments;
    }
```

Generator   A generator has to be defined that is used when HTML or LATEX
output is generated. This `IWord` could be treated specially by a custom transformation; however, for simple words that are just transformed to a string (as
is the case for `ArgRefWord`) it is sufficient to override a behavior method that
returns the string:

```
public string toTextString()
  overrides IWord.toTextString {
  "@arg(" + this.arg.name + ")";
}
```

---

*Summary — This chapter demonstrated the versatility of language modularization
and composition in MPS to the benefit of mbeddr. It shows that meaningful extensions
can be built without invasively changing the base language C. However some mbeddr
features go beyond implementing a language. These include verifications, refactorings
and the debugger. These, and others, are illustrated in the next chapter.*

Implementing the Non-Language Aspects of mbeddr

Abstract — *At the core,* Generic Tools, Specific Languages *and mbeddr rely on language extension to build domain-specific engineering tools. This is why language engineering has been covered extensively in the previous chapters. However, to make* mbeddr *useful,* some *extensions to the tool platform are required as well, all directly related to and closely integrated with languages. These tool extensions are discussed in this chapter. They include integrated verifications, debugging, IDE support, dataflow analysis, the visualizations, and the legacy code importer.*

9

9.1   VERIFICATION

This section first introduces mbeddr's approach to verification (also called formal analysis) in general, and then subsections 9.1.1 through 9.1.4 look at the various verifications supported by mbeddr. mbeddr implements an agile approach for combining DSLs and language extensions with verification. The methodology takes advantage of language engineering techniques provided by MPS, and has the following main characteristics:

- It relies on language fragments that can be easily analyzed and that are well-integrated with the rest of the code, and makes sure that analysis results can be lifted back to the domain level. For example, state machines can be model checked more easily than low-level implementations of state machine using, for example, `switch` statements.

- Users are made aware of whether a (part of a) program is currently analyzable or not. Users are given the choice between writing code that is analyzable or not. In the former case, they must use an analyzable, potentially restricted subset of a language, whereas in the latter case users can enjoy the full and more expressive language, but do not get analyzability. For example, a decision table can be marked as `verifiable`. In this case the condition expressions are restricted to logical and linear arithmetic expressions.

- The analyses are designed for users who are not experts in verification: properties can be expressed easily and the results are lifted back to the abstraction level of the DSL to make them easier to interpret. For example, the properties which a state machine should be checked for are specified using a set of high-level patterns, instead of using the LTL or CTL property specification languages.

- The integrated verification tools are decoupled from the verification use cases. This allows them to be used for a wide range of analyses of conceptually different C extensions. For example, the SMT solving infrastructure is used for verifying decision tables and feature models.

In terms of implementation, this methodology entails the following steps. They are implemented in some way for all verifications supported by mbeddr:

1. Choose the set of analyses that will be performed, and at the same time decide on the language abstractions that are necessary to make the analysis feasible and run in a reasonable time. This may include restriction of existing languages, or the definition of additional abstractions.

2. Choose an analysis tool to perform the actual analysis. Implement the input language of the analysis tool in MPS. Write a transformation that transforms programs expressed in the language abstractions identified above plus the properties to be verified to the specification language of the analysis tool.

3. Integrate the tool into MPS so that it can be run directly from a menu item, a button or something similar.

4. Finally, define a mapping from the analysis results provided by the analysis tool to the original language abstractions the user wrote. Integrate some kind of view that shows the results directly in MPS.

Incrementality   mbeddr's approach is incremental, both in defining the analyses as well as in using them. First, the supported language subset can be kept small, and enlarged over time, if the need arises, by allowing more constructs. The trade-offs between the complexity of implementing the analyses, their usefulness to application developers, and the size of the supported language subset can be continuously evaluated. Second, application developers can decide whether to use a restricted language subset that is analyzable, or to use the full language and lose the analyzability. While the language extensions are modular, they are nonetheless integrated into the IDE, enabling smooth migration between the two choices, avoiding tool integration headaches.

Soundness   Defining the analyses in an agile way, based on domain-specific extensions that inherently do not have formally defined semantics, can easily lead to unsound analyses. It might not always be clear what exactly is verified: since the DSL program is translated to the analysis tool *and* to a target language for implementation, keeping the two transformations consistent is challenging. This is currently addressed by manual reviews and some automated tests. Also, mbeddr currently does not claim to be suitable for safety-critical systems where formal analyses are mandatory. mbeddr considers the analyses as an additional means of testing.

9.1.1 SMT Solving for Decision Tables

Decision tables [Janicki et al., 1997] exploit MPS' projectional editor in order to represent two-level nested `if` statements as a table. Decision tables are discussed in Section 4.5; Figure 4.4 shows an example. Decision tables evaluate to different values for different combinations of input conditions. The rationale for tabular expressions is to let developers define the conditions more easily and to allow reviewers to directly gain an overview of varied sets of input conditions. Decision tables are translated into C essentially as an `if/else if` for the column headers, and nested in each branch, an `if/else if/else` for the row headers.

Verification Approach   As explained in Section 4.5, there are two obvious analyses for two-dimensional decision tables: *completeness* requires that every behavior of the table is explicitly modeled and no case is omitted. This requires listing all the possible combinations of the input conditions in the table. *Consistency* checks whether there are input conditions that overlap, meaning that several cases in the decision tables are applicable for one specific set of input values (non-determinism). If the language used for expressing the conditions is restricted to logical and linear arithmetic expressions, these two analyses can be reduced to SMT problems. Given a table with n rows (r_i) and m columns (c_j), its completeness can be verified by checking the satisfiability of the following formula (if satisfiable, then the table is incomplete):

$$\neg \bigvee_{i,j=1}^{n,m} (r_i \wedge c_j)$$

Similarly, the consistency of decision tables can be expressed by checking whether the following conjunctions are satisfiable. If they are satisfiable, then an inconsistency was found:

$$\forall i,k = 1..n \quad j,l = 1..m :$$
$$i \neq k \wedge j \neq l \Rightarrow r_i \wedge c_j \wedge r_k \wedge c_l$$

Decision tables in mbeddr generally allow arbitrary conditions. These may contain function calls, or they may not be in the subset of linear arithmetic, which makes them non-analyzable with Yices, the SMT solver used by mbeddr. If users wants a decision table to be verifiable, they must restrict the expressions to an analyzable subset, i.e. logical and linear expressions. The IDE reports an error for any decision table that is marked as `verifiable` and contains expressions that are not in this subset. This always keeps users informed as to whether their code is verifiable or not.

Implementation   mbeddr implements a language for specifying logical and arithmetic expressions; the language is essentially similar to the input language of Yices. Below is a partial example of the solver code generated for the decision table from Figure 4.4:

```
module decTab_1731059994647919839 {
  (set-evidence! true )
  (define-type Trackpoint (record id :: (subrange -128 127)
                                  timestamp :: (subrange -128 127)
                                  x          :: (subrange -128 127)
                                  y          :: (subrange -128 127)
                                  alt        :: (subrange 0 65535)
                                  speed      :: (subrange -32768 32767 )))
  (define tp :: Trackpoint)
  (assert+ !(or (select tp alt)    <= 2000 &&
                (select tp speed)  < 150 &&
                (select tp alt)    <= 2000 &&
                (select tp speed)  >= 150 &&
                (select tp alt)    >= 2000 &&
                (select tp speed)  < 150 &&
                (select tp alt)    >= 2000 &&
                (select tp speed)  >= 150))
  (check)
  {
    (retract 1)
    (assert+ (select tp alt)    <= 2000 &&
             (select tp speed) < 150 &&
             (select tp alt)    <= 2000 &&
             (select tp speed) >= 150
    (check)
  }
  ...
}
```

The solver input is written to a file, and Yices is executed as an external
process that reads the file and outputs the results into another file. This result
is shown to the user in MPS. In particular, as shown in Section 4.5, if the SMT
solver finds a problem, it generates an example of the table input values that
lead to the problem.

9.1.2 SAT Solving for Feature Models

Feature models are a well-known formalism for expressing product line variability at a conceptual level [Kang et al., 1990], i.e. independent of implementation artifacts (in the problem space as opposed to the solution space). A
feature is essentially a configuration option, and a feature model is a hierarchical collection of features, with constraints among them. Constraints include
mandatory (a feature *must* be in each product configuration), optional (it *may*
be in a product), or (*one or more* features from a set of related features must
be in a product) and xor (*exactly one* from a set of related features must be
in a product). In addition, there may be arbitrary cross-constraints between
any two features (such as requires-also and conflicts-with). A *configuration* of a feature model is a valid selection of the features in a feature model.
A *valid* configuration must not violate any of the constraints expressed in its

```
[verifiable]                                ;; each feature is declared as a boolean variable
feature model IntelligentSensorFamily       (define Root::bool)
  Root ! {                                   (define Diagnosis::bool)
    Diagnosis xor {                          ...
      Logging requires CAN ? {               ;; the root feature is always present
        Centralized                          (assert Root)
      }                                      ;; for each (sub-feature, feature) we have
      HeartBeat conflicts CAN ? {            ;;"sub-feature -> feature"
        ASIL_D                               (assert (or (not Diagnosis) Root))
      }                                      (assert (or (not Logging) Diagnosis))
    }                                        ...
    DataAquisition xor {                     ;; for each mandatory sub-feature we have
      Infrared                               ;; "feature -> sub-feature"
      Camera                                 (assert+ (or (not Root) Diagnosis))
    }                                        (assert+ (or (not Root) DataAquisition))
    CommProtocol ! {                         ;; for each feature with a Xor constraint
      CAN requires HeartBeat                 ;; we have "feature -> fold(xor, sub-features)"
      TCP_IP requires Logging ? {            (assert+ (or (not Diagnosis)
        IP_v5                                              (or (and (not Logging) HeartBeat)
      }                                                        (and Logging (not HeartBeat)))))
    }                                        ;; for each feature with requires another_feature
  }                                          ;; we have "feature -> another_feature"
                                             (assert+ (or (not Logging) CAN))
                                             ...
                                             ;; for each feature with conflicts another_feature
                                             ;; we have "feature xor another_feature"
                                             (assert+ (or (and (not HeartBeat) CAN)
                                                          (and HeartBeat (not CAN))))
                                             (set-evidence! true)
                                             (check)
```

Figure 9.1 Feature model analysis I: **Left:** example feature model expressed with mbeddr's feature model DSL **Right:** part of the encoding in Yices.

underlying feature model. Section 4.9 illustrates mbeddr's support for feature models.

Verification Approach   There are two obvious analyses for feature models. The first checks feature models for consistency, i.e. whether the set of constraints allows the definition of valid configurations at all. Conflicting constraints may prevent this (A requires B together with B conflicts with A). The second analysis checks a specific configuration for compliance with its feature model. As described by Mendonca et al., both of these analyses are easy to perform with the help of a SMT solver such as Yices [Mendonça et al., 2009].

Implementation   Technically, the implementation relies on the same integration of Yices as the previously described verification of decision tables. In particular, the same language is used to express the input to the solver. The generated input for the solver is of course different, to reflect the different domain-level semantics of the SMT problem. Figure 9.1 shows an example of a feature model and a part of its translation to Yices. Figure 9.2 shows the result of running the analysis and its lifted representation. Each of the assert ids from the unsat core given by Yices corresponds to a constraint from the feature model. This allows mbeddr to present the user with a list of those constraints that are violated.

```
> yices IntelligentSensorFamily.ys    FAIL: No valid configuration of: 'IntelligentSensorFamily'.
    id: 1                              The following constraints are conflicting:
    id: 2                                 -> 'Root' has mandatory child 'CommProtocol'
    id: 3                                 -> 'CommProtocol' has mandatory child 'CAN'
    id: 4                                 -> 'CAN' requires: 'HeartBeat'
    id: 5                                 -> 'HeartBeat' conflicts: 'CAN'

    ...
    unsat
    unsat core ids: 3 4 9 11
```

Figure 9.2 Feature model analysis II: **Left:** Yices verification output. **Right:** Results lifted to the domain level.

9.1.3 *Model-Checking State Machines*

State machines were introduced in Section 4.6. They are top level concepts and have in-events, out-events, states and transitions, as well as local variables. A transition is triggered by an in-event, and it may also have guard conditions that have to be `true` in order for the transition to fire if its triggering event is received by the state machine. The guard can refer to state machine-local variables as well as to in-event parameters. A state has entry and exit actions, and transitions have transition actions. As part of actions, local variables can be assigned and out-events can be fired. As a way of interacting with the remaining C program, an out-event can be bound to a C function call.

Verification Approach   Analyses based on symbolic model-checking are most suitable for the state machine language. There are numerous works (such as Clarke & Heinle [2000]) about model-checking different dialects of state machines. mbeddr support two kinds of analyses: *default analyses* are checked automatically for every state machine. They uncover typical bugs such as unreachable states and transitions that are never fired (dead code), sets of non-deterministic transitions, and over-/underflow detection for integer variables. *User-defined analyses* are defined specifically for a given state machine. To address the expectations of non-expert users, mbeddr supports specifications expressed with the well-known set of specification patterns[1] described by Dwyer et al. [1999]. Examples patterns include:

```
P is false After Q:              Q = <expr>    P = <expr>
always eventually reachable:     <state>
S Responds to P Before R:        P = <expr>    S = <expr>    R = <expr>
P is false After Q Until R:      Q = <expr>    P = <expr>    R = <expr>
P is false Between Q and R:      Q = <expr>    P = <expr>    R = <expr>
```

Implementation   As in the previous verification examples, mbeddr implements the input language to the NuSMV model checker. A transformation maps the high-level state machine to a representation in this input language[2], NuSMV is run, and the result is expressed in terms of the properties implied

---

[1] http://patterns.projects.cis.ksu.edu

[2] The input program is much too long to show in this thesis.

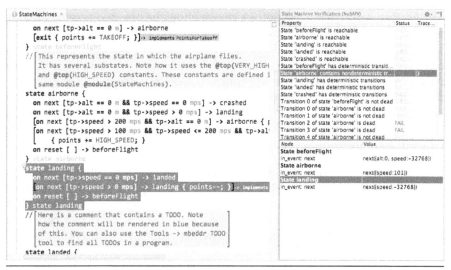

Figure 9.3 Model-checking a state machine: the left part shows the state machine, and the top right parts shows successful and failed property verifications. If the user selects a failed property, the top bottom part of shows an example execution trace that leads to the failed property.

by the state machine or specified by the user. Figure 9.3 shows the state machine discussed in Section 4.6, as well as the result of a model checking run.

By marking a state machine as `verifiable`, a set of constraints is activated that make sure that the state machine conforms to an analyzable language subset. Examples of constraints include: (1) a maximum of one update of a local variable inside a transition; (2) support for only range and Boolean types in local variables and input events; (3) external functions may only be called indirectly via out-event bindings (the code in external functions is not part of the verification). As with the other verifications, users can now choose between using a highly expressive variant of state machines (and thereby losing the analyzability of their code) or using a restricted subset that is verifiable.

9.1.4 Dataflow Analysis for Contract Checking

As shown in Section 4.4, interfaces and components are a backbone of mbeddr's version of C. Interfaces support the specification of behavior, and components make use of the interfaces by providing or requiring ports that conform to interfaces. Polymorphism is supported for interfaces, so different components can provide the same interface, implementing it in different but semantically compatible ways. To make this possible, an interface must specify its behavior with more than just signatures. To this end, interfaces support the specification of pre- and post-conditions for operations, as well as protocol state machines.

Verification Approach   Section 4.4 showed how the pre- and post-conditions as well as the protocol state machines on interfaces can be checked on implementing components, both at runtime and statically. Figure 4.3 showed an example of such a check. Both checks rely on the same (optionally generated) code that procedurally checks the contracts (see code snippet below). While the runtime check simply executed the `if` statement, the static analysis uses a reachability analysis based on dataflow checking: the CBMC bounded model checker for C is used to statically check whether the body of the `if` is ever entered; if so, the contract check failed.

Implementation   The implementation of this analysis is different than the previous ones because no special input format is required. Only the contract checks at the beginning and end of the functions generated from runnables have to be generated. The body of the `if` is only executed if a condition fails, and CBMC can verify statically whether reaching this code is possible for a given program. To facilitate lifting the result, a mapping is maintained between each label and the higher-level construct represented by the label.

```
void Components_InMemoryStorage_trackpointStore_store(
                            struct DataStructures_Trackpoint* tp,
                            void* ___instanceData) {
  struct ___InMemoryStorage_data* ___ci =
      (struct ___InMemoryStorage_data*)___instanceData;
  if (!InMemoryStorage_trackpointStore_isEmpty(___ci)) {
    pre_1731059994647814031__1731059994647814157:
    // output runtime error message
  }
  if (!(tp != 0)) {
    pre_1731059994647814055__1731059994647814157:
    // output runtime error message
  }
  // implementation of the runnable
  ___ci->field_storedTP = tp;
  if ( !(!(InMemoryStorage_trackpointStore_isEmpty(___ci))) ) {
    post_1731059994647814038__6514529288614093826:
    // output runtime error message
  } }
```

Running the reachability analysis with CBMC on the generated C results in a raw analysis result at the abstraction level of C. It specifies for each label whether it can be reached or not. If it can be reached the result includes an example execution trace through the C code. This raw result must be interpreted with regard to the higher-level conditions connected to a label. In addition, the trace must be related to the program that includes the higher-level constructs. Lifting the counterexample involves several steps:

1. Elimination of the generation noise from the C code: Part of the generated C code represents low-level encodings of higher-level concepts. For example, additional functions are generated that implement decision tables. In these cases, the corresponding part of the counterexample does

not make sense in terms of the higher-level construct; the part should not be visible in the lifted result[3].

2. Interpretation of the C-level parts of the counterexample: higher-level constructs are encoded in C via generation with the help of variables or function calls. These encodings need to be traced back. For example, the components are initialized in a specific function, recognizable by its name. If this function shows up in a C-level counterexample, it means that the components were initialized.

3. Rebuilding original names. Since mbeddr supports namespaces, the names of the C representation of higher-level program elements are prepended with module names. The original names of the higher-level abstractions must be recovered.

9.2 DEBUGGING

This section describes the mbeddr debugger. Like the mbeddr languages, the debugger is extensible. This section starts with a discussion of the requirements for mbeddr's extensible debugger (Section 9.2.1), then provides a simple example of how to specify the debugger for a language extension (Section 9.2.2), discusses the debugger architecture (Section 9.2.3), shows more examples of how this architecture solves challenges in extensible debuggers (Section 9.2.4) and concludes with a discussion that evaluates whether the approach addresses the requirements (Section 9.2.5).

9.2.1 Requirements for the Debugger

Debuggers for imperative languages[4] support at least the following features: *breakpoints* suspend execution on arbitrary statements; *single-step execution* steps over statements, and into and out of functions or other callables; and *watches* show values of variables, arguments or other aspects of the program state. *Stack frames* visualize the call hierarchy of functions or other callables.

As shown in Figure 9.4, two levels are distinguished in the mbeddr debugger: the *tree* representation of a program in MPS, and the generated *text* that is used by the C compiler and the debugger backend. A program in the tree representation can be separated into parts expressed in the base language (C in this case) and parts expressed using extensions. The latter is referred to as the *extension*-level or *DSL*-level. When debugging a program that contains extensions, breakpoints, stepping, watches and call stacks at the extension-level differ from their counterparts at the base-level. The debugger, which technically runs at the base-level, has to perform the mapping from the base-level

---

[3] As demonstrated in the next subsection, this problem is similar to the one encountered in debugging. However, no common approach is implemented currently.

[4] Debuggers for other behavioral paradigms may support very different ways of debugging, as discussed by Voelter et al. [2013].

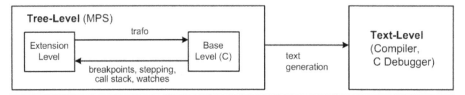

Figure 9.4 An extension-aware debugger maps the debug behavior from the base-level to the extension-level (an extension may also be mapped onto other extensions; this aspect is ignored in this section).

to the extension-level (Figure 9.4). In particular, an extensible debugger for mbeddr that supports debugging on the base-level and extension-level must address the following requirements:

- *Modularity* Language extensions in mbeddr are modular, so debugger extensions must be modular as well. No changes to the base language must be necessary to enable debugging for a language extension.

- *Framework Genericity* In addition, new language extensions must not require changes *to the core debugger infrastructure* (not just the base language).

- *Simple Debugger Definition* Creating language extensions is an integral part of using mbeddr. Hence, the development of a debugger for an extension should be simple and not require too much knowledge about the inner workings of the framework, or even the C debugger backend.

- *Limited Overhead* As a consequence of embedded software development, the additional, debugger-specific code generated into the binary has to be limited. Additional code increases the size of the binary, potentially making debugging on a small target device infeasible.

- *Debugger Backend Independence* Embedded software projects use different C debuggers, depending on the target device. This prevents modifying the C debugger itself: changes would have to be re-implemented for every C debugger used.

9.2.2 *An Example Extension*

The starting point is developing a simple `foreach` extension to mbeddr C. The `foreach` statement can be used to conveniently iterate over C arrays. Users have to specify the array as well as its size. Inside the `foreach` body, `it` acts as a reference to the current iteration's array element[5]:

---

[5] Note that for the sake of the example, this example does not consider nested `foreach` statements, so unique names for various (generated) variables are not a problem.

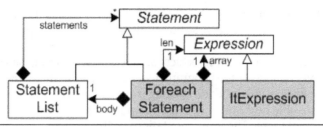

Figure 9.5 UML class diagram showing the structure of the `ForeachLanguage`. Concepts from the C base language are in white boxes, new concepts are gray.

```
int8 sum = 0;
int8[] a = {1, 2, 3};
foreach (a sized 3) {
    sum += it;
}
```

The code generated from this piece of extended C is shown in the next snippet. The `foreach` statement is expanded into a regular `for` statement and an additional variable `__it`:

```
int8 sum = 0;
int8[] a = {1, 2, 3};
for (int __c = 0; __c < 3; __c++) {
    int8 __it = a[__c];
    sum += __it;
}
```

Developing the Language Extension   To make the `foreach` extension modular, it lives in a separate language named `ForeachLanguage`. The new language extends C, since concepts defined in C will be reused. The structure can be seen from Figure 9.5. The extensions defines an editor, a `can be child` constraint to restrict the `it` expression to within `foreach` statements, type system rules for the various expressions and a generator to plain C.

Developing the Debug Behavior   The implementation of the debugger extension for `foreach` resides completely in the `ForeachLanguage`; this keeps the debugger definition for the extension local to the extension language.

To set a breakpoint on a concept, it must implement the `IBreakpointSupport` marker interface provided by the mbeddr debugger infrastructure. `Statement` already implements this interface, so `ForEachStatement` implicitly implements this interface as well.

Stepping behavior is implemented via `ISteppable`. The `ForeachStatement` implements this interface indirectly via `Statement`, but the methods that define the step over and step into behavior have to be overridden. Assume the debugger is suspended on a `foreach` and the user invokes *step over*. If the array is empty or the iteration is finished, a step over ends up on the statement that follows *after the whole foreach* statement. Otherwise the debugger ends up on the first line of the `foreach` body (`sum += it;`). This is the first line of the mbeddr program, *not* the first line of the generated base program (which would be `int8 __it = arr[__c];`).

The debugger cannot guess which alternative will occur, since it would need to know the state of the program, evaluating the expressions in the (generated) `for`. Instead the mbeddr debugger infrastructure sets breakpoints on *each* of the possible next statements and then resumes execution until the program hits one of them. The implementations of the `ISteppable` methods specify strategies for setting breakpoints on these possible next statements. The `contributeStepOverStrategies` method collects strategies for the *step over* case:

```
void contributeStepOverStrategies(list<IDebugStrategy> res) {
  ancestor
  statement list: this.body
}
```

The method is implemented using a DSL for debugger specification, which is part of the mbeddr debugger framework. The DSL simplifies the implementation of debuggers significantly. It is an extension of MPS' BaseLanguage. The `ancestor` statement delegates to the `foreach`'s ancestor; this will lead to a breakpoint on the subsequent statement. The second line results in a breakpoint on the first statement of the `body` statement list.

Since the `array` and `len` expressions can be arbitrarily complex and may contain invocations of callables (such as function calls), the *step into* behavior has to be specified as well. This requires the debugger to inspect the expression trees in `array` and `len` and find any expression that can be stepped into. Such expressions implement `IStepIntoable`. If it finds any, the debugger has to step into each of them, in turn. Otherwise the debugger falls back to *step over*. An additional method configures the expression trees which the debugger must inspect:

```
void contributeStepIntoStrategies(list<IDebugStrategy> res) {
  subtree: this.array
  subtree: this.len
}
```

By default, the Watch window contains all C symbols (global and local variables, arguments) as supplied by the native C debugger. In the case of the `foreach`, this means that `it` is not available, but `__it` and `__c` are. This is exactly the wrong way around: the Watch window should show `it`, but not `__it` and `__c`. To customize watches and resolve this problem, a concept has to implement `IWatchProvider`. Here is the code for `foreach`, also expressed in the debugger definition DSL:

```
void contributeWatchables(list<UnmappedVariable> unmapped,
                                list<IWatchable> mapped) {
  hide "__c"
  map "__it" to "it"
    type: this.array.type:ArrayType.baseType
```

```
    category: WatchableCategories.LOCAL_VARIABLES
    context: this
}
```

The first line hides __c. The rest maps a base-level C variable to a watchable. It finds a C variable named __it (inserted by the foreach generator) and creates a watch variable named it. At the same time, it hides the base-level variable __it. The type of it is the base type of the array over which the foreach iterates. The it watchable is assigned to the local variables section and the foreach node is associated with it. Double-clicking on the it in the Watch window will highlight the foreach in the code.

Stepping into the foreach body does not affect the call stack, since the concept represents no cal(for details, see the next subsection). No stack frame related functionality is necessary.

9.2.3 Debugger Framework Architecture

The central idea of the debugger architecture is this: from the C code in MPS and its extensions (tree level), C text is generated (text level). This text is the basis for the debugging process by a native C debugger. Trace data is used to find out how the generated text maps back to the tree level in MPS.

Execution Architecture   The Mapper is at the core of the execution architecture. It is driven by the Debugger UI (and through it, by the user) and controls the C debugger via the Debug Wrapper. It uses the Program Structure and the Trace Data. The Mapper also uses a language's debug specification, discussed below. Figure 9.6 shows the components and their interfaces.

The IDebugControl interface is used by the Debugger UI to control the Mapper. For example, it provides a resume operation. IBreakpoints allows the UI to set breakpoints on program nodes. IWatches lets the UI retrieve the

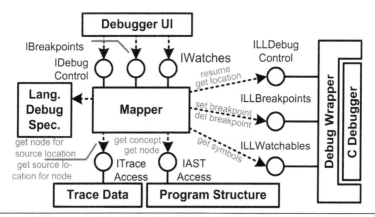

Figure 9.6 The Mapper is the central component of the debugger execution architecture. It is used by the Debugger UI and, in turn, uses the Debug Wrapper, the Program Structure and the Trace Data.

data items for the Watch window. The `Debug Wrapper` essentially provides the same interfaces, but on the level of C (prefixed with `LL`, for "low level"). In addition, `ILLDebugControl` lets the `Mapper` find out about the program location of the `C Debugger` when it is suspended at a breakpoint. `IASTAccess` lets the `Mapper` access program nodes. Finally, `ITraceAccess` lets the `Mapper` find out the program node (tree level) that corresponds to a specific line in the generated C source text (text level), and vice versa.

To illustrate the interactions of these components, the list below describes a *step over*. After the request has been handed over from the UI to the `Mapper` via `IDebugControl`, the `Mapper` performs the following steps:

1. Asks the current node's concept for its *step over* strategies; these define all possible locations where the debugger could end up after the *step over*.

2. Queries `TraceData` for the corresponding lines in the generated C text for those program locations.

3. Uses the debugger's `ILLBreakpoints` to set breakpoints on those lines in the C text.

4. Uses `ILLDebugControl` to resume program execution. It will stop at any of the breakpoints just created.

5. Uses `ILLDebugControl` to get the C call stack.

6. Queries `TraceData` to find out, for each C stack frame, the corresponding nodes in the tree-level program.

7. Collects all relevant `IStackFrameContributor`s (see the next section). The `Mapper` uses these to construct the tree-level call stack.

8. Gets the currently visible symbols and their values via `ILLWatchables`.

9. Queries the nodes for all `WatchableProvider`s and use them to create a set of watchables.

At this point, execution returns to the `Debugger UI`, which then gets the current location and watchables from the `Mapper`, to highlight the statement on which the debugger is suspended and populate the Watch window.

In mbeddr's implementation, the `Debugger UI`, `Program Repository` and `Trace Data` are provided by MPS. In particular, MPS builds a trace from the program nodes (tree level) in MPS to the generated text-level source. The `Debug Wrapper` is part of mbeddr and relies on the Eclipse CDT Debug Bridge[6], which provides a Java API to `gdb`[7] and other C debuggers.

Debugger Specification   The debugger specification resides in the respective language module. As shown in the `foreach` example, the specification

---

[6] www.eclipse.org/cdt

[7] www.gnu.org/software/gdb/documentation/

relies on a set of interfaces and a number of predefined strategies, as well as the debugger specification DSL.

The interface `IBreakpointSupport` is used to mark language concepts on which breakpoints can be set. C's `Statement` implements this interface. Since all statements – including `foreach` – inherit from `Statement`, breakpoints can be set on all statements by default.

When the user sets a breakpoint on a program node, the mapper uses `ITraceAccess` to find the corresponding line in the generated C text. A statement defined by an extension may be expanded to several base-level statements, so `ITraceAccess` actually returns a range of lines, and the breakpoint is set on the first one.

Stack frames represent the nesting of invoked callables at runtime. A *callable* is a language concept that contains statements and can be called from multiple call sites. Stack frames for a language concept are created if it has callable semantics. The only callables in C are functions, but in mbeddr, test cases, state machine transitions and component methods are callables as well. Callable semantics on the extension level do not necessarily imply a function call on the base level. There are cases in which an extension-level callable is *not* mapped to a function, and where a non-callable *is* mapped to a function. Consequently, the C call stack may differ from the extension call stack shown to the user. Concepts with callable semantics on the extension level or base level implement `IStackFrameContributor`. The interface provides operations that determine whether a stack frame has to be created in the debugger UI and what the name of the stack frame should be.

Stepping behavior is configured via the following set of concept interfaces: `IStackFrameContributor, ISteppable, ISteppableContext, IStepIntoable` as well as `IDebugStrategy`. The left part of Figure 9.7 shows an overview. The methods defined by these interfaces return *strategies* that determine where the debugger may have to stop next if the user selects a stepping operation (remember that the debugger framework sets breakpoints to implement stepping). New strategies can be added without changing the generic execution aspect of the framework.

Strategies implement `IDebugStrategy` and are responsible for setting breakpoints to implement a particular stepping behavior. Language extensions can either implement their own strategies or use predefined ones. The predefined ones include setting a breakpoint on a particular node, searching for `IStepIntoables` in expression subtrees (step into), or delegating to the outer stack frame (step out).

To support *watches*, language concepts implement `IWatchProvider` if they directly contribute items into the Watch window. An `IWatchProviderContext` contains zero or more watch providers. Typically these are concepts that own statement lists, such as `Functions` or `IfStatements`. If the debugger is suspended on any particular statement, the visible watches can be found by iterating through all ancestor `IWatchProviderContext`s and asking them for their `IWatchProviders`. The right part of Figure 9.7 shows the typical structure of the concepts.

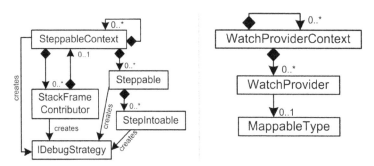

Figure 9.7 **Left:** The structure of language concepts implementing the stepping-related interfaces. The boxes represent language concepts implementing the interfaces discussed in the text. Those concepts define the containments, so this figure represents a typical setup. **Right:** Typical structure of language concepts implementing the watches-related interfaces.

An `IWatchProvider` implements the `contributeWatchables` operation. It has access to the C variables available in the native C debugger. Based on those, it creates a set of watchables. The method may hide a base-level C variable (because it is irrelevant to the extension-level), promote C variable to a watchable or create additional watchables based on the values of C variables. The representation of a watchable often depends on the variable's type as expressed in the *extension program*. This type may be different from the one in the C program. For example, values of type `Boolean` are represented with *true* and *false*, even though they are represented as `int`s in C. As the watchable is created, the type that should be used in the Watch window is specified. Types that should be used in this way must implement `IMappableType`. Its method `mapVariable` is responsible for computing a type-appropriate representation of a value.

9.2.4 *More Examples*

To illustrate mbeddr's approach to extensible debuggers further, we have implemented the debugging behavior for mbeddr C and most default extensions. Some interesting cases are discussed below.

In many cases it is impossible to know statically which piece of code will be executed when *stepping into* a callable. Consider polymorphic calls on interfaces. The mbeddr components extension provides interfaces with operations, as well as components that `provide` and `use` these interfaces. The component methods that implement interface operations are generated to base-level C functions. The same interface can be implemented by *different* components, each implementation ending up in a *different* C function. A client component only specifies the *interface* it uses, not the component. Hence it is not known statically which C function will be called if an operation is invoked on the interface. However, it is known statically which components implement the interface, so it is known which functions *may* be invoked. A strategy implemented specifically for this case sets breakpoints on the first line *of each of these functions* to make sure the debugger stops in the first line of any of them if the user *steps into* an operation invocation. A similar challenge exists in state machines: as an event is fired into a state machine, it is not known which transition will be triggered. Consequently, breakpoints are set in all transitions (translated to `case` branches in a `switch` statement) of the state machine.

In many cases a single statement on the extension level is mapped to several statements or whole blocks on the base level. *Stepping over* the single extension-level statement must step over the whole block or list of statements in terms of C. An example is the `assert` statement used in test cases. This is mapped to an `if` statement. The debugger has to step over the complete `if` statement, independent of whether the condition in the `if` evaluates to `true` or `false`. Note that this behavior is automatic: the `assert` statement sets a breakpoint on the base-level counterpart of the *next tree-level statement*. It is irrelevant how many lines of C text further down this is.

Extensions may provide custom data types that are mapped to one or more data types or structures in the generated C. The debugger has to reconstruct the representation in terms of the extension from the base level data. For example, the state of a component is represented by a `struct` that has a member for each of the component fields. Component operations are mapped to C functions. In addition to the formal arguments declared for the respective operation, the generated C function also takes this `struct` as an argument. However, to support the polymorphic invocations discussed earlier, the type of this argument is `void*`. Inside the operation, the `void*` is cast down to allow access to the component-specific members. The debugger performs the same downcast to be able to show watchables for all component fields.

9.2.5 *Discussion*

To evaluate the suitability of the solution for mbeddr's purposes, the following list revisits the requirements described earlier.

- *Modularity* The approach discussed in this chapter requires no changes to the base language or its debugger implementation to specify the debugger for an extension. Also, independently developed extensions retain their independence if they contain debugger specifications. In particular, MPS' capability of incrementally including language extensions in a program *without defining a composite language first* is preserved in the face of debugger specifications.

- *Framework Genericity* The extension-dependent aspects of the debugger behavior are extensible. In particular, stepping behavior is factored into strategies, and new strategies can be implemented by a language extension. Also, the representation of watch values can be customized by making the respective type implement `IMappableType` in a suitable way.

- *Simple Debugger Definition* This challenge is solved by the debugger definition DSL. It supports the definition of stepping behavior and watches in a declarative way, without concerning the user with implementation details of the framework or the debugger backend.

- *Limited Overhead* The solution generates no debugger-specific code at all (except the debug symbols added by compiling the C code with debug options). Instead, the debugger relies on trace data to map the extension level to base level and ultimately to text. This is a trade-off: first, the language workbench must be able to provide trace information. Second, the generated C text cannot be modified by a text processor before it is compiled and debugged, since this would invalidate the trace data (the C preprocessor works, since it is handled correctly by the compiler and debugger). The approach has another advantage: the existing transformations do not have to be changed to generate debugger-specific code. This keeps the transformations independent of the debugger.

- *Debugger Backend Independence* The Eclipse CDT Debug Bridge is used to wrap the particular C debugger, so any compatible debugger can be used without changing the infrastructure. The approach requires no changes to the native C debugger itself, but since breakpoints are used for stepping, the debugger must be able to handle a reasonable number of breakpoints. Most C debuggers support this, so this is not a serious limitation. The debugger also has to provide an API for setting and deleting breakpoints, for querying the currently visible symbols and their values, as well as for querying the code location at which the debugger suspended execution.

9.3 IDE SUPPORT

Section 4.10 described various aspects of IDE support provided by MPS and mbeddr. This section discusses the implementation of two of them: customizing Find Usages and Refactorings.

9.3.1 *Customized Find Usages*

In many cases, there are different kinds of references to any given element. For example, for an `Interface` in the mbeddr C components extension, references to that interface can either be sub-interfaces (`ISomething extends IAnother`) or components, which can either *provide* an interface or *require* an interface. When finding references, the user may want to distinguish between these different cases.

MPS provides *Finders* to support such functionality. The left part of Figure 9.8 shows the resulting Find Usages dialog for an `Interface` after two custom finders are implemented in the language: one for components providing the interface, and one for components requiring the interface.

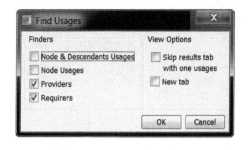

Figure 9.8 **Left:** The Find Usages dialog for `Interfaces`. The two additional Finders in the left box are contributed by the language. **Right:** The result of Find Usages: notice the two additional categories.

To implement custom Finders, MPS provides a DSL. The following code shows the implementation for the finder of interface providers:

```
finder findProviders for concept Interface
  description: Providers

  find(node, scope)->void {
    nlist<> refs = execute NodeUsages ( node , <same scope> );
    foreach r in refs.select(it|it.isInstanceOf(ProvidedPort))
      add result r.parent ;
  }

  getCategory(node)->string {
    "Providers";
  }
```

A name is specified for the finder (`findProviders`) as well as the type to which it applies (i.e., references to which it will find: `Interface` in the example). Next is the implementation of the `find` method. Notice how in the first line of the implementation an existing existing finder, `Node Usages`, is called, which finds *all* references. These are then filtered by whether the referencing element is a `ProvidedPort`, and if so, the parent of the port, i.e. the `Component`, is added to the result. Finally, `getCategory` returns a string that is use to structure the result. The right part of Figure 9.8 shows an example of such a result.

9.3.2 *Refactorings*

A very typical refactoring for a procedural language such as C is to introduce a new local variable. Consider the following code:

```
boolean isAtLimit(int8 v, lim) {
  int8 val = measure(v * FACTOR);
  val = calibrate(val, v * FACTOR);
  return val >= lim;
}
```

The first two lines contain the expression v * FACTOR twice. A nicer version of this code might look like this:

```
boolean isAtLimit(int8 v) {
  int8 product = v * FACTOR;
  int8 val = measure(product);
  val = calibrate(val, product);
  return val >= lim;
}
```

The *Introduce Local Variable* refactoring performs this change. MPS provides a DSL for refactorings, based on which the implementation is about 20 lines of code. The code below is the declaration of the refactoring itself:

```
refactoring introduceLocalVariable ( "Introduce Local Variable" )

keystroke: <ctrl+alt>+<V>
target: node<Expression>
allow multiple: false

isApplicableToNode(node)->boolean {
    node.ancestor<Statement>.isNotNull;
}
```

The code above specifies the refactoring's name (introduceLocalVariable), the label used in the refactoring menu, the keystroke to execute it directly (Ctrl-Alt-V) as well as the target, i.e. the language concept on which the refactoring can be executed. In the example, Expressions should be refactored, but only if these expressions are used in a Statement. An expression cannot be refactored if it is used, for example, as the init expression for a global constant. This is determined by checking whether the Expression has a Statement among its ancestors. Next, a parameter is defined for the refactoring:

```
parameters:
  varName chooser: type: string
                   title: Name of the new Variable

init(refactoringContext)->boolean {
  return ask for varName;
}
```

The parameter varName represents the name of the newly introduced variable. In the refactoring's init block, the user is queried for this parameter. The ask for expression returns false if the user selects Cancel in the dialog that prompts the user for the name. The execution of the refactoring stops in this case. Next is the implementation of the refactoring algorithm itself in the refactor block:

```
node<Expression> targetExpr = refactoringContext.node;
node<Statement> targetStmt = targetExpr.ancestor<Statement>;
int index = targetStmt.index;
```

The algorithm first declares a local variable that represent the expression on which the refactoring is invoked. It is obtained from the `refactoringContext`. The code also defines a variable that captures the `Statement` under which this expression is located. The `index` of this `Statement` is stored. Finally, the code iterates over all `siblings` of the statement in which the expression lives:

```
nlist<Expression> matchingExpressions = new nlist<Expression>;
sequence<node<>> siblings =
    targetStmt.siblings.union(new singleton<node<Statement>>(stmt));
foreach s in siblings {
  if (s.index >= index) {
    foreach e in s.descendants<Expression> {
      if (MatchingUtil.matchNodes(targetExpr, e)) {
        matchingExpressions.add(e);
} } } }
```

The loop above finds all expressions that are structurally similar to the one for which the refactoring is executed (using `MatchingUtil.matchNodes`). The matching expression is remembered if it occurs in a statement that is *after* the one that contains the target expression. The next step is to actually introduce the new local variable:

```
node<LocalVariableDeclaration> lvd =
            new node<LocalVariableDeclaration>();
lvd.name = varName;
lvd.type = targetExpr.type.copy;
lvd.init = targetExpr.copy;
targetStmt.add prev-sibling(lvd);
```

This code creates a new `LocalVariableDeclaration` and sets the `name` to the one obtained earlier from the user, its type is set to a copy of the type calculated by the type system for the target expression, and the variable is initialized with a copy of the target expression itself. This new variable is then added to the list of statements, just *before* the statement that contains the target expression.

One more step is required: all occurrences of the target expression have to be replaced with a reference to the newly introduced local variable. These occurrences have earlier been collected in the `matchingExpressions` collection:

```
foreach e in matchingExpressions {
  node<LocalVarRef> ref = new node<LocalVarRef>();
  ref.var = lvd;
  e.replace with(ref);
}
```

The actual replacement is performed with the `replace with` built-in function. This is very convenient since it avoids manually finding out in which property or collection the expression lives in order to replace it.

Dataflow analysis can be used to detect dead code, null access, unnecessary `if`s (because it can be shown statically that the condition is always true or false) or read-before-write errors. The foundation for dataflow analysis is the *dataflow graph*. This is a data structure that describes the flow of data through a program's code. Consider the following example:

```
int i = 42;
j = i + 1;
someMethod(j);
```

The `42` is "flowing" from the `init` expression in the local variable declaration into the variable `i` and then, after adding `1`, into `j`, and then into `someMethod`. dataflow analysis consists of two tasks: building a dataflow graph for a program, then performing analyses on this dataflow graph to detect problems in the program.

MPS comes with predefined data structures for dataflow graphs, a DSL for defining how the graph is derived from language concepts (and hence, programs) and a set of default analyses that can be integrated into a language. This section looks at all these ingredients. MPS also comes with a framework for developing custom analyses; however, this is beyond the scope of this section.

Building a Dataflow Graph   dataflow is specified in the *Dataflow* aspect of language definitions, which contains dataflow builders (DFBs) for language concepts. These are programs expressed in MPS' dataflow DSL that build the dataflow graph for instances of those concepts in programs. Here is the DFB for `LocalVariableDeclaration`:

```
dataflow builder for LocalVariableDeclaration {
  (node)->void {
    if (node.init != null) {
      code for node.init
      write node = node.init
    } else {
      nop
} } }
```

If the `LocalVariableDecaration` has an `init` expression (it is optional), then the DFB for the `init` expression has to be executed using the `code for` statement. Next is an actual dataflow definition: the `write node = node.init` specifies that write access is performed on the current node. The statement also expresses that whatever value was in the `init` expression is now in the node itself. If there is no `init` expression, the `LocalVariableDeclaration` node still has to be marked as visited by the dataflow builder using the `nop` statement. A subsequent analysis reports all program nodes that have *not* been visited by a DFB as dead code.

The `LocalVariableRef` expression serves as an example of the `read` statement, since it read-accesses the variable it references. Its dataflow is defined

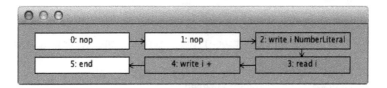

Figure 9.9 An example of a dataflow for a simple C function. The dataflow graph for a program element can be shown by selecting `Language Debug -> Show dataflow Graph` from the element's context menu. This will render the dataflow graph graphically and constitutes a good debugging tool when building custom dataflow graphs and analyses.

as `read node.var`, where `var` is the name of the reference that points to the referenced variable.

An `AssignmentStatement` first executes the DFB for the `rvalue` and then "flows" the `rvalue` into the `lvalue` – the purpose of an assignment:

```
dataflow builder for AssigmentStatement {
  (node)->void {
    code for node.rvalue
    write node.lvalue = node.rvalue
} }
```

The dataflow definition for a `StatementList` simply marks the list as visited and then execute the DFBs for each statement in the list. Figure 9.9 shows the dataflow graph for the simple function below:

```
void trivialFunction() {
  int8 i = 10;
  i = i + 1;
}
```

Analyses   MPS supports a number of dataflow analyses out of the box. These analyses operate only on the dataflow graph, so the same analyses can be used for any language, once the DFBs for that language map programs to dataflow graphs. The following utility class uses the unreachable code analysis:

```
public class DataflowUtil {

  private Program prog;

  public DataflowUtil(node<> root) {
    // build a program object and store it
    prog = DataFlow.buildProgram(root);
  }

  public void checkForUnreachableNodes() {
    // grab all instructions that
```

```
    // are unreachable (predefined functionality)
    sequence<Instruction> all =
      ((sequence<Instruction>) prog.getUnreachableInstructions());

    // remove those that may legally be unreachable
    sequence<Instruction> filtered =
          all.where({~instruction =>
              !(Boolean.TRUE.equals(instruction.
                    getUserObject("mayBeUnreachable")))); });

    // get the program nodes that correspond
    // to the unreachable instructions
    sequence<node<>> unreachableNodes = filtered.
      select({~instr => ((node<>) instr.getSource()); });

    // output errors for each of those unreachable nodes
    foreach n in unreachableNodes {
      error "unreachable code" -> n;
} } }
```

The class builds a `Program` object in the constructor. `Program`s are wrappers around the dataflow graph and provide access to a set of predefined analyses on the graph. One of them is used here in the `checkForUnreachableNodes` method. This method extracts all unreachable nodes from the graph (see comments in the code above) and reports errors for them. To actually run the check, this method is called from a checking rule for C functions:

```
checking rule check_DataFlow forFunction as fct {
  new DataflowUtil(fct.body).checkForUnreachableNodes();
}
```

9.5 VISUALIZATIONS

mbeddr supports visualizations (i.e., read-only diagrams) of various language constructs. Examples include the visualization of component dependencies (Figure 4.2) or of state machines (Figure 4.6).

The visualization infrastructure consists of three ingredients. The first one is PlantUML[8], which is used to render SVG images from textual descriptions. PlantUML itself is a Java application, so the renderer can be called directly from within MPS. Internally it uses Graphviz[9] for some of the diagrams, so Graphviz must be installed on the user's computer.

The second ingredient is a custom SVG viewer based on Batik, Apache's SVG toolkit[10]. The existing Batik SVG renderer component is embedded in an MPS plugin, so the pictures can be displayed directly in MPS. SVG in general, and Batik in particular, support the association of URLs with shapes; when

---

[8] plantuml.sourceforge.net

[9] http://graphviz.org/

[10] http://xmlgraphics.apache.org/batik/

the user clicks on the shape, the URL is "activated". What activation means is determined in Batik by a customizable handler. mbeddr's handler selects the node associated with the shape in the MPS editor. A custom URL scheme encodes the node's unique ID.

The third ingredient are language concepts that contribute visualizations. Their task is simply to create the textual input for PlantUML based on the structure of (part of) a program. Language concepts that contribute visualizations implement the `IVisualizable` interface. This contributes two behavior methods for language concepts to implement:

```
concept behavior IVisualizable {
  public virtual abstract string[] getCategories();
  public virtual abstract VisGraph getVisualization(string cat);
}
```

A visualizable concept can contribute several different visualizations, called *categories*. The `getCategories` method returns an array of strings that represent the currently available categories (the list may depend on the particular program structure). `getVisualization` returns the actual visualization for a given category. The `VisGraph` return type is essentially a wrapper around the textual PlantUML input.

The interface is also connected to an action in MPS that contributes a *Visualize* menu item to the context menu of visualizable program nodes. When selected, the SVG viewer opens, showing the image corresponding to the first category. A drop-down box in the viewer lets the user select other categories.

An Example The transitive dependencies of modules can be visualized as a box-and-line diagram. PlantUML's class diagrams[11] are (mis)used for this purpose. The `Module` concept implements `IVisualizable` in the following way:

```
public string[] getCategories() {
  new string[]{"transitive dependencies"};
}

public VisGraph getVisualization(string category) {
  if ("transitive dependencies".equals(category)) {
    VisGraph g = new VisGraph();
    set<node<Module>> visited = new hashset<node<Module>>;
    renderDependentModules(this, g, visited);
    return g;
  } else return null;
}
```

Since the creation of the diagram specification is done using a recursive algorithm (to handle the *transitive* dependencies), most of the code resides in `renderDependentModules`. This is called initially with the current module, the `Visgraph` that represents the result, and a set `visited` to detect cycles. The implementation of `renderDependentModules` looks as follows:

---

[11] http://plantuml.sourceforge.net/classes.html

```
private void renderDependentModules(node<Module> m, VisGraph g,
                                    set<node<Module>> visited) {
  if (visited.contains(m)) { return; }
  visited.add(m);
  g.add("component " + m.name + " <<module>>");
  g.add("url of " + m.name + " is " + IVisualizable.makeURL(m));
  foreach mi in m.imports.filter<ModuleImport> {
    renderDependentModules(mi.module, g, visited);
    g.add(m.name + ".>" + mi.module.name);
  }
}
```

The method first returns in case a cycle is detected. Otherwise it adds a
component statement to the graph, using the name of the current module and
the «module» stereotype. The next line associates a URL with the shape; it
uses a utility method IVisualizable.makeURL that encodes the unique ID of
the module node. The method then iterates over all ModuleImports of the
current module. It calls renderDependentModules recursively on the imported
module, then adds a dotted line (.>) from the current module to the imported
one.

9.6   LEGACY CODE IMPORTER

Importing textual code into MPS is simple in principle, assuming a parser
for the textual language exists. In this case, this parser can be called directly
from within MPS, and the resulting AST can be mapped to the instances
of corresponding language concepts in the MPS language definition. Such a
mapping transformation can be implemented in Java or any DSL developed in
MPS specifically for this purpose. MPS itself uses this approach for importing
exiting Java code.

As a consequence of the preprocessor, importing C code is harder; the problem is described in the context of refactoring C code by Garrido & Johnson
[2002]. There are two alternatives. The first alternative imports C code after
the preprocessor has run. The resulting C program can be parsed easily, and
the approach discussed above can be used. However, as a consequence, any
abstractions built with preprocessor directives such as constants or macros are
lost – the remaining code is much harder to read and may not really resemble
the original textual source. Also, running the preprocessor resolves all #ifdef
directives, removing any product line variability expressed this way. So, to
import C code in a meaningful way, #ifdef variability has to be lifted into
feature models and presence conditions based on mbeddr's native support
for expressing product line variability. In addition, all other preprocessor abstractions must be kept intact. Parsing C code while taking into account the
preprocessor in general and #ifdef variability in particular is a hard problem
that is, for example, discussed by Badros & Notkin [2000]. Providing IDE
support, such as type checking for variable code, is a related challenge that is
implemented as part of TypeChef [Kenner et al., 2010].

244

As part of mbeddr, we had tried to solve this problem ourselves, but we underestimated the complexity of building a robust solution. The effort ultimately failed. We have since decided to rely on an established industry-strength solution for this problem[12]. In particular, we are in the process of integrating with Semantic Designs C frontend[13], which is in turn based on the work described by Baxter & Mehlich [2001]. This tool works with a C grammar that includes preprocessor statements and outputs a completely resolved and typed AST that includes preprocessor statements. Semantic Designs can handle ca. 95% of preprocessor statements correctly; they are working on the remaining 5%. In terms of integration into mbeddr, we have to write code that transforms an XML representation of the C AST as produced by Semantic Designs' tool into an mbeddr AST, factoring `#ifdefs` into presence conditions and feature models. The integration of this tool is still in progress, so this topic is not discussed any further in this thesis.

Summary — Generic Tools, Specific Languages *emphasizes the idea of using* language engineering *to build domain-specific tools instead of classical* tool engineering. *While this chapter shows that some tool extensions are necessary, most of them are either directly related to languages (debuggers, dataflow, legacy code importer) or are generic in the sense that they can be used for arbitrary languages (such as the visualizations). To conclude the thesis, the next chapter evaluates* Generic Tools, Specific Languages *from the language engineering perspective.*

---

[12] Solving this problem is not part of the contribution of mbeddr and this thesis, so we think this is a reasonable approach.

[13] http://semanticdesigns.com/Products/FrontEnds/CFrontEnd.html?Home=CTools

Validation II: The Language Engineer's Perspective

Abstract — Generic Tools, Specific Languages *exploits language engineering and language workbenches over tool construction. To evaluate the feasibility of this approach, this chapter evaluates the process of* building *mbeddr based on language engineering with MPS. In particular, it discusses domain-specific extensibility, modularity and projectional editing, MPS' scalability, the effort to build mbeddr, as well as MPS' learning curve. The chapter concludes that* Generic Tools, Specific Languages *is a productive approach for developing domain-specific tools and that MPS is a good fit for the purpose, despite a few limitations.*

10

10.1 DOMAIN-SPECIFIC EXTENSIBILITY

A cornerstone of *Generic Tools, Specific Languages* and mbeddr is the ability to extend languages in meaningful ways, while retaining tight syntactic and semantic integration with C and existing extensions. Of course, the mbeddr default extensions, discussed in Chapter 4, are the most significant example: they constitute domain-specific extensions of C. The evaluation in Chapter 5 shows that the resulting tool seems to be useful for embedded software development.

The remainder of this section evaluates whether and how mbeddr and its extensions can be extended as part of application development projects. Some of the example systems introduced in Section 5.1 are used for the evaluation.

Smartmeter: The Smartmeter project was staffed partially by members of the mbeddr team. Consequently, the threshold for building language extensions was particularly low, and a number of extensions have been built during the project. The target processor has *special-purpose registers*: when a value is written to such a register, a hardware-implemented computation is automatically triggered based on the value supplied by the programmer. The result of the computation is then stored in the register. Running code that works with these registers on the PC for testing purposes leads to two problems: first, the header files that define the addresses of the registers are not valid for the PC's processor. Second, there are no special-purpose registers on the PC, so no automatic computations would be triggered. Smartmeter solves this problem with a language extension that supports the definition of registers as first-class entities and allows read and write access from C code (see code below). The extension also supports specifying an expression that performs the computation. When the code is translated for the real device, the real registers are accessed based on the addresses defined in the processor header files. In the emulated case used in testing, generated `struct`s are used to hold the register data; the expressions are inserted into the code that updates the struct, simulating the hardware-based computation.

```
exported register8 ADC10CTL0 compute as val * 1000
```

```
void calculateAndStore( int8 value ) {
    int8 result = // some calculation with value
    ADC10CTL0 = result; // stores result * 1000 in register
}
```

Many aspects of the Smartmeter system are driven by *interrupts*. To integrate the component-based architecture used in Smartmeter with interrupts, it is necessary to be able to trigger component runnables via an interrupt. To this end, Smartmeter has implemented a language extension that allows the declaration of interrupts. In addition, the extension provides runnable triggers that express that a runnable is triggered by an interrupt. The following example declares two interrupts, and the component runnable `interruptHandler` is declared to be triggered by an interrupt:

```
module Processor {
    exported interrupt USCI_A1
    exported interrupt RTC
}
```

```
exported component RTCImpl {
    void interruptHandler() <- interrupt {
        hw->pRTCPS1CTL &= ~RT1PSIFG;
    }
}
```

Note that this code does not specify *which* interrupt triggers the runnable, because this is done as part of component instantiation (not shown). Instantiation also checks that each interrupt-triggered runnable has at least one interrupt assigned to it. In addition, for testing purposes on the PC, there are language constructs that simulate the occurrence of an interrupt: the test driver simulates the triggering of interrupts based on a test-specified schedule and checks whether the system reacts correctly. ◄

ASIC Testing: In this system, mbeddr's C extensions were not used. Instead, a new DSL was built that describes ASIC test cases. When building this DSL, parts of the existing C language were reused, including expressions and the primitive types, simplifying the development of the DSL. An importer was built to read the test descriptions from the legacy Excel format into instances of the DSL. As a consequence of the stricter specification of the language, several inconsistencies were uncovered in existing test cases. Finally, a generator was developed to generate C code that implements the test cases in a way that can be executed by the target device. Developing the generator was efficient because of the fact that C was already available in MPS. Summing up, the developers report that, [..]

```
#include "implementation.oil"
 CPU ATMEL_AT91SAM7S256 {
  OS LEJOS_OSEK {
    STATUS = EXTENDED;              APPMODE  appmode1 {
    STARTUPHOOK = FALSE;            };
    ERRORHOOK = FALSE;
    SHUTDOWNHOOK = FALSE;           TASK OSEK_Task_Background  {
    PRETASKHOOK = FALSE;             PRIORITY = 1;
    POSTTASKHOOK = FALSE;            SCHEDULE = FULL;
    USEGETSERVICEID = FALSE;         ACTIVATION = 1;
    USEPARAMETERACCESS = FALSE;      STACKSIZE = 512;
    USERESSCHEDULER = FALSE;         AUTOSTART = TRUE
  };                                };
                                   };
```

Figure 10.1 An example OIL file used to configure the Lejos OSEK operating system. OIL files declare the memory model, events, tasks and other OS entities necessary for a given application. Program code reference these declarations. An OSEK-specific generator creates the specific implementation of the operating system based on this configuration.

mbeddr and MPS are a very appropriate tooling for Model Driven Software Development when working in a C [..] environment. [C is] extensively supported by the IDE, not only when writing solutions [..], but also when developing code generators. Using mbeddr C in our code generator prevented us from having any syntax errors in generated code – starting with the first iteration. The idea of custom refactorings was very appealing to us. With mbeddr and MPS one can manipulate a model very easily and [..] with full IDE support. Refactorings are basically written in Java, any Java package can be accessed including file I/O and access to the IDE user interface (e.g., file chooser, message boxes). ◀

Park-o-Matic: The Park-o-Matic system did not significantly extend the mbeddr languages, but provided an additional generator. The Park-o-Matic has to be deployed as an AUTOSAR component. This has two consequences. First, the component's external structure (names, interfaces, ports) must be described in an AUTOSAR-specific XML format, to enable deployment tools to work with the component. This additional generator has been integrated with the mbeddr component generator and is run for all components marked as AUTOSAR. The second consequence is that all invocations of operations on required ports that are marked as AUTOSAR must go through the AUTOSAR-specific middleware, i.e., special API functions have to be called from inside the component. The generator was integrated with the existing components generator. Both of these generator extensions have been built without changes to the existing generators, validating the extensibility in terms of generators. ◀

Lego Mindstorms: The Lego Mindstorms system was an early attempt at validating the extensibility of mbeddr, and consequently, a number of extensions were built. The OSEK operating system has to be configured for each application with regards to the memory model, tasking, scheduling, and memory allocation. These configurations are expressed in OIL (OSEK Implementation Language) files. To be able to define these OIL files, we have implemented the OIL language in MPS. This is rather trivial, since OIL files are essentially nested name-value pairs. An example is shown in Figure 10.1. The language to express OIL files is *not* a C extension, it is a separate, stand-alone (external) DSL. In OSEK, OIL files are text files with a predefined set of possible entries. In the mbeddr extension, the IDE knows about the possible contents and can provide code completion and consistency checking.

A major reason why the OIL file declares tasks and events is that the operating system instance generated from an OIL file then schedules tasks and manages events for the programmer. However, it is of course necessary to provide *implementations* of tasks that specify the behavior of the task when it executes. A new top-level concept for C called `task` is available to serve this purpose:

```
module ... {
  task (SirenTask) {
    if ( siren.isOn() ) {
      siren.playOnce();
    }
    TerminateTask();
  }
}
```

`SirenTask` in the code above is actually a reference to the task node declared in the OIL file of the particular system. This ensures that only implementations for tasks declared in the OIL file are possible. Conversely, the system reports a warning in the OIL file if there is no task implementation for any particular task declaration in the OIL file.

The OSEK API provides various functions for managing events; the code below uses a few of them:

```
task (Shoot) {
  while ( true ) {
    WaitEvent(ShootEvt);
    ClearEvent(ShootEvt);
    if ( ... ) {
      SetEvent(PoliceCarDriver, SignalHit);
    }
  }
  TerminateTask();
}
```

In OSEK, the arguments passed into these API functions are simply integers. In mbeddr, we have built an extension, `EventMaskType`, which directly acts as a reference to the events declared in the OIL file; pressing `Ctrl-Space` shows the available events (`ShootEvent` and `SignalHit` are examples in the code above). This has obvious advantages for program consistency. The code below shows the declaration of these functions:

```
external module kernel resources header: "kernel.h"
                                 header: <osek.h> {
   void TerminateTask();
   void ActivateTask(TaskType task_type);
   void ChainTask(TaskType task_type);
   void ShutdownOS(StatusType status);
   StatusType SignalCounter(CounterType counter);
   StatusType WaitEvent(EventMaskType event);
   StatusType GetEvent(TaskType task, EventMaskType* event);
   StatusType ClearEvent(EventMaskType event);
   StatusType SetEvent(TaskType task, EventMaskType event);
}
```

Note how this external module "wraps" the header files that define the API provided by OSEK. It redefines the functions using the more specific `TaskType` and `EventMaskType`. The reason why this works is that these types, when generated to C, are reduced to the same `int` types used by the original API. This ensures that, while providing better IDE support and error checking in the IDE, the generated code is still compatible with the original API, without any overhead.

Lejos-OSEK comes with its own particular flavor of `make` files for building executables. Also, there are some peculiarities about how binaries are configured. For this reason we have built a new platform (mbeddr's abstraction of the build process) which specifies the OIL file to be used for a given system and specifies the path to the build infrastructure provided by Lejos-OSEK. Also, a new generator for `BuildConfigurations` is provided which translates `BuildConfigurations` into valid Lejos-OSEK `make` files. ◀

Pacemaker: The core behavior of the pacemaker is specified as a state machine. To verify this state machine and to prove correctness of the code, two additional C extensions have been developed. One supports the specification of nondeterministic environments for the state machine (simulating the human heart), and another one allows the specification of temporal properties (expressing the correctness conditions for the state machine in the face of its nondeterministic environment).

This is an example of domain-specific extension of the existing verification. The verification of the state machine relies on the existing integration of CBMC. Since CBMC works on (instrumented) C code, new verifications can be integrated into mbeddr with the following three ingredients. First, domain-specific language extensions are developed that allow users to express the system, the verification conditions, and if necessary, its environment. Second, these extensions are then generated to CBMC-compatible C code (for example, calling specially-named pseudo functions to obtain nondeterministic values). Third, the results have to be lifted back and shown to the application developer in terms of the domain-specific extensions. The pacemaker verification used this approach. ◄

Summing up, the various project-specific extensions clearly demonstrate the feasibility of defining custom extensions to mbeddr. The effort required to define these extensions was limited and they clearly improved readability and IDE support for the language (some of the efforts are discussed in Section 10.4).

10.2 MODULARITY & PROJECTIONAL EDITING

Language modularity, extension and composition is central to mbeddr in two ways. First it enables third parties to create C extensions without having to agree about how to invasively change C. Second, modular language extension also helps to scale the system from the perspective of the language engineer. At this point, mbeddr consists of 51 separate languages with clear dependencies on each other. Putting all the language concepts from these languages into one single language would quickly become unmaintainable.

The integration of formal verification, a problem typically associated with *tool* extension and integration, has been reduced mostly to a *language* integration problem. We implemented the NuSMV and Yices input languages in MPS, reusing part of the C expression language. Then we implemented a transformation from domain-specific abstractions to these input languages. Only the execution of the verification tool, the lifting of the verification results and their representation in the UI remained as *tool* integration problems. This approach substantially reduced the effort for the integration.

While users can make use of the existing extensions that come with mbeddr (see the next subsection), they are encouraged to build their own modular extensions specific to their system context, as discussed in the previous section. Based on these extensions, preliminary conclusions can be drawn regarding the feasibility of incremental, modular language extension.

Modularity   Building an extension should not require changes to the base language. This, in turn, requires that the base language is built with extension in mind to some degree, since only entities of a certain granularity can be extended or overwritten. This is similar to object-oriented programming where one cannot override lines 10 to 12 in a 20-line method. In addition to being useful in their own right, the implementation of the default extensions also served to verify that the C base language is extensible; the extensions for Smartmeter demonstrate this further. The registers extension (Section 10.1) requires new top-level module contents (the register definitions themselves), new expressions (for reading and writing into the registers), and embedding expressions into new contexts (the code that simulates the hardware computation when registers are written). All these have been built without changing

C. Similarly, the interrupt-based runnable triggers have been hooked into the generic trigger facility that is part of the components language. The latter is an example of where a base language (the components extension in this case) has been built with extensibility in mind: an abstract concept `AbstractTrigger` had been defined, which has been extended to support interrupts. Even the units extension, which provides new types, new literals, overloaded typing rules for operators and some adapted code generators. has been developed in a modular way, without changing the C base language[1].

Special care has to be taken in the definition of type system rules. Regular typing rules cannot be overridden in a sublanguage. Only the overloaded operations container can be overloaded (as their name suggests) in a sublanguage. As a consequence it requires some thought when designing a language to make the type system extensible in meaningful ways.

To orchestrate the generation of the final C code, language designers specify a partial ordering among generators using priorities. It is not easily possible to "override" an existing generator, but generators can run *before* or *after* existing ones. Generator extension is not possible directly. This sometimes requires placeholders (see Section 7.4.2), put in by earlier generators to be reduced by later ones. Obviously this requires pre-planning on the part of the developer of the generator that adds the placeholder (or later invasive redesign).

Reuse   Once a language is designed in a reasonable way (as discussed in the previous item), the language (or parts of it) should be reusable in contexts that had not been specifically anticipated in advance. Embedding state machines into components (discussed in Section 8.3) is an example. The C expression language is reused inside the guard conditions in a state machine's transitions; constraints prevent the use of those C expression that are not allowed inside transitions (for example, references to global variables). Decision tables are also used in components. The Smartmeter system contains more examples: expressions have been embedded in the register definition for simulating the hardware behavior, and types with measurement units have been used in decision tables. Again, no change to the existing languages has been necessary.

Combination   Ideally, independently developed extensions should not interact in unexpected ways (extension composition, Section 7.4.7). We have not seen such interactions so far, in the default extensions or in Smartmeter. While there is no automatic way to detect such interactions or declare incompatibility between languages or extensions, the following steps can be taken to minimize the risk of unexpected interactions. Names of generated C elements (variables, functions) should be qualified to make sure that no name clashes occur. Also, an extension should avoid making specific assumptions about or changing the environment in which it is used. For example, it is

---

[1]   During the implementation of the default extensions we found a few bugs in the C base language that prevented modular extension. These were not conceptual problems, but real bugs. They have been fixed, so C can now be extended meaningfully in a modular way.

a bad idea for a new `Statement` to change the return type of the containing function during transformation, because two such badly designed statements could not be used together in a single function; they may require *different* return types for that function. Finally, in traditional parser-based systems, there may be syntactic interactions between independently developed extensions. As discussed at length, this *never* happens in MPS.

In terms of concrete syntax, combination of independently developed language extensions in one program can never lead to ambiguities from the perspective of the tool. Potential ambiguities are resolved by the user as he enters the program (discussed at the end of Section 7.4.7) – once entered, a program is always unambiguous. However, extension combination may lead to syntactic ambiguities *for the developer* as he reads the code, because different language concepts may use the same syntax. Since MPS 3.0 it has been possible to define several editors for the same language concept, and override editors for existing concept from a new language. This could allow the concrete syntax ambiguity to be solved by changing the notation (or color or font) of existing concepts if they are used together with a particular other language. Such a new concrete syntax would be defined in the respective adapter language.

Projectional editing as implemented in MPS is a suitable foundation for implementing *Generic Tools, Specific Languages*. As mentioned above, mbeddr currently consists of 51 language modules integrated in terms of syntax, type system, semantics and IDE. Modularization, reuse and combination largely works in the way it was expected to work.

As discussed in Section 10.4 below, the effort of building such a system is acceptable. Based on the literature research performed as part of this thesis, and based on my industry experience, a modular language system of comparable size and complexity has not been built before with other tools; in particular, not with parser-based systems. This leads to the conclusion that projectional editing has advantages in this space.

Projectional editing also has advantages in terms of notational freedom. mbeddr exploits this to the advantage of the end users in the following ways:

- Tables are used in several places, among them in decision tables (Section 4.5) and in state machines (Section 4.6).

- Optional projection, the ability to optionally not show contents even though they are in the program tree, is used for requirements traces (Section 4.8) and product line variability (Section 4.9).

- Semi-structured content, where unstructured prose text is mixed with program elements, is used in requirements (Section 4.8) as well as in comments and the documentation language (Section 4.7).

Projectional editing is the enabler for these notations – they cannot be provided by parser-based systems. While we have not performed a systematic usability study to uncover whether these notations lead to productivity advantages, the feedback we received from our users was positive. The user survey already mentioned in Chapter 5 indicates (in Figure 10.2) that users

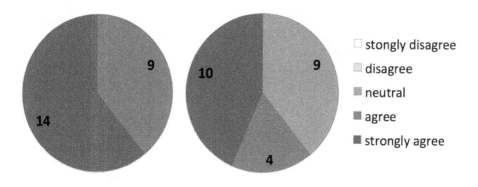

Figure 10.2 These diagrams show the degree to which users agree with the statement that they benefit from modular languages (left) and flexible, non-textual notations (right). None of the users disagreed or disagreed strongly.

benefit from language modularity and the flexible notations afforded by projectional editing.

10.3 TOOL SCALABILITY

The scalability of MPS as a language workbench can be measured in different
ways, including its ability to manage the complexity associated with large or
many languages, the learning curve, working in teams and in terms of supported language sizes and tool performance. This section looks at language
size and tool performance. The others are discussed below.

Typically, lines of code (LOC) are used to describe the size of a program.
In a projectional editor like MPS, a "line" is not necessarily meaningful. However, it is feasible to estimate the equivalent LOC number by counting the
occurrences of certain language definition ingredients and associating a LOC
factor with them. For example, the statements that are used in the imperative
parts of a language definition (for example, in scopes or type system rules)
have a LOC factor of 1.2, since many statements embed higher-order functions and would span more than one line. 1.2 turned out to be a reasonable
average. Another example for a LOC factor is an intention: an intention declares the concept it applies to, a label and an applicability condition. These
are one line each. It also contains a number of statements which are counted
separately, as statements. Hence, the LOC factor for intentions is 3. A similar argument holds for constraints or reference scopes. As a final example,
consider editor cells. An editor definition contains a large number of cells,
and we found that on average, 4 occur per "line" of editor definition, leading
to a LOC factor of 0.25. The third column of the table in Table 10.1 shows
the factors for all kinds of ingredients involved in language definition. While
this approach is an approximation, we have made several manual checks and
found that it is accurate enough to get a feel for the size of various language
implementations.

Table 10.1 shows the result of the LOC count for the mbeddr core, i.e. C itself plus unit test support, decision tables and build/make integration. According to the metric discussed above, the core comprises about 8,640 lines of code. This includes all aspects of language definition (including syntax, type system, to-text-generators) as well as the IDE (code completion, syntax highlighting, quick fixes). Using the same metric, the components extension (interfaces, components, pre- and post-conditions, support for mock components and a generator back to plain C) is ca. 3,000 LOC. The state machines extension is ca. 1,000 LOC. These numbers are an indication that MPS supports very concise definition of languages, an observation that is also confirmed by the comparison of language implementation sizes by Erdweg et al. [2013]. While we have not implemented C with other language workbenches, some of the authors have experience with other tools. For example, implementing C and its IDE with Xtext would require significantly more code, since many language aspects are not supported first class (for example, type systems), or must be implemented using more verbose Java code that relies on Xtext APIs.

Element	Count	LOC Factor	LOC Equivalent
Language concepts	260	3.00	780
Property declarations	47	1.00	47
Link declarations	156	1.00	156
Editor cells	841	0.25	210
Reference constraints	21	2.00	42
Property constraints	26	2.00	52
Behavior methods	299	1.00	299
Typesystem rules	148	1.00	148
Generation rules	57	10.00	570
Statements	4,919	1.20	5,903
Intentions	47	3.00	141
Text generators	103	2.00	206
Total approximate LOC:			8,640

Table 10.1 Number of instances of various language definition elements in the mbeddr core; a factor is used to translate them into equivalent lines of code.

To be able to deal with a large set of evolving languages, it is crucial that building and testing be automated. We use the Teamcity[2] integration server for this. This automatically builds MPS plugins from all mbeddr languages and also automatically runs the tests. We have two kinds of test cases (details of how these work in MPS can be found in Chapter 14 of Voelter et al. [2013]):

- Executable test cases test the execution semantics of the languages. This is done by expressing test cases in the mbeddr language, then generating C code that is then executed.

---

[2] http://www.jetbrains.com/teamcity/

- Type system tests verify that constraints, scopes and type system rules work correctly.

Both kinds of test cases have proved essential. It is impossible to keep a large set of languages stable unless automated testing is used.

10.4 EFFORT

The core C implementation was developed in ca. four person-months, divided between three people, resulting in roughly 2,200 LOC per person month. Extrapolated to a year, this would be 26,400 LOC per person. According to McConnell[3], in a project of up to 10,000 LOC, a developer can typically write between 2,000 and 25,000 LOC per year, so the mbeddr implementation is just slightly above the typical range. The state machines extension (including the generator and the integration with the NuSMV model checker) and components extension (including a generator to C with polymorphic and static wiring options, testing support, pre- and post conditions and protocol state machines) were both implemented in about a month. The unit testing extension and the support for decision tables were implemented in a few days.

The effort for incremental, project-specific extensions is also interesting. The registers and interrupt extensions for the Smartmeter project were built in 3 hours each (plus some bug fixing when they were first used). The custom verifications for the Pacemaker were built and integrated in ca. 2 days. In the context of a development project which, like Smartmeter, is planned to run a few person-years, these efforts can easily be absorbed. Furthermore they lead to benefits in terms of the improved safety and testability, as shown in Section 5.

10.5 MPS LEARNING CURVE

MPS is a comprehensive environment for building and composing languages. In addition to defining the structure, syntax and an IDE, it also supports advanced features such as type systems, refactorings and debuggers. Consequently, the learning curve for the language developer (not the application developer) is significant. Our experience with several novice MPS language developers is that it takes around four weeks of full-time training and practice to become a decent MPS language developer, and months to become really proficient. With improved documentation and some cleanup of MPS itself, this effort may be reduced, but it is still a significant investment. Note that these numbers apply to people who are already experienced software developers and already have at least a basic understanding of languages, modeling or meta programming.

This effort may seem high, but it has to be put into perspective: once a developer has mastered the learning curve, MPS scales well in the sense that

---

[3] http://codinghorror.com/blog/2006/07/diseconomies-of-scale-and-lines-of-code.html

increasingly large and complex languages are *not* overly more complex to build. This is in sharp contrast to our experiences with some other, parser-based language workbenches, where, with increasing language complexity, the accidental complexity of the language implementation increases significantly. Also, it is well known that becoming proficient in a programming language can take months to years. MPS is essentially a set of languages to build languages – so it is not a surprise that the effort to learn the system is of the same magnitude.

10.6 LIMITATIONS OF MPS

Even though MPS, with its projectional editor is fit for purpose for *Generic Tools, Specific Languages* and mbeddr, there are still a number of problems MPS has to address in the future. These are discussed in this section.

Editor Usability   MPS' approaches to editor usability was discussed in Section 6.2.1, and Section 5.3.2 reported on the experience of application developers with this editor. Generally, the editor works for users after getting used to it for a few days. However, there are still a number of remaining issues, including the following:

- The TAB order cannot be explicitly defined by the language engineer. For notations other than text, such as tables or mathematical symbols, this makes editing unnecessarily hard.

- There are still a number of cases, especially in the DSLs used for defining languages, in which the cursor jumps to random places after editing actions, requiring the user to manually go back to the current editing location. This is annoying and confusing.

- References to symbols are not always automatically rebound if the referenced symbol's identity is changed. A reference contains name information about the target, so that, if the target's ID changes, for example, because the element is deleted and recreated, the reference can be rebound based on the name. However, this does not work in some cases, requiring the user to press `Ctrl-Space` + `Enter` for all references broken in this way.

- If different aspects of language definition override the text or background color of a program node in different ways, it is not clear which one wins, and the color changes randomly.

All of these issues have been reported to the MPS team and will be solved in the near future.

Cross-Model Generation   MPS stores data in models. Each model is essentially an XML file that contains program nodes. Models can import each other, making (some) nodes from the imported model visible to the importing model. Large systems, such as the Smartmeter, are spread out over many models. This means that, when code is generated, the to-be-generated AST may span several models – references cross the model boundary. As a consequence of an architectural problem in the MPS generator, generating code from ASTs that cross multiple models does not work. As a workaround, mbeddr automatically imports all the program nodes from referenced models into the model for which the code generator is invoked. While this works, it is not efficient, and it leads to the regeneration of C files that have already been generated from other model files. Rearchitecting the generator and fixing this problem is scheduled for 2014.

Type System Tests   The support for testing constraints, scopes and type system rules is very nice in principle: developers write example programs that contain errors, marking program nodes that are expected to have errors with special annotations. However, executing such tests takes too long – in the background, a new instance of MPS is started, so it takes ca. one minute before the first test is even run. Also, the way failed assertions are reported to the developer is flawed, and it is sometimes hard to work out which assertion has actually failed.

Language Evolution   Language evolution refers to the problem of what to do with existing models when the underlying language changes. Section 6.2.2 explains how, by using a disciplined approach to language evolution as well as MPS mechanisms such as quick fixes and migration scripts, this challenge has been addressed in mbeddr. However, more direct support by MPS would be useful: languages should be versioned, programs should declare to which version of a language they comply, and migration of "old" programs should be automated, as far as possible. This is currently not supported, but addressing this problem is on the MPS roadmap.

A related problem occurs with language composition. Composing languages leads to coupling. In the case of referencing and extension the coupling is direct, in the case of reuse and embedding the coupling is indirect via the adapter language. As a consequence of a change of the referenced/base/context/host language, the referencing/extending/reused/embedded language may have to change as well. With the planned language versioning support, this problem should be simplified; however, some process discipline will always have to be established in which dependent languages are migrated to new versions of a changed language they depend on.

Graphical Editors   The ability to work with arbitrary notations under the same architectural framework is a clear advantage of projectional editors. At the time of writing, MPS supports textual notations, tables, semi-structured prose as well as symbols – and all of these are used by mbeddr and have been discussed throughout this thesis. Graphical editors are not yet available. However, as of early 2014, a prototype framework for graphical editors in MPS has become available, and support for box-and-line diagrams will become available in 2014. State machines diagrams, as well as a graphical notation for components and connectors, will be added to mbeddr in 2014 as well.

Summary *— This chapter evaluates mbeddr from the perspective of language engineering. By looking at extensibility, modularity, projectional editing, scalability, effort spent and the learning curve for MPS, this chapter also implicitly evaluates the* Generic Tools, Specific Languages *approach itself. The next chapter provides an overall conclusion of the thesis.*

Conclusion

Abstract — *While not every possible aspect of mbeddr and* Generic Tools, Specific Languages *has been researched as part of this thesis, mbeddr seems to be a useful tool, and* Generic Tools, Specific Languages *in general seems to be a useful approach for tool development. This is reinforced by the fact that mbeddr has been chosen by a major vendor as the basis of the forthcoming controls engineering tool. I conclude the thesis with a general outlook on the role of languages and language engineering in software development and areas outside of embedded software in which* Generic Tools, Specific Languages *is starting to get applied: requirements engineering and business applications.*

11

11.1 *GENERIC TOOLS, SPECIFIC LANGUAGES* REVISITED

In the introduction to this thesis, *Generic Tools, Specific Languages* was defined in the following way:

> *Generic Tools, Specific Languages* is an approach for developing tools and applications in a way that supports easier and more meaningful adaptation to specific domains. To achieve this goal, *Generic Tools, Specific Languages* generalizes programming language IDEs to domains traditionally not addressed by languages and IDEs. At its core, *Generic Tools, Specific Languages* represents applications as documents/programs/models expressed with suitable languages. Application functionality is provided through an IDE that is aware of the languages and their semantics. The IDE provides editing support, and also directly integrates domain-specific analyses and execution services. Applications and their languages can be adapted to increasingly specific domains using language engineering; this includes developing incremental extensions to existing languages or creating additional, tightly integrated languages. Language workbenches act as the foundation on which such applications are built.

The core of this thesis is the demonstration and evaluation of *Generic Tools, Specific Languages* for the example domain of embedded software development based on the mbeddr tool. Part II of the thesis demonstrates mbeddr and discusses the degree to which it is useful to application developers. Part III explains how language engineering with the MPS language workbench is used to implement mbeddr. The evaluation chapters (5 and 10) draw an overall positive picture regarding the usefulness of mbeddr for application developers, and regarding *Generic Tools, Specific Languages* as an approach to building domain-specific development tools.

This positive picture is reinforced by the ACCEnT project. mbeddr has been selected as the basis for the ACCEnT controls and embedded engineering tool by Siemens PL (LMS). As part of ACCEnT, mbeddr is being extended with dataflow blocks for controls development, data dictionaries that describe names, types, units, values and constraints of important data items, cross-cutting support for tying managed names to program elements, constant groups for managing sets of constants in a PLE-aware way, refactoring support from plain C to dataflow blocks and integration of dataflow models with mbeddr's components, among other things. The extensions for ACCEnT have been added to mbeddr without invasive changes to mbeddr and its languages, with the exception of introducing a few abstract base concepts in mbeddr to serve as hooks.

While ACCEnT will be a commercial tool that builds on mbeddr, mbeddr itself remains an open source platform. It continues to be used in several projects, the smart meter mentioned earlier being the biggest one. In early 2014 mbeddr has been contributed to the Eclipse foundation as part of the technology project[1].

11.2 OPEN ISSUES AND FUTURE WORK

Some aspects of *Generic Tools, Specific Languages* and mbeddr were not researched in the context of this thesis and/or the LW-ES research project. This section briefly looks at some of these.

Additional Abstractions   There are several relatively obvious extensions of C that have not been built, mainly because we didn't have the resources. The first one is more specific numeric types; `float` and `double` types are generally avoided in embedded software. Instead, a numeric type should be able to specify its value range and its precision, and should be mapped to an appropriately-sized integer type. The type system and the operators have to be extended correspondingly. The second area is concurrency. Language abstractions for shared memory and locking as well as for message passing should be added. Languages for specifying tasks and their schedules would be useful as well. This area is also amenable to verification. For example, in a message passing system, verification could be used to show that the sender does not access a message data structure after it has been sent. In this case, copying of the data (to avoid shared access to the message) can be avoided, combining message passing semantics with shared memory performance. This approach is similar to what has been done in the Microsoft Singularity operating system [Hunt & Larus, 2007], but, in line with mbeddr's philosophy, the verification could be simplified by suitable language extensions and/or restrictions.

Performance and Overhead   Abstraction and subsequent automatic generation typically involves an overhead in terms of runtime performance, memory

---

[1] http://www.eclipse.org/proposals/technology.mbeddr/

consumption or the size of the binary. Whether this is relevant depends on the domain in which *Generic Tools, Specific Languages* is applied. It is certainly relevant in the domain of embedded software. Section 5.2.1 discusses performance and overhead for mbeddr. However, this discussion is based on selective evidence from a few systems built with mbeddr; a systematic study has not been performed. To make mbeddr viable for real-world use, prospective users have to clearly understand the consequences for performance and overhead of the different extensions. In the future, we are planning to conduct a more systematic study on this topic. In addition, there are ideas of integrating performance prediction and runtime monitoring facilities into mbeddr, to at least make the trade-off transparent to users.

Maintenance   The long-term maintainability of applications written with mbeddr as well as the long-term evolution of mbeddr itself were not studied. In general, decoupling the description of application behavior from the generated implementation through DSLs and generation has the advantage that both of them can be changed independently: new language constructs can be added (through extension or evolution), which generate to the same target platform. Similarly, by exchanging or evolving the generator, new target platforms can be supported for the same language abstractions. However, in practice, the two dimensions are often not completely independent; assumptions on the target platform may unconsciously find their way into the DSLs, or performance considerations may limit the degree to which abstractions can be used sensibly. In addition, the DSL(s) and IDE itself must be maintained, and because of the fact that a good DSL incorporates knowledge about its domain, language changes may be necessary as the domain changes. This requires language engineering experience. An organization must keep language engineering experience available, in addition to the expertise in the domain. This can be a challenge in some organizations. Van Deursen and Klint discuss the question of maintenance of DSLs based on a DSL in the insurance domain [Van Deursen & Klint, 1998]. They conclude that,

> DSLs are no panacea for solving all software engineering problems, but a DSL designed for a well-chosen domain and implemented with adequate tools may drastically reduce the costs for building new applications as well as for maintaining existing ones.

However, the authors also warn that

> [..] an application domain may not be sufficiently understood to warrant the design of a DSL for it or adequate technology may not be available to support the design and implementation of the DSL.

The first concern has to be evaluated for each domain separately, but the ability to incrementally extend languages may help: the DSL can initially define abstractions only for those aspects of the domain that are understood, and then grow over time as the understanding of the domain involves. The concern about adequate technology has certainly been addressed to some extent in the fifteen years since the paper was written. MPS has proven to be a capable language engineering platform for the purposes of *Generic Tools, Specific Languages*.

Usability and User Acceptance   We clearly perceive initial prejudice, irritation and rejection towards projectional editing by many people who are asked to use MPS. However, as illustrated by our preliminary experience with our users' acceptance of projectional editing and mbeddr discussed in Section 5.3.2, the opinion becomes much more positive after a few days. We also perceive a difference between different user groups. Developers who currently use textual IDEs (such as embedded software developers) are much more skeptical than users who currently use tools like Word or Excel (prospective users of business applications developed with MPS; see Section 11.3). To better understand the challenges of projectional editing, we are currently conducting a more systematic study (together with Janet Siegmund and Thorsten Berger).

11.3   BEYOND EMBEDDED SOFTWARE

The history of programming is shaped by the abstractions available to developers when building systems. The better these abstractions reflect the domain for which the developer writes code, the easier a developer's job is, and the more productive he becomes. The abstractions are the tools (in the sense of hammer or wrench, not in the sense of IDE) we use to build our products: the better the tool, the more sophisticated the product, and the more efficient its development.

Abstractions come in various forms, from functions over classes to libraries and frameworks. However, the cleanest way to make abstractions available to developers is through a suitable language. A language is a set of abstractions and consistency constraints, plus nice syntax and IDE support. Well-designed languages let us compose new abstractions from those supplied by the language. Language engineering now lets us evolve the language itself by defining extensions or by combining extensions with each other. And as a community, we bootstrap ourselves by defining languages and IDEs that help us build languages: the language workbenches.

As this thesis shows, projectional editors are a significant step forward for language workbenches. They support essentially unconstrained language extension and composition (at least from a structural and syntactic perspective). But more importantly, they support diverse syntactic forms in an integrated way. In this thesis I have focused on text and tables. However, as I write this conclusion in March of 2014, an early version of a fully integrated graphical editor is available in an MPS early access preview. We are in the process of integrating it into mbeddr for instantiating and connecting components, and into ACCEnT for data flow editing. In addition, the mbeddr and MPS teams are working on mathematical notations. An early version is shown in Figure 11.2, and much more elegant looking formulas are currently being implemented.

MPS itself is planned to evolve in 2014 in significant ways. The graphical editor and the mathematical notations will be added. A way to strip MPS down to a much simpler UI to not confuse end users is being developed. And a number of usability enhancements are scheduled for the editor.

Also, language engineering and language workbenches are an active research area. I am particularly interested in seeing progress in the formalisms and languages used for language definition. For example, Eelco Visser's team is working on declarative rules for name binding [Konat et al., 2013] and for type system definition. The mbeddr and MPS teams are looking into more closely integrating the specification of generators and debuggers and at more grammar-like specification of the concrete syntax of language concepts in order to automatically derive parsers for legacy code import (at least for languages that do not have preprocessors).

In the long term, I see the importance of languages and language engineering grow significantly because it will allow new groups stakeholders to directly contribute to software development. Today, many important stakeholders enter their knowledge into Word or Excel documents in a way that is only semi-structured and is very hard to check for consistency and completeness. Developers have to understand these descriptions and then manually encode them in programming language. Tools built according to the *Generic Tools, Specific Languages* approach, can do much better, by using language workbench technology to create structured, checkable languages that retain much of the friendly syntax people know from today's Office products. Specifically, I see two domains in which this approach makes sense: requirements engineering and business applications. We currently work on both of these, and I want to discuss them as the conclusion of the thesis.

Requirements Engineering   As discussed in Section 4.8, mbeddr comes with a language for requirements engineering. While this language is a part of mbeddr, the requirements management solution is sufficiently different from domain-specific extensions of C that it can be seen as a validation of *Generic Tools, Specific Languages* in it own right – this time in the domain of requirements engineering. For example, during the development of ACCEnT, the mbeddr requirements language has been used by non-programmers to collect the requirements for ACCEnT. The language was extended in various ways:

- Various requirements properties such as `state` (`new`, `accepted`, `tbd`) and `priority` were added.

- A way to associate work packages with requirements was defined. A work package contains a target milestone, a responsible party and an effort estimate, as well as a short description.

- The starting point for the requirements elaboration process was a set of scenarios, essentially lists of activities users will perform with the

```
Assessment: EffortsOfWorkPackages
query:      workpackages for scope <none> responsible <none> status any prio >= <none>
sorted:     true
must be ok: false   hide ok ones: false
```

FlightJudgementRules

▌ FasterThan100.impl (1)	24	○
▌ FasterThan200.impl (1)	32	○
▌ InitialNoPoints.inital (1)	8	○
▌ PointsFactor.prototype (1)	24	○
▌ PointsForTakeoff.impl1 (1)	80	○
▌ PointsForTakeoff.impl2 (1)	40	○

`total 6, new 1, ok 0`

Figure 11.1 An assessment that shows an overview of the efforts spent for work packages associated with requirements. The number is the estimated effort for the work package. The progress bar shows the degree of completion, and the color highlights the effort spent relative to the estimated effort: green = finished with estimated or less effort, blue = in progress, percentage of effort spent is less than percentage finished, yellow = in progress, percentage of effort spent is more than percentage finished, red = effort spent more than estimated. Note how the projectional editor is used to render graphical progress bars in the editor of an assessment.

tool. These scenarios were given to the mbeddr team as a text file. An MPS language was developed to capture these scenarios. The language also supported tracing to the requirements as a means of expressing the fact that the requirements cover a particular scenario. Coverage analysis helped us make sure that the requirements cover all scenarios.

- Various assessments were developed to gain an overview of the requirements. Examples include: which requirements are still in status *tbd*, what is the total effort for a given party and milestone, which requirements have no work packages associated with them, which scenario steps have no requirements associated with them.

- As the implementation of the system proceeds based on the requirements, actual effort is associated with the work packages. Assessments provide an overview of the degree of completion and actual effort. See Figure 11.1 for an example.

We received extremely positive feedback for this approach to requirements engineering from our non-programmer users. They said several times that this was the most productive tool for requirements engineering they ever worked with. They suggested it be used in another project immediately.

The ability to integrate structured and formal parts into prose requirements also makes this tool a great basis for the kinds of highly structured requirements found in safety-critical systems. Mathematical expressions can be embedded directly, expression and calculations can be type checked and/or tested with test cases directly in the IDE, and various tabular formalisms for

266

$$anui = \begin{cases} \text{CATV equals D1} & \left(\displaystyle\sum_{i=1}^{k} \left[\frac{anui * 6}{prs} + prd * \left(\frac{i}{3} + 12 \right) \right] + 42 \right) * arb \\\\ \text{CATV equals D2} & \displaystyle\sum_{i=1}^{arb} \left[INFWP\ [\ i\ ] + local \right] \\\\ \text{<<condition>>} & \displaystyle\sum_{i=1}^{12} \left[cal\ [\ 1\ ] + local \right] \end{cases}$$

<<Rule>>

Figure 11.2 This is an example of something akin to a `switch` statement. Depending on the condition in the second column, the value calculated by the mathematical expression in the third colum is assigned to the variable in the first column. Using some graphical elements, placeholders (such as «condition» and «Rule») and mathematical notations helped with the acceptance of the language by end users.

behavioral specifications[2] can be directly integrated into requirements documents, and cross-linked from prose text with embeddable words. We will explore this direction in the future.

Business Applications *Generic Tools, Specific Languages* is also applied in the field of business applications. MPS is currently used to develop product configuration systems in the financial domain, an area that has seen productive use of DSLs for a long time, as illustrated, for example, by the Risla language discussed by Van Deursen & Klint [1998] or the Intentional's Pension Workbench discussed earlier[3]. While I am not able to disclose more information about the specific project, it makes use of some of the same features as mbeddr, in particular varied but integrated notations and modular extension. The system replaces a traditional form-oriented business application, responding to the inherent "language-ness" of the domain. The following characteristics of *Generic Tools, Specific Languages* and projectional editing seem most important, based on our preliminary experience:

- The ability to use tabular notations that resemble Excel (to a degree) is very useful to meet the expectations of current Excel users. In addition, mathematical notations are very useful for any number of business calculations. Figure 11.2 illustrates the kind of calculations used in the financial system.

- Business users want to play with, test and debug their systems. Similar to test-driven development, business rules are accompanied by unit tests. Ideally these are run directly in the IDE using an interpreter for

---

[2] https://cs.uwaterloo.ca/~jmatlee/talks/parnas01.pdf

[3] http://www.infoq.com/presentations/DSL-Magnus-Christerson-Henk-Kolk

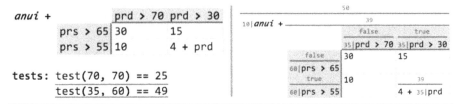

Figure 11.3 **Left, Top:** An expression used in insurance rules using an mbeddr-inspired decision table. **Left, Bottom:** Two test cases; the first argument is `prd`, the second one is `prs`. **Right:** The same expression in debug mode, where intermediate result of every subexpression (computed by an interpreter for a given test case) are annotated over or to the left of the expression.

the business rule language. An integrated debugger is useful as well. Figure 11.3 shows an example debugger for a purely functional expression language that exploits projectional editing by showing the values of all intermediate expressions inline.

- Business users, such as actuaries in the financial domain, do not consider themselves programmers and they do not want to be given "programming tools". So it is important to make the tools look friendly. Figure 11.2 illustrates how projectional editors can blur the boundary between languages and what the users know from their existing applications.

- It turned out to be important that users are never presented with an empty editor in which they can then use code completion to "write programs". It is much better if the editor has some fixed scaffolding, into which users can enter data, a little bit like forms. Projectional editors can render such scaffolding as read-only editor contents.

- For some (novice) users it is useful to make the available editor actions explicit. To achieve this, an alternative projection can be defined that contains buttons for the most important actions. Once users get used to code completion and intentions, they can switch the editor mode to not show buttons, resulting in a much more compact notation.

- The ability to mix formal/structured aspects with prose is also useful. Many business applications integrate a lot of prose for documentation, and the ability to make prose first class, mixed with other languages is very useful.

Bibliography

Amelunxen, C., Klar, F., Königs, A., Rötschke, T., & Schürr, A. (2008). Metamodel-based Tool Integration with Moflon. In *Proceedings of the 30th International Conference on Software Engineering*, ICSE '08, (pp. 807–810)., New York, NY, USA. ACM. (Cited on pages 14 and 23.)

Andalam, S., Roop, P., Girault, A., & Traulsen, C. (2009). PRET-C: A new language for programming precision timed architectures. In *Proocedings of the Workshop on Reconciling Performace with Predictability (RePP), Embedded Systems Week.* (Cited on page 45.)

Arcaini, P., Gargantini, A., & Riccobene, E. (2010). Automatic Review of Abstract State Machines by Meta Property Verification. In *Proceedings of the Second NASA Formal Methods Symposium.* NASA. (Cited on page 50.)

Arnoldus, J., Bijpost, J., & van den Brand, M. (2007). Repleo: a syntax-safe template engine. In *GPCE.* (Cited on page 182.)

Axelsson, E., Claessen, K., Devai, G., Horvath, Z., Keijzer, K., Lyckegard, B., Persson, A., Sheeran, M., Svenningsson, J., & Vajda, A. (2010). Feldspar: A domain specific language for digital signal processing algorithms. In *MEMOCODE 2010.* (Cited on page 45.)

Bachrach, J. & Playford, K. (2001). The Java syntactic extender (JSE). In *OOPSLA '01: Proceedings of the 16th ACM SIGPLAN conference on Object-oriented programming, systems, languages, and applications.* (Cited on page 182.)

Badros, G. J. & Notkin, D. (2000). A framework for preprocessor-aware C source code analyses. *Software Practice and Experience, 30(8),* 907–924. (Cited on page 244.)

Ball, T., Cook, B., Levin, V., & Rajamani, S. K. (2004). SLAM and Static Driver Verifier: Technology Transfer of Formal Methods inside Microsoft. In *IFM'04.* (Cited on page 50.)

Batory, D., Johnson, C., MacDonald, B., & von Heeder, D. (2002). Achieving extensibility through product-lines and domain-specific languages: a case study. *ACM Trans. Softw. Eng. Methodol., 11(2),* 191–214. (Cited on page 54.)

Batory, D. S. (2005). Feature Models, Grammars, and Propositional Formulas. In Obbink, J. H. & Pohl, K. (Eds.), *Software Product Lines, 9th International Conference, SPLC 2005, Rennes, France, September 26-29, 2005, Proceedings,* volume 3714 of *Lecture Notes in Computer Science.* Springer. (Cited on page 106.)

Baxter, I. D. & Mehlich, M. (2001). Preprocessor conditional removal by simple partial evaluation. In *Reverse Engineering, 2001. Proceedings. Eighth Working Conference on,* (pp. 281–290). IEEE. (Cited on page 245.)

Ben-Asher, Y., Feitelson, D. G., & Rudolph, L. (1996). ParC - An Extension of C for Shared Memory Parallel Processing. *Software: Practice and Experience*, 26(5). (Cited on page 45.)

Beuche, D., Papajewski, H., & Schroeder-Preikschat, W. (2004). Variability management with feature models. *Science of Computer Programming*, 53(3). (Cited on pages 30 and 101.)

Beuche, D. & Weiland, J. (2009). Managing Flexibility: Modeling Binding-Times in Simulink. In R. Paige, A. Hartman, & A. Rensink (Eds.), *Model Driven Architecture - Foundations and Applications*, volume 5562 of *Lecture Notes in Computer Science* (pp. 289–300). Springer Berlin Heidelberg. (Cited on page 40.)

Beyer, D., Henzinger, T., Jhala, R., & Majumdar, R. (2004). An eclipse plug-in for model checking. In *IWPC'04*. (Cited on page 50.)

Binder, R. (2000). *Testing Object-oriented Software Testing: Models, Patterns, and Tools*. Addison-Wesley Professional. (Cited on pages 61 and 73.)

Blanc, X., Gervais, M.-P., & Sriplakich, P. (2005). Model Bus: Towards the Interoperability of Modelling Tools. In U. Aßmann, M. Aksit, & A. Rensink (Eds.), *Model Driven Architecture*, volume 3599 of *Lecture Notes in Computer Science* (pp. 17–32). Springer Berlin Heidelberg. (Cited on page 15.)

Bock, C. (2004). UML 2 composition model. *Journal of Object Technology*, 3(10), 47–73. (Cited on page 66.)

Booch, G., Rumbaugh, J., & Jacobson, I. (1998). The Unified Modeling Language (UML). *World Wide Web: http://www. rational. com/uml/(UML Resource Center)*, 94. (Cited on page 80.)

Börger, E., Cavarra, A., & Riccobene, E. (2000). Modeling the Dynamics of UML State Machines. In Y. Gurevich, P. Kutter, M. Odersky, & L. Thiele (Eds.), *Abstract State Machines - Theory and Applications*, volume 1912 of *Lecture Notes in Computer Science* (pp. 223–241). Springer Berlin Heidelberg. (Cited on page 79.)

Boussinot, F. (1991). Reactive C: An Extension of C to Program Reactive Systems. *Software: Practice and Experience*, 21(4). (Cited on page 45.)

Bravenboer, M., Dolstra, E., & Visser, E. (2010). Preventing injection attacks with syntax embeddings. *Science of Computer Programming*, 75(7), 473–495. (Cited on pages 156 and 181.)

Bravenboer, M., Kalleberg, K. T., Vermaas, R., & Visser, E. (2008). A language and toolset for program transformation. *Science of Computer Programming*, 72(1-2). (Cited on pages 145 and 184.)

Bravenboer, M., Vermaas, R., Vinju, J. J., & Visser, E. (2005). Generalized Type-Based Disambiguation of Meta Programs with Concrete Object Syntax. In Glueck, R. & Lowry, M. R. (Eds.), *Generative Programming and Component Engineering, 4th International Conference, GPCE 2005*, volume 3676 of *Lecture Notes in Computer Science*, (pp. 157–172)., Tallinn, Estonia. Springer. (Cited on page 164.)

Bravenboer, M. & Visser, E. (2004). Concrete syntax for objects: domain-specific language embedding and assimilation without restrictions. In *Proceedings of the 19th Annual ACM SIGPLAN Conference on Object-Oriented Programming, Systems, Languages, and Applications, OOPSLA 2004*, Vancouver, BC, Canada. ACM. (Cited on page 181.)

Bravenboer, M. & Visser, E. (2007). Designing Syntax Embeddings and Assimilations for Language Libraries. In *MoDELS 2007*, volume 5002 of *LNCS*. Springer. (Cited on page 182.)

Brown, A. W. (1993). Control integration through message-passing in a software development environment. *Software Engineering Journal, 8(3)*, 121–131. (Cited on page 15.)

Brown, A. W. (1996). *Component-Based Software Engineering: Selected Papers from the Software Engineering Institute* (1st ed.). Los Alamitos, CA, USA: IEEE Computer Society Press. (Cited on page 66.)

Brown, A. W. & Penedo, M. H. (1992). An Annotated Bibliography on Integration in Software Engineering Environments. *SIGSOFT Softw. Eng. Notes, 17(3)*, 47–55. (Cited on page 14.)

Broy, M. (2006). Challenges in automotive software engineering. In *Proceedings of the 28th international conference on Software engineering*, ICSE '06, (pp. 33–42)., New York, NY, USA. ACM. (Cited on pages 28 and 29.)

Broy, M., Feilkas, M., Herrmannsdoerfer, M., Merenda, S., & Ratiu, D. (2010). Seamless Model-Based Development: From Isolated Tools to Integrated Model Engineering Environments. *Proceedings of the IEEE, 98(4)*. (Cited on page 11.)

Broy, M., Kirstan, S., Krcmar, H., & Schätz, B. (2011). What is the Benefit of a Model-Based Design of Embedded Software Systems in the Car Industry? In *Emerging Technologies for the Evolution and Maintenance of Software Models*. ICI. (Cited on page 44.)

Bruckhaus, T., Madhavii, N., Janssen, I., & Henshaw, J. (1996). The impact of tools on software productivity. *Software, IEEE, 13(5)*, 29–38. (Cited on page 11.)

Burch, J., Clarke, E., McMillan, K., Dill, D., & Hwang, L. (1992). Symbolic model checking: 10$\overset{.}{2}$0 States and beyond. *Information and Computation, 98(2)*, 142 – 170. (Cited on page 19.)

Burmester, S., Giese, H., Niere, J., Tichy, M., Wadsack, J. P., Wagner, R., Wendehals, L., & Zündorf, A. (2004). Tool integration at the meta-model level: the Fujaba approach. *International Journal on Software Tools for Technology Transfer*, 6(3), 203–218. (Cited on pages 14 and 23.)

Buschmann, F., Meunier, R., Rohnert, H., Sommerlad, P., & Stal, M. (1996a). A Systems of Patterns: Pattern-Oriented Software Architecture. (Cited on page 117.)

Buschmann, F., Meunier, R., Rohnert, H., Sommerlad, P., & Stal, M. (1996b). *Pattern-Oriented Software Architecture: A System of Patterns*. Wiley. (Cited on page 171.)

Calder, M., Kolberg, M., Magill, E. H., & Reiff-Marganiec, S. (2003). Feature interaction: a critical review and considered forecast. *Computer Networks*, 41(1), 115–141. (Cited on page 41.)

Clarke, E. (1997). Model checking. In *Foundations of Software Technology and Theoretical Computer Science*, volume 1346 of *LNCS* (pp. 54–56). Springer. (Cited on page 85.)

Clarke, E., Kroening, D., & Lerda, F. (2004). A Tool for Checking ANSI-C Programs. In K. Jensen & A. Podelski (Eds.), *Tools and Algorithms for the Construction and Analysis of Systems*, volume 2988 of *Lecture Notes in Computer Science* (pp. 168–176). Springer Berlin Heidelberg. (Cited on pages 19 and 74.)

Clarke, E. M., Emerson, E. A., & Sistla, A. P. (1986). Automatic verification of finite-state concurrent systems using temporal logic specifications. *ACM Trans. Program. Lang. Syst.*, 8(2), 244–263. (Cited on page 85.)

Clarke, E. M. & Heinle, W. (2000). Modular Translation of Statecharts to SMV. Technical report, Carnegie Mellon University. (Cited on pages 50 and 224.)

Cleland-Huang, J., Settimi, R., Romanova, E., Berenbach, B., & Clark, S. (2007). Best practices for automated traceability. *Computer*, 40(6), 27–35. (Cited on page 54.)

Clements, P. C. (1995). From Subroutines to Subsystems: Component-Based Software Development. (Cited on page 66.)

Combemale, B., Gonnord, L., & Rusu, V. (2011). A Generic Tool for Tracing Executions Back to a DSML's Operational Semantics. In *ECMFA'11*. (Cited on page 50.)

Corbett, J. C., Dwyer, M. B., Hatcliff, J., Laubach, S., Păsăreanu, C. S., Robby, & Zheng, H. (2000). Bandera: extracting finite-state models from Java source code. In *Proceedings of the International Conference of Software Engineering (ICSE)*. (Cited on page 49.)

Cox, R., Bergan, T., Clements, A. T., Kaashoek, M. F., & Kohler, E. (2008). Xoc, an extension-oriented compiler for systems programming. In *ASPLOS 2008*. (Cited on page 45.)

Czarnecki, K. & Antkiewicz, M. (2005). Mapping Features to Models: A Template Approach Based on Superimposed Variants. In R. Glueck & M. Lowry (Eds.), *Generative Programming and Component Engineering*, volume 3676 of *Lecture Notes in Computer Science* (pp. 422–437). Springer Berlin Heidelberg. (Cited on pages 37 and 54.)

Czarnecki, K. & Pietroszek, K. (2006). Verifying feature-based model templates against well-formedness OCL constraints. In *Proceedings of the 5th international conference on Generative programming and component engineering*, GPCE '06, (pp. 211–220)., New York, NY, USA. ACM. (Cited on page 54.)

Czarnecki, K. & Wasowski, A. (2007). Feature Diagrams and Logics: There and Back Again. In *Software Product Lines, 11th International Conference, SPLC 2007, Kyoto, Japan, September 10-14, 2007, Proceedings*. IEEE Computer Society. (Cited on page 106.)

Damm, W., Achatz, R., Beetz, K., Daembkes, H., Grimm, K., Liggesmeyer, P., et al. (2010). Nationale Roadmap Embedded Systems. In *Cyber-Physical Systems* (pp. 67–136). Springer. (Cited on page 27.)

David H. Lorenz, Boaz Rosenan (2011). Cedalion: A Language for Language Oriented Programming. In *Proceedings of OOPSLA/SPLASH 2011*. (Cited on page 186.)

Dearle, A., Kirby, G. N. C., & McCarthy, A. (2010). A Middleware Framework for Constraint-Based Deployment and Autonomic Management of Distributed Applications. *CoRR, abs/1006.4733*. (Cited on page 29.)

Dhungana, D., Rabiser, R., Grünbacher, P., Lehner, K., & Federspiel, C. (2007). DOPLER: An Adaptable Tool Suite for Product Line Engineering. In *Software Product Lines, 11th International Conference, SPLC 2007, Kyoto, Japan, September 10-14, 2007, Proceedings. Second Volume (Workshops)*. Kindai Kagaku Sha Co. Ltd., Tokyo, Japan. (Cited on page 101.)

Dhurjati, D., Kowshik, S., Adve, V., & Lattner, C. (2003). Memory Safety Without Runtime Checks or Garbage Collection. *SIGPLAN Not., 38(7)*, 69–80. (Cited on page 29.)

Douglass, B. P. (2010). *Design Patterns for Embedded Systems in C: An Embedded Software Engineering Toolkit*. Elsevier. (Cited on page 27.)

Dunkels, A., Schmidt, O., Voigt, T., & Ali, M. (2006). Protothreads: simplifying event-driven programming of memory-constrained embedded systems. In *Proceedings of the 4th international conference on Embedded networked sensor systems*, SenSys '06, New York, NY, USA. ACM. (Cited on page 47.)

Dwyer, M., Avrunin, G., & Corbett, J. (1999). Patterns in property specifications for finite-state verification. In *Proceedings of the International Conference of Software Engineering (ICSE)*. (Cited on pages 50, 85, and 224.)

Dziobek, C., Loew, J., Przystas, W., & Weiland, J. (2008). Functional variants handling in Simulink models. In *MathWorks Virtual Automotive Conference, Stuttgart*. (Cited on page 15.)

Ebert, C. & Jones, C. (2009). Embedded Software: Facts, Figures, and Future. *Computer, 42(4)*. (Cited on page 42.)

Efftinge, S., Eysholdt, M., Köhnlein, J., Zarnekow, S., von Massow, R., Hasselbring, W., & Hanus, M. (2012). Xbase: implementing domain-specific languages for Java. In *Proceedings of the 11th International Conference on Generative Programming and Component Engineering*, (pp. 112–121). ACM. (Cited on page 185.)

El-khoury, J., Redell, O., & Torngren, M. (2005). A tool integration platform for multi-disciplinary development. In *Software Engineering and Advanced Applications, 2005. 31st EUROMICRO Conference on*, (pp. 442–449). (Cited on page 14.)

Eles, C. & Lawford, M. (2011). A tabular expression toolbox for Matlab/Simulink. In *Proceedings of the Third international conference on NASA Formal methods*. (Cited on page 50.)

Engler, D. & Ashcraft, K. (2003). RacerX: effective, static detection of race conditions and deadlocks. In *Proceedings of the nineteenth ACM symposium on Operating systems principles*, SOSP '03, (pp. 237–252)., New York, NY, USA. ACM. (Cited on page 29.)

Erdweg, S., Giarrusso, P. G., & Rendel, T. (2012). Language Composition Untangled. In *Proceedings of LDTA*. to appear. (Cited on page 180.)

Erdweg, S., Kats, L. C. L., Kastner, C., Ostermann, K., & Visser, E. (2011). Growing a Language Environment with Editor Libraries. In *Proceedings of the 10th ACM international conference on Generative programming and component engineering (GPCE 2011)*, New York, NY, USA. ACM. (Cited on page 184.)

Erdweg, S., Rendel, T., Kästner, C., & Ostermann, K. (2011). SugarJ: library-based syntactic language extensibility. In *OOPSLA 2011*, OOPSLA '11, New York, NY, USA. ACM. (Cited on page 184.)

Erdweg, S., van der Storm, T., Völter, M., Boersma, M., Bosman, R., Cook, W. R., Gerritsen, A., Hulshout, A., Kelly, S., Loh, A., et al. (2013). The state of the art in language workbenches. In *Software Language Engineering* (pp. 197–217). Springer. (Cited on page 256.)

Ernst, M. D., Badros, G. J., & Notkin, D. (2002). An Empirical Analysis of C Preprocessor Use. *IEEE Trans. Softw. Eng., 28*. (Cited on page 58.)

Favaro, J., de Koning, H.-P., Schreiner, R., & Olive, X. (2012). Next Generation Requirements Engineering. In *Proc. 22nd Annual INCOSE International Symposium (Rome, Italy, July 2012)*. (Cited on page 53.)

Fehnker, A., Huuck, R., Jayet, P., Lussenburg, M., & Rauch, F. (2007). Goanna: a static model checker. In *FMICS'06/PDMC'06*. (Cited on page 50.)

Ferguson, R., Parrington, N., Dunne, P., Hardy, C., Archibald, J., & Thompson, J. (2000). MetaMOOSE - an object-oriented framework for the construction of CASE tools. *Information and Software Technology*, 42(2). (Cited on page 186.)

Flatt, M., Barzilay, E., & Findler, R. B. (2009). Scribble: closing the book on ad hoc documentation tools. In *Proceedings of the 14th ACM SIGPLAN international conference on Functional programming*, ICFP '09, (pp. 109–120)., New York, NY, USA. ACM. (Cited on page 52.)

Fowler, M. (2004). Inversion of control containers and the dependency injection pattern. (Cited on page 67.)

Fowler, M. (2005). Language Workbenches: The Killer-App for Domain Specific Languages? (Cited on pages 6 and 139.)

Fowler, M. & Beck, K. (1999). *Refactoring: improving the design of existing code*. Addison-Wesley Professional. (Cited on page 107.)

Fuentes-Fernández, L. & Vallecillo-Moreno, A. (2004). An introduction to UML profiles. *UML and Model Engineering*, 2. (Cited on page 25.)

Gamma, E., Helm, R., Johnson, R., & Vlissides, J. (1995). *Design patterns: elements of reusable object-oriented software*. Addison-Wesley Professional. (Cited on pages 149, 167, and 191.)

Garrido, A. & Johnson, R. (2002). Challenges of refactoring C programs. In *Proceedings of the international workshop on Principles of software evolution*, (pp. 6–14). ACM. (Cited on page 244.)

Goddard, P. (1993). Validating the safety of embedded real-time control systems using FMEA. In *Reliability and Maintainability Symposium, 1993. Proceedings., Annual*, (pp. 227–230). (Cited on page 30.)

Goddard, P. (2000). Software FMEA techniques. In *Reliability and Maintainability Symposium, 2000. Proceedings. Annual*, (pp. 118–123). (Cited on page 30.)

Gokhale, A. S., Balasubramanian, K., Krishna, A. S., Balasubramanian, J., Edwards, G., Deng, G., Turkay, E., Parsons, J., & Schmidt, D. C. (2008). Model driven middleware: A new paradigm for developing distributed real-time and embedded systems. *Science of Computer Programming*, 73(1). (Cited on page 45.)

Graaf, B., Lormans, M., & Toetenel, H. (2003). Embedded Software Engineering: The State of the Practice. *IEEE Softw.*, *20*(6). (Cited on page 45.)

Grünbacher, P., Rabiser, R., Dhungana, D., & Lehofer, M. (2009). Model-Based Customization and Deployment of Eclipse-Based Tools: Industrial Experiences. In *Proceedings of the 2009 IEEE/ACM International Conference on Automated Software Engineering*, ASE '09, Washington, DC, USA. IEEE Computer Society. (Cited on page 186.)

Grundy, J. & Hosking, J. (2007). Supporting Generic Sketching-Based Input of Diagrams in a Domain-Specific Visual Language Meta-Tool. In *Proceedings of the 29th international conference on Software Engineering*, ICSE '07, Washington, DC, USA. IEEE Computer Society. (Cited on page 186.)

Hammond, K. & Michaelson, G. (2003). Hume: a domain-specific language for real-time embedded systems. In *GPCE 03*, GPCE '03. (Cited on page 45.)

Harel, D. (1987). Statecharts: A visual formalism for complex systems. *Science of computer programming*, *8*(3), 231–274. (Cited on page 79.)

Harel, D. & Rumpe, B. (2004). Meaningful Modeling: What's the Semantics of "Semantics"? *IEEE Computer, Volume 37*(10), 64–72. (Cited on page 158.)

Hayes, J. H., Dekhtyar, A., & Osborne, J. (2003). Improving requirements tracing via information retrieval. In *Requirements Engineering Conference, 2003. Proceedings. 11th IEEE International*, (pp. 138–147). IEEE. (Cited on page 54.)

Hedin, G. & Magnusson, E. (2003). JastAdd—an aspect-oriented compiler construction system. *Science of Computer Programming*, *47*(1). (Cited on page 183.)

Heitmeyer, C. (2006). Developing Safety-Critical Systems: the Role of Formal Methods and Tools. In *Australian Computer Society, Inc.* (Cited on page 11.)

Hemel, Z. & Visser, E. (2011). Declaratively Programming the Mobile Web with Mobl. In *Proc. of the 2011 ACM Int. Conference on Object oriented programming systems languages and applications*, OOPSLA 2011, (pp. 695–712). ACM. (Cited on page 186.)

Humble, J. & Molesky, J. (2011). Why Enterprises Must Adopt Devops to Enable Continuous Delivery. *Cutter IT Journal*, *24*(8), 6. (Cited on page 12.)

Hunt, G. C. & Larus, J. R. (2007). Singularity: Rethinking the Software Stack. *SIGOPS Oper. Syst. Rev.*, *41*(2), 37–49. (Cited on page 262.)

Ivanicic, F., Shlyakhter, I., Gupta, A., & Ganai, M. K. (2005). Model Checking C Programs Using F-SOFT. In *ICCD'05*. (Cited on page 29.)

Jackson, E. K. & Sztipanovits, J. (2006). Correct-ed through Construction: A Model-based Approach to Embedded Systems Reality. In *Proceedings of International Conference on Engineering of Computer Based Systems (ECBS)*. (Cited on page 49.)

Janicki, R., Parnas, D. L., & Zucker, J. (1997). *Tabular representations in relational documents*. Springer-Verlag New York, Inc. (Cited on page 221.)

Jarke, M. (1998). Requirements tracing. *Commun. ACM*, *41*(12), 32–36. (Cited on pages 20 and 37.)

Jim, T., Morrisett, J. G., Grossman, D., Hicks, M. W., Cheney, J., & Wang, Y. (2002). Cyclone: A Safe Dialect of C. In *USENIX 2002*. USENIX Association. (Cited on page 42.)

Jr., G. L. S. (1999). Growing a Language. *Higher-Order and Symbolic Computation*, *12*(3). (Cited on page 182.)

Kang, K., Cohen, S., Hess, J., Nowak, W., & Peterson., S. (1990). Feature-oriented domain analysis (FODA) feasibility study. Technical report, SEI. (Cited on page 222.)

Karthik, S. & Jayakumar, H. G. (2005). Static Analysis: C Code Error Checking for Reliable and Secure Programming. In *International Enformatika Conference '05*. (Cited on page 47.)

Kästner, C. (2007). CIDE: Decomposing Legacy Applications into Features. In *Software Product Lines, 11th International Conference, SPLC 2007, Kyoto, Japan, September 10-14, 2007, Proceedings. Second Volume (Workshops)*. Kindai Kagaku Sha Co. Ltd., Tokyo, Japan. (Cited on page 105.)

Kästner, C. (2010). *Virtual separation of concerns*. PhD thesis, PhD thesis, University of Magdeburg. (Cited on page 54.)

Kats, L. C. L. & Visser, E. (2010). IDEs. In *Proceedings of the 25th Annual ACM SIGPLAN Conference on Object-Oriented Programming, Systems, Languages, and Applications, OOPSLA 2010, October 17-21, 2010, Reno/Tahoe, Nevada, USA*, (pp. 444–463). ACM. (best student paper award). (Cited on page 184.)

Kats, L. C. L., Visser, E., & Wachsmuth, G. (2010). Pure and declarative syntax definition: paradise lost and regained. In *Proceedings of the 25th Annual ACM SIGPLAN Conference on Object-Oriented Programming, Systems, Languages, and Applications, OOPSLA 2010*, Reno/Tahoe, Nevada. ACM. (Cited on pages 155 and 181.)

Kenner, A., Kästner, C., Haase, S., & Leich, T. (2010). TypeChef: toward type checking# ifdef variability in C. In *Proceedings of the 2nd International Workshop on Feature-Oriented Software Development*, (pp. 25–32). ACM. (Cited on page 244.)

Khare, R., Guntersdorfer, M., Oreizy, P., Medvidovic, N., & Taylor, R. (2001). xADL: enabling architecture-centric tool integration with XML. In *System Sciences, 2001. Proceedings of the 34th Annual Hawaii International Conference on*, (pp. 9 pp.–). (Cited on page 14.)

Kliemannel, F., Mann, S., & Rock, G. (2010). A custom approach for variability management in automotive applications. In *Proc. 4th Int. Workshop on Variability Modeling of Software-intensive Systems (VAMOS 2010)*, volume 37, (pp. 155–158). (Cited on page 40.)

Klint, P. (1993). A Meta-Environment for Generating Programming Environments. *ACM Transactions on Software Engineering Methodology*, 2(2). (Cited on page 184.)

Klint, P., van der Storm, T., & Vinju, J. J. (2009). RASCAL: A Domain Specific Language for Source Code Analysis and Manipulation. In *Ninth IEEE International Working Conference on Source Code Analysis and Manipulation, SCAM 2009, Edmonton, Alberta, Canada, September 20-21, 2009*. IEEE Computer Society. (Cited on page 184.)

Knuth, D. E. (1984). Literate Programming. *The Computer Journal*, 27(2), 97–111. (Cited on page 52.)

Konat, G., Kats, L., Wachsmuth, G., & Visser, E. (2013). Declarative Name Binding and Scope Rules. In K. Czarnecki & G. Hedin (Eds.), *Software Language Engineering*, volume 7745 of *Lecture Notes in Computer Science* (pp. 311–331). Springer Berlin Heidelberg. (Cited on page 265.)

Königs, A. & Schürr, A. (2006). Tool Integration with Triple Graph Grammars - A Survey. *Electronic Notes in Theoretical Computer Science*, 148(1), 113 – 150. Proceedings of the School of SegraVis Research Training Network on Foundations of Visual Modelling Techniques (FoVMT 2004). (Cited on page 14.)

Kopetz, H. (2011). *Real-time systems: design principles for distributed embedded applications*. Springer. (Cited on page 27.)

Krahn, H., Rumpe, B., & V"olkel, S. (2010). MontiCore: a framework for compositional development of domain specific languages. *STTT*, 12(5), 353–372. (Cited on page 182.)

Kramler, G., Kappel, G., Reiter, T., Kapsammer, E., Retschitzegger, W., & Schwinger, W. (2006). Towards a Semantic Infrastructure Supporting Model-based Tool Integration. In *Proceedings of the 2006 International Workshop on Global Integrated Model Management*, GaMMa '06, (pp. 43–46)., New York, NY, USA. ACM. (Cited on page 14.)

Kuhn, A., Murphy, G., & Thompson, C. (2012). An Exploratory Study of Forces and Frictions Affecting Large-Scale Model-Driven Development. In R. France, J. Kazmeier, R. Breu, & C. Atkinson (Eds.), *Model Driven Engineering Languages and Systems*, volume 7590 of *Lecture Notes in Computer Science* (pp. 352–367). Springer Berlin Heidelberg. (Cited on pages 28, 30, 53, 63, and 133.)

Lee, E. (2000). What's ahead for embedded software? *Computer*, 33(9), 18–26. (Cited on pages 28 and 29.)

Lee, E. (2008). Cyber Physical Systems: Design Challenges. In *Object Oriented Real-Time Distributed Computing (ISORC), 2008 11th IEEE International Symposium on*, (pp. 363–369). (Cited on page 28.)

Lee, W. S., Grosh, D., Tillman, F., & Lie, C. (1985). Fault Tree Analysis, Methods, and Applications 2013; A Review. *Reliability, IEEE Transactions on*, R-34(3), 194–203. (Cited on page 30.)

Levy, M. & Conte, T. M. (2009). Embedded Multicore Processors and Systems. *Micro, IEEE*, 29(3), 7–9. (Cited on page 29.)

Liggesmeyer, P. & Trapp, M. (2009). Trends in Embedded Software Engineering. *IEEE Softw.*, 26. (Cited on pages 28, 29, 44, and 45.)

Liskov, B. & Wing, J. M. (1994). A Behavioral Notion of Subtyping. *ACM Transactions on Programming Languages and Systems*, 16(6), 1811–1841. (Cited on page 157.)

Loer, K. & Harrison, M. (2002). Towards Usable and Relevant Model Checking Techniques for the Analysis of Dependable Interactive Systems. In *In Proceedings of the International Conference on Automatic Software Engineering (ASE)*. (Cited on page 49.)

Loughran, N., Sanchez, P., Garcia, A., & Fuentes, L. (2008). Language Support for Managing Variability in Architectural Models. In C. Pautasso & E. Tanter (Eds.), *Software Composition*, volume 4954 of *Lecture Notes in Computer Science* (pp. 36–51). Springer Berlin Heidelberg. (Cited on page 54.)

Mali, Y. & Wyk, E. V. (2011). Building Extensible Specifications and Implementations of Promela with AbleP. In *Model Checking Software - 18th International SPIN Workshop, Proceedings*, volume 6823 of *Lecture Notes in Computer Science*. Springer. (Cited on page 182.)

Medina-Mora, R. & Feiler, P. H. (1981). An Incremental Programming Environment. *IEEE Trans. Software Eng.*, 7(5). (Cited on page 183.)

Mendonça, M., Wasowski, A., & Czarnecki, K. (2009). SAT-based analysis of feature models is easy. In Muthig, D. & McGregor, J. D. (Eds.), *Software Product Lines, 13th International Conference, SPLC 2009, San Francisco, California, USA, August 24-28, 2009, Proceedings*, volume 446 of *ACM International Conference Proceeding Series*. ACM. (Cited on pages 50, 106, and 223.)

Mernik, M., Heering, J., & Sloane, A. M. (2005). When and how to develop domain-specific languages. *ACM Comput. Surv.*, 37(4), 316–344. (Cited on pages 54 and 179.)

Mernik, M., Lenic, M., Avdicausevic, E., & Zumer, V. (2002). LISA: An Interactive Environment for Programming Language Development. In *Compiler Construction, 11th International Conference, CC 2002, Part of ETAPS 2002, Proceedings*, volume 2304 of *Lecture Notes in Computer Science*. Springer. (Cited on pages 183 and 185.)

Mernik, M. & Zumer, V. (2005). Incremental programming language development. *Computer Languages, Systems & Structures, 31*(1). (Cited on page 185.)

Meyer, B. (1992). Applying 'design by contract'. *Computer, 25*(10), 40–51. (Cited on page 36.)

Meyer, B. (1998). Design by Contract: The Eiffel Method. In *TOOLS 1998: 26th Int. Conference on Technology of Object-Oriented Languages and Systems*, (pp. 446). IEEE CS. (Cited on page 66.)

Mine, A. (2011). Static Analysis of Run-Time Errors in Embedded Critical Parallel C Programs. In *ESOP 2011*, volume 6602 of *LNCS*. Springer. (Cited on page 47.)

MISRA (2004). Guidelines for the Use of the C Language in Critical Systems. (Cited on pages 28 and 42.)

Naumann, D. A. & Barnett, M. (2004). Towards Imperative Modules: Reasoning about Invariants and Sharing of Mutable State. In *19th IEEE Symposium on Logic in Computer Science*. IEEE CS. (Cited on page 47.)

Notkin, D. (1985). The GANDALF project. *Journal of Systems and Software, 5*(2). (Cited on page 183.)

Nystrom, N., Clarkson, M. R., & Myers, A. C. (2003). Polyglot: An Extensible Compiler Framework for Java. In *Compiler Construction, 12th International Conference, CC 2003, Part of ETAPS 2003, Proceedings*, volume 2622 of *Lecture Notes in Computer Science*. Springer. (Cited on page 182.)

Palopoli, L., Ancilotti, P., & Buttazzo, G. C. (1999). A C Language Extension for Programming Real-Time Applications. In *6th International Workshop on Real-Time Computing and Applications (RTCSA 99)*. IEEE CS. (Cited on page 45.)

Parr, T. J. & Quong, R. W. (1995). ANTLR: A Predicated-LL(k) Parser Generator. *Software: Practice and Experience, 25*(7). (Cited on pages 181 and 185.)

Pavletic, D., Raza, A. S., Voelter, M., Kolb, B., & Kehrer, T. (2013). Extensible Debuggers for Extensible Languages. In *GI/ACM WS on Software Reengineering, 2013*. (Cited on page 10.)

Porter, S. W. (1988). Design of a Syntax Directed Editor for PSDL (Prototype Systems Design Language). Master's thesis, Naval Postgraduate School, Monterey, CA, USA. (Cited on page 183.)

Puccetti, A. (2010). Static Analysis of the XEN Kernel using Frama-C. *J. UCS*, *16*(4). (Cited on page 47.)

Ratiu, D., Voelter, M., Kolb, B., & Schaetz, B. (2013). Using Language Engineering to Lift Languages and Analyses at the Domain Level. In *Proceedings the 5th NASA Formal Methods Symposium (NFM'13)*. (Cited on page 9.)

Ratiu, D., Voelter, M., Molotnikov, Z., & Schaetz, B. (2012). Implementing Modular Domain Specific Languages and Analyses. In *Proceedings the 9th Workshop on Model-Driven Engineering, Verification, and Validation (Modevva'12)*. (Cited on page 9.)

Ratiu, D., Voelter, M., Schaetz, B., & Kolb, B. (2012). Language Engineering as Enabler for Incrementally Defined Formal Analyses. In *Proceedings of the Workshop on Formal Methods in Software Engineering: Rigorous and Agile Approaches (FORMSERA'2012)*. (Cited on page 9.)

Renggli, L., Girba, T., & Nierstrasz, O. (2010). Embedding Languages Without Breaking Tools. In *ECOOP'10*. (Cited on page 185.)

Reps, T. W. & Teitelbaum, T. (1984). The Synthesizer Generator. In *First ACM SIGSOFT/SIGPLAN software engineering symposium on Practical software development environments*. ACM. (Cited on pages 183 and 184.)

Roos-Frantz, F. (2009). A Preliminary Comparison of Formal Properties on Orthogonal Variability Model and Feature Models. In Benavides, D., Metzger, A., & Eisenecker, U. W. (Eds.), *Third International Workshop on Variability Modelling of Software-Intensive Systems, Seville, Spain, January 28-30, 2009. Proceedings*, volume 29 of *ICB Research Report*. Universitat Duisburg-Essen. (Cited on page 101.)

S. Andalam, P. S. Roop, A. G. (2010). Predictable multithreading of embedded applications using PRET-C. In *Proc. of ACM-IEEE Int. Conference on Formal Methods and Models for Codesign (MEMOCODE)*,. (Cited on page 47.)

Samek, M. (2002). *Practical statecharts in C/C++: Quantum programming for embedded systems*. CMP. (Cited on page 79.)

Schmidt, D. C. (2006). Guest Editor's Introduction: Model-Driven Engineering. *Computer*, *39*(2), 25–31. (Cited on page 13.)

Simon, D. E. (1999). *An Embedded Software Primer: Text*, volume 1. Addison-Wesley. (Cited on page 27.)

Simonyi, C., Christerson, M., & Clifford, S. (2006). Intentional Software. In *OOPSLA 2006*. ACM. (Cited on pages 24, 141, and 183.)

Stahl, T. T. & Voelter, M. (2006). *Model-driven software development*. John Wiley & Sons Chichester. (Cited on page 11.)

Sztipanovits, J. & Karsai, G. (2001). Embedded Software: Challenges and Opportunities. In T. Henzinger & C. Kirsch (Eds.), *Embedded Software*, volume 2211 of *Lecture Notes in Computer Science* (pp. 403–415). Springer Berlin Heidelberg. (Cited on page 28.)

Tatsubori, M., Chiba, S., Itano, K., & Killijian, M.-O. (1999). OpenJava: A Class-Based Macro System for Java. In *1st Workshop on Reflection and Software Engineering, OOPSLA '99*, volume 1826 of *LNCS*. (Cited on page 182.)

Thaker, S., Batory, D., Kitchin, D., & Cook, W. (2007). Safe composition of product lines. In *Proceedings of the 6th international conference on Generative programming and component engineering*, GPCE '07, (pp. 95–104)., New York, NY, USA. ACM. (Cited on page 54.)

Thomas, D. & Hunt, A. (2002). Mock objects. *Software, IEEE*, 19(3), 22–24. (Cited on page 73.)

Thomas, I. & Nejmeh, B. (1992). Definitions of tool integration for environments. *Software, IEEE*, 9(2), 29–35. (Cited on page 14.)

Tolvanen, J.-P. & Kelly, S. (2005). Defining Domain-Specific Modeling Languages to Automate Product Derivation: Collected Experiences. In H. Obbink & K. Pohl (Eds.), *Software Product Lines*, volume 3714 of *Lecture Notes in Computer Science* (pp. 198–209). Springer Berlin Heidelberg. (Cited on page 54.)

Tolvanen, J.-P. & Kelly, S. (2009). MetaEdit+: defining and using integrated domain-specific modeling languages. In *Proceedings of the 24th ACM SIGPLAN conference companion on Object oriented programming systems languages and applications*, OOPSLA '09, New York, NY, USA. ACM. (Cited on page 186.)

Tomassetti, F. & Ratiu, D. (2013). Extracting variability from C and lifting it to mbeddr. In *1st International Workshop on Reverse Variability Engineering (REVE 2013)*, (pp.ŋ). (Cited on page 109.)

Tratt, L. (2005). Model transformations and tool integration. *Software & Systems Modeling*, 4(2), 112–122. (Cited on page 14.)

Van Deursen, A. & Klint, P. (1998). Little languages: Little maintenance? *Journal of software maintenance*, 10(2), 75–92. (Cited on pages 263 and 267.)

Visser, E. (1997). *Syntax Definition for Language Prototyping*. PhD thesis, University of Amsterdam. (Cited on page 181.)

Visser, E. (2007). A Case Study in Domain-Specific Language Engineering. In *GTTSE 2007*, volume 5235 of *Lecture Notes in Computer Science*, (pp. 291–373). (Cited on page 186.)

Voelter, M. (2010). Embedded Software Development with Projectional Language Workbenches. In *Model Driven Engineering Languages and Systems, 13th International Conference, MODELS 2010, Oslo, Norway, October 3-8, 2010. Proceedings*, Lecture Notes in Computer Science. Springer. (Cited on page 8.)

Voelter, M. (2011). Language and IDE Development, Modularization and Composition with MPS. In *GTTSE 2011*, LNCS. Springer. (Cited on page 9.)

Voelter, M. (2013). Integrating Prose as First-Class Citizens with Models and Code. In *7th International Workshop on Multi-Paradigm Modeling MPM 2013*, (pp.ĩ7). (Cited on page 10.)

Voelter, M., Benz, S., Dietrich, C., Engelmann, B., Helander, M., Kats, L., Visser, E., & Wachsmuth, G. (2013). *DSL Engineering – Designing, Implementing and Using Domain-Specific Languages*. CreateSpace Publishing Platform. (Cited on pages 10, 227, and 256.)

Voelter, M., Ratiu, D., Kolb, B., & Schaetz, B. (2013). mbeddr: instantiating a language workbench in the embedded software domain. *Automated Software Engineering, 20*(3), 1–52. (Cited on page 9.)

Voelter, M., Ratiu, D., Schaetz, B., & Kolb, B. (2012). mbeddr: an Extensible C-based Programming Language and IDE for Embedded Systems. In *Proceedings of SPLASH Wavefront 2012*. (Cited on page 9.)

Voelter, M., Ratiu, D., & Tomassetti, F. (2013). Requirements as first-class citizens: Integrating requirements closely with implementation artifacts. In *ACESMB@MoDELS*. (Cited on page 10.)

Voelter, M. & Visser, E. (2011). Product Line Engineering using Domain-Specific Languages. In de Almeida, E. S. & Kishi, T. (Eds.), *Software Product Line Conference (SPLC), 2011 15th International*, (pp. 70–79). CPS. (Cited on pages 9 and 101.)

von Hanxleden, R. (2009). SyncCharts in C - A Proposal for Light-Weight, Deterministic Concurrency. In *Proceedings of the International Conference on Embedded Sofware (EMSOFT'09)*. (Cited on page 47.)

Wasserman, A. (1990). Tool integration in software engineering environments. In F. Long (Ed.), *Software Engineering Environments*, volume 467 of *Lecture Notes in Computer Science* (pp. 137–149). Springer Berlin Heidelberg. (Cited on page 14.)

Watkins, R. & Neal, M. (1994). Why and how of requirements tracing. *Software, IEEE, 11*(4), 104–106. (Cited on pages 20 and 53.)

White, J., Benavides, D., Schmidt, D. C., Trinidad, P., Dougherty, B., & Ruiz-Cortes, A. (2010). Automated diagnosis of feature model configurations. *Journal of Systems and Software, 83*(7), 1094–1107. (Cited on page 106.)

Whittle, J., Hutchinson, J., Rouncefield, M., Burden, H., & Heldal, R. (2013). Industrial Adoption of Model-Driven Engineering: Are the Tools Really the Problem? In *Proceedings of the 16th International Conference on Model Driven Engineering Languages and Systems (MODELS) 2013*. ACM. (Cited on pages 13, 31, and 32.)

Winkler, S. & Pilgrim, J. (2010). A survey of traceability in requirements engineering and model-driven development. *Software and Systems Modeling, 9*, 529–565. (Cited on pages 53 and 93.)

Woodward, M. V. & Mosterman, P. J. (2007). Challenges for embedded software development. In *Circuits and Systems, 2007. MWSCAS 2007. 50th Midwest Symposium on*, (pp. 630–633). IEEE. (Cited on page 28.)

Wyk, E. V., Bodin, D., Gao, J., & Krishnan, L. (2008). Silver: an Extensible Attribute Grammar System. *ENTCS, 203*(2). (Cited on pages 181, 183, and 184.)

Wyk, E. V., de Moor, O., Backhouse, K., & Kwiatkowski, P. (2002). Forwarding in Attribute Grammars for Modular Language Design. In *Compiler Construction, 11th International Conference, CC 2002, Held as Part of the Joint European Conferences on Theory and Practice of Software, ETAPS 2002, Proceedings*, volume 2304 of *Lecture Notes in Computer Science*. Springer. (Cited on page 184.)

Wyk, E. V., Krishnan, L., Bodin, D., & Schwerdfeger, A. (2007). Attribute Grammar-Based Language Extensions for Java. In *ECOOP 2007 - 21st European Conference on Object-Oriented Programming, Proceedings*, volume 4609 of *Lecture Notes in Computer Science*. Springer. (Cited on page 182.)

Yang, Z. & Jiang, M. (2007). Using Eclipse as a Tool-Integration Platform for Software Development. *Software, IEEE, 24*(2), 87–89. (Cited on page 15.)

Yannakakis, M. (2000). Hierarchical State Machines. In J. Leeuwen, O. Watanabe, M. Hagiya, P. Mosses, & T. Ito (Eds.), *Theoretical Computer Science: Exploring New Frontiers of Theoretical Informatics*, volume 1872 of *Lecture Notes in Computer Science* (pp. 315–330). Springer Berlin Heidelberg. (Cited on page 79.)

Yoshimura, K., Forster, T., Muthig, D., & Pech, D. (2008). Model-Based Design of Product Line Components in the Automotive Domain. In *Software Product Line Conference, 2008. SPLC '08. 12th International*, (pp. 170–179). (Cited on page 40.)

Zalila, F., Crégut, X., & Pantel, M. (2012). Leveraging formal verification tools for DSML users: a process modeling case study. In *ISoLA'12*. (Cited on page 50.)

26
1B/4806

5 0 0 3 5 9 4 3 0 *